For my son Quincey

Katrin Stumptner (ed.)

Group Analysis and Psychodynamic Group Therapy with Children and Adolescents

Creative, Innovative, and Practical Inspiration

VANDENHOECK & RUPRECHT

Bibliographic information published by the Deutsche Nationalbibliothek:
The Deutsche Nationalbibliothek lists this publication in the Deutsche
Nationalbibliografie; detailed bibliographic data available online: https://dnb.de.

© 2024 Vandenhoeck & Ruprecht, Robert-Bosch-Breite 10, D-37079 Göttingen,
an imprint of the Brill-Group
(Koninklijke Brill BV, Leiden, Netherlands; Brill USA Inc., Boston MA, USA; Brill Asia Pte Ltd,
Singapore; Brill Deutschland GmbH, Paderborn, Germany; Brill Österreich GmbH, Vienna,
Austria)
Koninklijke Brill BV includes the imprints Brill, Brill Nijhoff, Brill Schöningh,Brill Fink,
Brill mentis, Brill Wageningen Academic, Vandenhoeck & Ruprecht, Böhlau and V&R unipress.

All rights reserved. No part of this work may be reproduced or utilized in any form
or by any means, electronic or mechanical, including photocopying, recording,or any
information storage and retrieval system, without prior written permission from
the publisher.

The German edition is also published by Vandenhoeck & Ruprecht under the title "Gruppenanalytisch arbeiten mit Kindern und Jugendlichen. Impulse für eine kreative und vielfältige Praxis" (ISBN: 978-3-525-46285-0)

Cover image: Paul Klee, Fischzauber, 1925/akg-images

Translations from the German:
Jeremy Gaines (the articles by Katrin Stumptner, Anja Khalil & Carla Weber, Matthias Wenck, Beate Schnabel, Gerhild Ohrnberger, Andreas Opitz, Horst Wenzel; Eva Aralikatti (the article by Christoph Radaj); Reema Jones (the article by Furi Khabirpour); Tom Kelley (the article by Ballhausen-Scharf et al.); Mevsim Kücükakyüz (the article by Dietlind Köhncke).
All other translations were provided to the publishers by the respective authors.
Editing and proofreading: Jeremy Gaines

Typesetting: SchwabScantechnik, Göttingen
Printed and bound: ⊕ Hubert & Co, Ergolding
Printed in the EU

Vandenhoeck & Ruprecht Verlage | www.vandenhoeck-ruprecht-verlage.com

ISBN 978-3-525-40037-1

"Where novel ideas arise they belong neither to me nor to the other person. They arise between us."

(Waldenfels, 1997, p. 53)

Table of Contents

Editorial 11
Katrin Stumptner

Conceptual Developments and Vocational Policy Trends in Group Analysis for Children and Young People in Germany, Austria, and Switzerland

Group-analytical Work with Children and Adolescents: Insights into an
Unusual Kind of Advanced Training 25
Birgitt Ballhausen-Scharf, Christoph F. Müller, Hans Georg Lehle, Dietrich Winzer

Can Cooperation Models Help to Integrate Psychodynamic Group Therapy
with Children and Adolescents into Institutional Further Training?
An Experience-based Report 37
Thomas Schneider

Interdisciplinary Groups with Children and Young People

Parent-child Groups with Children under Six Years Old 69
Anke Mühle

From Holocaust Denial to a Personal Family Tableau: "Narrative Group Work" –
How to Apply Group Analysis in Schools to Support Democratic Skills
Europe-wide 91
Harald Weilnböck

Playing

On Playing 109
Dietlind Köhncke

Hansel and Gretel 122
Furi Khabirpour

When the Jubjub Bird Freezes Everything around Himself – Pain Treatment with Families in Group Psychotherapy with the Use of Digital Media 130
Christoph Radaj

Destructive Processes in Groups – The Stance of Group Leaders

"Must I become a Villain?" – On the Significance of Destruction in Existential Conflicts 145
Anja Khalil, Carla Weber

A Suicide Fantasy – Confusion, Speechlessness, and Projective Identification as Defenses of Tabooed Issues in Group-Analytical Psychotherapy with Late Adolescent Women Aged 18–21 158
Franziska Schöpfer

The Dynamic Links between Groups of Children and those of Primary Carers

Drudgery and Duty or Findings and Freedom?! Reflections and Experiences from a Parents' Group Accompanying Analytical Children's Group Therapy 183
Matthias Wenck

Children's Group for Primary School Children – Group Analysis in a Family and Educational Counseling Center under the Aegis of Diakonisches Werk 193
Horst Wenzel

The Rhythmic-Triadic Setting in Group Analysis 208
Katrin Stumptner

The Dynamic Network Provided by the Institutional Context of Schools, Youth Welfare Agencies and Hospitals

The Meaning of Shame in the Context of School Groups 223
Ursula Proebsting

Group-analytical Approach in Inpatient Educational Support 233
Tilman Sprondel

Group Analysis in Child and Adolescent Psychiatry –
Experiences and Significance 248
Andreas Opitz

Membership of a Range of Identities

What's it Like to Arrive in Germany? Experiences in Group Analyses
with Unaccompanied Refugee Minors 261
Gerhild Ohrnberger

Psychotherapy and Psychoanalysis in the Counseling Center 274
Kadir Kaynak

Opening Transcultural Spaces in Group-analytical Processes with Refugees 288
Beate Schnabel

To finish with a story 305
Christina Selle

Word of Thanks 306

Information on authors 308

Editorial

Katrin Stumptner

1 The WE in the ME – the ME in the WE

> *"To assist a child we must provide him with
> an environment which will enable him to develop freely."*
> (Maria Montessori, 1870–1952)

This book invites you to take a walk through landscapes of group analysis with children and adolescents (GACA). Twenty-two colleagues will introduce you to the pedagogical-interdisciplinary and psychodynamic fields of group analysis with children and adolescents, with the 18 contributions offering insights into the theoretical, professional, and conceptual work of GACA. The colleagues present their practical work in various institutional contexts and in outpatient practice. This book is intended to help emphasize the crucial importance of the social space that is the *group* in work with children, adolescents, and their caregivers, who are either parents or other significant persons in a caring role, such as foster parents, adoptive parents, grandparents, siblings, guardians, etc.

2 GACA turns 18

The conceptual development of group analysis with children, adolescents, and caregivers, as it is practiced in the German-speaking world today, can be understood as a complex transgenerational process from its beginning in 2003 until the present (Stumptner, 2019). Four group analysts from different institutes met in 2003 with the idea of bringing together colleagues working in groups with children and adolescents, and in 2005 these four[1] established a workshop that still takes place annually in September. Subsequently, a group of committed col-

---

1 Veronika Dietrichs-Paeschke, Pieter Hutz, Willi Meyer, and Gerhard Rudnitzki.

leagues[2] came together to work on an extension of group analysis on an ongoing basis from 2006 onwards. The members of this working group came from different institutional cultures of group analysis, and in a long-term process they developed a common theory and practice of group analysis with children and adolescents and their caregivers, drawing on their diversity of perspectives. In 2016 they established the Working Group for Group Analysis with Children and Adolescents (*Arbeitsgemeinschaft Gruppenanalyse mit Kindern und Jugendlichen e. V.*, abbreviated in German to *GaKiJu*).

In the German-speaking world, GACA has gone through many evolutionary processes in its conceptual development with ongoing effort towards a lived diversity. We have the protagonists to thank for "essential developmental steps towards an independent profession and theory formation alongside [and in connection with; K. S.] group analysis with adults" (Schneider, 2021, p. 16). In the meantime, GACA has become known in the international group-analytic space: in 2017 at the international symposium of the Group Analytic Society International (GASi) in Berlin, and in 2021 at the first international workshop of the GaKiJu working group, also in Berlin.

For this 16th workshop, the revised edition (by Ballhausen-Scharf, Lehle, Müller, Winzer) of the Guide to Competence Development in GACA was published (*Leitfaden zur Kompetenzentwicklung in der GaKiJu,* Arbeitsgemeinschaft GaKiJu, 2021). In the first contribution in the book – "Group-analytic work with children and adolescents. Insights into an unusual kind of further training" – *Birgitt Ballhausen-Scharf, Christoph F. Müller, Hans Georg Lehle,* and *Dietrich Winzer* provide a condensed summary and give insights into this revised edition of the Guide (curriculum) to Competence Development in GACA.

There is growing interest in professional exchange regarding GACA. In terms of professional policy, psychodynamic group therapy is anchored in the German health care system and has been included in the new professional development regulations as a mandatory component of ongoing training for child and adolescent psychotherapists and specialists in child and adolescent psychiatry and psychotherapy. In his contribution "Can cooperation models help to integrate psychodynamic group therapy with children and adolescents into institutional further training?", *Thomas Schneider* discusses the integration of psychodynamic group therapy in the current, professionally complex process of change in further training guidelines from a personal point of view.

---

2   Ilse Adami-Himmel, Birgitt Ballhausen-Scharf, Susan Herzog, Elisabeth Hofmann, Thomas Jung, Furi Khabirpour, Robert Mayerle, Christoph Müller, Gerhild Ohrnberger, Gerhard Rudnitzki, Thomas Schneider, Katrin Stumptner, Matthias Wenck, Ursula Wienberg, Dietrich Winzer.

3 The group and mental health

Since the beginning of the corona pandemic, the existential importance of the *group* as an important social learning and development space for children and adolescents has increasingly penetrated the awareness of those responsible in politics, culture, and society. Dealing with the phenomenon of the group in its social dimension more comprehensively and penetrating more of the complex interrelationships and the manifold dynamic effective factors are crucially important for group-analytic work with children, adolescents, and caregivers. People interact, move, and engage continuously in and between small, medium, and large groups, and within these "we" spaces they continuously form a sense of the ego feeling, thinking, and acting. According to Werner Knauss, "every human interaction can be understood on an unconscious level as a group interaction" (Knauss, 2006, p. 50). Inner conceptions of oneself as a member of a group, a society, are formed by early internalized relational and interactional experiences within the small group of the family and are supplemented, expanded, confirmed, and modified by further cultural-social experiences in communities such as kindergarten, kibbutz, school, village community, sports club, refugee camp, home, boarding school, asylum-seeker housing, etc. Basic experiences in the relational network of the family matrices[3] form the internalized field of tension, the dynamic matrix of predominantly unconscious experiences, in which the ego in the "we" continuously evolves and attempts to give its own meaning to life as a member of communities.

"Mental health", says the World Health Organization, "should be seen as a valued source of human capital or well-being in society. We all need good mental health to thrive, to care for ourselves, and to interact with others, so it is important not only to address the needs of people with defined mental disorders, but also to protect and promote the mental health of all people and to recognize its inherent value. Mental health and well-being are influenced not only by individual characteristics, but also by the social circumstances in which people find themselves and the environments in which they live. These determinants interact dynamically and can threaten or protect a person's mental state" (WHO, 2019).

The WHO's wording makes it clear that "mental health" is not a matter of course, but an important prerequisite and "source" for well-being and self-care

---

3   Family matrix refers to the transcultural-transgenerational-family communication and relationship fabric with all its habitually created rituals, socio-societal habits, language cultures, beliefs, traditional notions, etc.

in the responsible coexistence of a society. During the SARS-CoV-2 pandemic, we experienced what it means to be asked to limit our contacts in order to protect each other. This radical restriction in social togetherness provokes in various ways the need of us humans for connection, communication, and emotional exchange. The "mental health" of everyone in society, as a "source of well-being," is being put to the test in this pandemic, with children and adolescents particularly affected here. They find themselves constantly under attack in their sensitive developmental phases and needs due to the limitations on social contact.

Irrespective of the current pandemic situation, it is the responsibility of adults to create suitable framework conditions in the private and public-social environment in order to fulfill the duty of care for younger generations. Such framework conditions should be designed with the involvement of children and adolescents according to their age-related needs, "because they are the most important stakeholder group for decision-making processes and action concepts that affect their health and future" (WHO, 2020). It would be desirable to focus socio-political awareness more on "public spirit, that is, community spirit" (Foulkes, 1978, p. 28), "insofar as the attempt at resolution involves all those who are actually involved anyway," namely all people – children, adolescents, and adults.

4   Some of the ideas underpinning GACA

Children and adolescents are always looking for spaces of action in which they can engage in the confrontations necessary for their psychosexual development and share experiences with each other according to their age and psychological makeup. In this regard, cultural diversity influences and shapes their developing sense of self and ability to imagine possible roles in society. In the Western world, the emphasis is on individual development toward autonomy and self-reflection, and the focus is on discussion within the parent-child relationship. A notable aspect here is that social relationships and experiences at the sibling level and in peer groups are still given less attention in individual development. Yet these experiences play a significant role in overcoming developmental crises, acquiring social skills, and in the desire to communicate, become independent, engage, and participate. These levels are effective dynamic factors in pedagogical as well as therapeutic-group-analytical work with children and adolescents.

Group-analytical work with children and adolescents in both the pedagogical and the therapeutic context covers the entire range, from infancy to young adulthood. In GACA, caregivers are included in the dynamic work process according to the psychosexual development and age of the children, as well as the respective institutional conditions of the group work taking place. In the following contributions the work with three age groups – toddlers, school children, and adolescents – is presented in three different contextual settings and with three different conceptual-interdisciplinary approaches:

Anke Mühle, in her article "Parent-child groups with children under six years old", takes us into complex, interdisciplinary-interactional group work in a family counseling center.

Ursula Pröbsting, meanwhile, takes us into the institution of school with her text "The meaning of shame in the context of school groups". As the head of an elementary school, she describes the complex psychodynamics between the institution of school, the teacher, the child, and the parents with a group-analytical perspective.

And *Harald Weilnböck,* in "From Holocaust denial to personal family tableau", presents his concept of narrative conversation groups as an interdisciplinary application of group analysis, as intensive political education work in schools, as youth work, and as prevention of right-wing extremism.

***

If the framework of the social context is experienced as safe, a play space opens up for children and adolescents in which they begin to negotiate conflicts with and among one another. This leads to a fundamental element of GACA – *play*.

Playful communication, a universal, natural form of expressing oneself as already described by Winnicott (2006), is crucial in this regard. "[N]on-verbal signals and the precise observation of the social situation" (Keller, 2019, p. 114) play an important role here. Children, adolescents, and adults create a shared space of relationships and meaning according to their age in the simultaneity of "analogic and digital communication" (Watzlawick, 2021, p. 36).

In her article "On playing", *Dietlind Köhncke* examines the essential importance of play in the development of children. In doing so, she takes a close look at the facets, the complexity, and the effectiveness of play and reveals its inherent potential, including for group-analytic self-awareness in further training as a group analyst.

According to Winnicott, *play* enables maturation processes; it is an "expression of mental health and leads to group relationships" (Winnicott, 2006, p. 52). According to Brandes, those who play together create a "collective context" (Brandes, 2008, p. 124). As "actors," they form a network of diverse relationships in the simultaneity of rapidly changing communication in interaction between themselves and others. The group, he says, is a "complex phenomenon of simultaneity and interweaving of the social and the individual" (Brandes, 2008, p. 124). In his theoretical discourse, Brandes addresses the tension between individual and group and between developmental need and ability in the self-education process of children: "We are accustomed to talking about children's self-education from a pedagogical-constructivist perspective. In this context, the focus is on the individual child and his or her self-actively controlled learning process. If the social context of this learning is included and the importance of the children's group for learning processes is taken into account" (Brandes, 2008, p. 123), we can extend this perspective in a group-analytical understanding to self-education in and through groups.

Furi Kharbipour writes about the interweaving of dynamic effectiveness of complex world events in the microcosm of a group-analytic children's group with an accompanying parents' group. His contribution "Hansel and Gretel (a fairy tale by the Brothers Grimm)" includes a touching poem by Sa'di from "The Rose Garden": *"Human beings are body parts of each other…".*

Meanwhile, the contribution by *Christoph Radaj* – "When the Jubjub bird freezes everything around himself – Pain treatment with families in group psychotherapy with the use of digital media" focuses on the integration of digital media in group psychotherapy for young people with pain amplification syndrome (PAS). He explores the treatment setting of a group of children and the parent group sessions that run concurrently.

***

The *group leader* – as the above suggests – plays a significant role in group-analytic work with children and adolescents. As an adult, in a parental transference she assumes responsibility for the framework and the "dynamic administration" (Foulkes, 1992) and is responsible for all organizational matters in the course of the group process.

According to the *group-analytic approach,* the group leader participates observantly, looking on from the group boundary between inside and outside, and is responsible for maintaining communication in the group. She is an advisor, a co-player, and a translator according to the diversity of transmission within the group. The group leader witnesses destructive, shameful relational and interactional experiences without evaluating or judging. She repeatedly marks the boundaries between experiences of conflict and violence and protects the group as a whole, as well as each individual wherever there is destructive pressure to act. In an atmosphere of safety, reliability, and tolerance, conflicts can be negotiated between one another and empathies can be formed. As Foulkes writes, "the group situation in and of itself becomes a therapeutic," as well as pedagogical, "effective factor" (Foulkes, 1992, p. 105). The group becomes an exploratory space of play and training involving "I", "you", and "we" experiences. "Reality is not, after all, constructed by the individual in an irregular and arbitrary way; it is an agreement of communication" (Watzlawick, 2021, p. 24), in which affectively marked experiences of meaning are co-constructed, transformed, shared, shaped, and translated.

In their contribution "'Must I become a villain?' On the meaning of destruction in existential conflicts", *Anja Khalil* and *Carla Weber* lead us into an ever-threatened space of experiencing power and powerlessness and allow us to participate in the process with a group of children in the struggle for support and connection in the "we" context.

Franziska Schöpfer takes up the topic of existential confrontation in detachment processes using the example of an outpatient, analytic group with late adolescent women. In her contribution "A suicide fantasy. Confusion, speechlessness, and projective identification as defenses of tabooed topics in analytic group psychotherapy," she invites us to likewise participate in a tense group process in which phenomena of resistance and defense are negotiated in the group space and become accessible to language.

5 The dynamic network between the children's and the parents' groups

In our work with children and adolescents, we cannot avoid the caregivers, or rather we are dependent on always taking them into consideration too, and, as far as possible and reasonable, involving them in the process. Behr and Hearst emphasize the importance of support from caregivers in the work with their children: "As with other types of therapy in child and adolescent services, group therapy must be actively supported by parents and caregivers to be truly effective" (Behr and Hearst, 2009, p. 207).

In his contribution "Drudgery and duty or findings and freedom?! Reflections and experiences from a parents' group accompanying analytical children's group therapy", *Matthias Wenck* sheds light on both the group-analytic effective factors and the effectiveness of a parent group accompanying the children's group, which he leads together with his colleague Ursula Wienberg.

The group leader's view of and into the family matrix opens up a complex understanding of unconsciously acting family themes in the interaction and communication among the children and adolescents within the play and communication space of the group. Norbert Elias, who, as a sociologist working on the meaning of the individual and society, made a decisive contribution to the development of group analysis according to S. H. Foulkes, formulated that all interactions of people are "based on their unintentional interdependencies" (Elias, 2015, p. 45). In work with children and adolescents, access to this knowledge plays an important role in the ability to translate interactions as narratives of relational experiences that have so far operated in their context with caregivers but could not yet be understood.

Families, especially in their formative stages, are fragile entities. Becoming a parent releases long-ago memories of one's own childhood and reminds us again and again of "quasi unsatisfied needs and unresolved conflicts" (Schon, 1995, p. 111) with parental caregivers. In the confrontation and emerging conflict with their own children, unconscious, unresolved conflicts from their own childhood are often unintentionally negotiated. Children bring caregivers "to their limits, which now call for expansion" (Martens, 1989, p. 30). "It should be emphasized that these conflicts arise within the mother-father-child triangle and, if not resolved, arise again within such a triangle (namely, in the next generation) until one day they can be resolved within the triangle" (Schon, 1995, p. 112). What Schon dubbed the "triangle" can be equated with the family matrix, the transgenerationally effective network of relationships and communication within which each actor depends on the continuously shared resonance exchange for the development of self-perception and identity (or identities).

Children react according to the mental overload of their caregivers and often stand out in the extended social spaces (daycare center, school, etc.) due to disruptive behavior or significant withdrawal. The mental overload of the fragile family matrix and their resulting emotional neediness are shifted to corresponding side scenes. In severe emergencies, such as mental illness, life-threatening disease, separation and flight experiences, or in the face of death, caregivers are emotionally overwhelmed to the highest degree. The affective-regulating protective space within the community, which is significant for children (Dornes, 2004), loses reliability in its function of providing emotional support. The *family vessel* becomes full of holes. In the case of long-term crises and traumatic events, depending on the age of the children and their cognitive-emotional maturity, these stresses lead to behavioral problems, psychological, psychosomatic as well as somatic disorders and illnesses such as eating problems, wetting the bed, sleep disorders, silence, absence from school, self-injuries, suicidal crises, and others. Support from *external,* professionally reliable help in connection with an accompanying *group-analytic intervention* in an outpatient or institutional context can be of existential importance if one is to be able to translate the messages of the worrying behavior of the children and adolescents diagnosed as psychosomatic illness.

S. H. Foulkes (1992) understands illness to be a communication disturbance in the network of relationships. In her article "Ins Auge fassen – Deutsche Wurzeln der Gruppenanalyse" ("In the mind's eye – German roots of group analysis"), Dietlind Köhncke (1991, p. 3 f.) likewise presents the historical perspective of this attitude thus: Inspired by his experience as a resident in the neurological clinic of Kurt Goldstein in Berlin, S. H. Foulkes developed his thoughts on group-analytic theory. Goldstein concluded, based on his study of patients with brain injuries, that the individual neuron in the central nervous system is part of a communication system and responds only in the context of that system. The healthy organism always responds to a stimulus as a whole. Only where the organism is damaged does the reaction of a single isolated part occur. Goldstein understood disease as a communication disturbance in the organism. Foulkes adopts these ideas and transfers them to the interdependence of social relations. In his developed theory for group analysis, "the group becomes a holistic organism: If a free exchange between all members takes place in the healthy social organism, the sick organism shows the symptom of isolation" (Köhncke, 1991, p. 4).

It is against this background, then, that Foulkes introduces the notion of the *matrix* and thus makes the link to the group as a self-functioning organism of communication and connection. He writes: "The matrix is the hypothetical fabric of communication and relationships in a given group. It is the basis that ultimately determines the meaning and significance of all events and upon which all communications, whether verbal or nonverbal, are based" (Foulkes, 1992, p. 33).

In his article "Children's group for primary school children – group analysis in a family and educational counseling center under Protestant sponsorship", *Horst Wenzel* describes in excerpts a group process with elementary school children and the parallel group of caregivers in a group-analytical setting.

In his contribution "Group analysis in child and adolescent psychiatry – experience and significance", *Andreas Opitz* presents the dynamic interaction, within the institution of psychiatry, of the multi-professional team, the therapy group, and his position as head of the adolescent group, offering insight into the group process in a day clinic.

Tilman Sprondel's contribution "Group-analytical approach in inpatient educational support" deals with the close and multi-layered interconnections of the dynamic relationship work of youth groups and team groups on the basis of practical examples.

And in her contribution "The rhythmized-triadic setting", *Katrin Stumptner* introduces the complexity of a setting as a group-analytical effective factor in the detachment process between adolescents and caregivers. The background to this model comes from many years of experience with outpatient groups and the knowledge that detachment is only possible where there is first a feeling of connection.

In groups, children, adolescents, and caregivers can have the liberating experience of a "resumption of relationship" and thereby experience a "re-establishment of the imaginary space in between" (Köhncke, 1997, p. 121). In the artificially established network of relational and communicative experiences, "what was experienced as destructive" and is currently being felt can "become productive" (Köhncke, 1997, p. 121) and, in the best case, can be mentalized, processed, tested, and better understood in the developing dynamic matrix of the group. The transfer of "old interaction patterns to the current situation" (Köhncke, 1997, p. 120) of the group is modulated by unexpected mirror and resonance reactions. It enables the participants to develop changed ideas of themselves in relation to others in the group and to recognize their own active role within it more self-confidently. In the back and forth between the levels of "I am", "You are", "We are", an inner dance begins in the negotiation space of communication within the group. Conflicts and questions about what connects and what separates, about belonging in the diversity of identities, emerge again and again. The continuous self-awareness in the perspective and the exchange with others transforms the "I am" into the "we are" in an affecting way. According to Liesel Hearst, in and after the processing of cultural memories, there emerges a unique individuality that can be recognized and shared by all, along with a sense of belonging to the community, "whatever the different cultures from which the individual may come. That which is common, it seems to me, has its roots in early childhood, [...] which, however different its social and cultural manifestations may have been, consists of the same ingredients (or lack thereof): empathy, trust, continuity, constancy in 'holding', and a non-pressuring nurturing environment. These are the fundamental basal, unavoidable, and entirely universal needs of a child, regardless of cultural heritage. The way they were handled [in the respective cultural community; K. S.] in childhood influences the core of individuality. This core is at once individual and universal and therefore recognizable and shareable by all" (Hearst, 1998, p. 45). In this vein, the final three articles in this volume deal with ruptures in self-experience and the experience of belonging:

In her text "What's it like to arrive in Germany? Group-analytical experiences with unaccompanied refugee minors", *Gerhild Ohrnberger* leads us into a complex group process taking place in a psychiatric practice. Like a string instrument, she picks up the vibrations of the young people who speak in the languages of their families of origin and whose words she, as a group analyst, only understands in substance through the simultaneous interpreting performed by her colleague.

Another contextual perspective is formulated by *Kadir Kaynak* in his contribution "Psychotherapy and psychoanalysis in the counseling center". In his report, he elaborates the necessity and importance of a multi-professional, intercultural team at the counseling center in the intercultural society of a Berlin neighborhood and gives us insights into the dynamic complexity of understanding using practical examples.

Beate Schnabel, meanwhile, contributes "Opening of transcultural spaces in group-analytical processes with refugees", in which she approaches the requirements of transcultural processes from a theoretical perspective and concretizes the complexity of transcultural understanding in a differentiated and empathetic way on the basis of a group process with young refugees.

***

In all the contributions in this book, a central factor in group analysis is the *trust* of the group leader *in the group.* A sufficiently self-explored and stable group introject by the group leader opens up the professional ability to engage in group processes as a co-player and to reliably maintain the boundaries between inside and outside. It is "a balance between minimal structuring and appropriate leadership presence within a setting that provides support and security with clearly defined rules and agreements" (Lehle, 2018, p. 147) that enables participants to establish a connection to the "we" and to discover and train the ego within it.

Bibliography

Arbeitsgemeinschaft Gruppenanalyse mit Kindern und Jugendlichen (Hrsg.) (2021). *Gruppenanalyse mit Kindern und Jugendlichen – Ein Leitfaden zur Kompetenzentwicklung.* Göttingen: Vandenhoeck & Ruprecht

Behr, H., Hearst, L. (2009). *Gruppenanalytische Psychotherapie. Menschen begegnen sich.* Eschborn: Verlag Dietmar Klotz

Brandes, H. (2008). *Selbstbildung in Kindergruppen. Die Konstruktion sozialer Beziehungen.* München: Ernst Reinhardt

Dornes, M. (2004). Über Mentalisierung, Affektregulierung und Entwicklung des Selbst. *Forum der Psychoanalyse,* 20 (2): 175–99

Elias, N. (2015). Soziologie und Psychiatrie. *Gruppenpsychotherapie und Gruppendynamik – Zeitschrift für Theorie und Praxis der Gruppenanalyse,* 51 (1): 28–45

Foulkes, S. H. (1978). *Praxis der gruppenanalytischen Psychotherapie*. München/Basel: Reinhardt

Foulkes, S. H. (1992). *Gruppenanalytische Psychotherapie*. Mit einem Nachwort von Georg R. Gfäller. München: Pfeiffer.

Hearst, L. (1998). Der Wandel unseres historischen und kulturellen Erbes in der Gruppenanalyse. *Luzifer – Amor,* 11 (21): 30–47

Keller, H. (2019). *Mythos Bindungstheorie. Konzept-Methode-Bilanz.* Weimar: Verlag das Netz

Knauss, W. (2005). Die Gruppe im Unbewußten – eine Brücke zwischen Individuum und Gesellschaft. *Jahrbuch für Gruppenanalyse,* 11: 49–58

Köhncke, D. (1991). Ins Auge fassen – Deutsche Wurzeln der Gruppenanalyse. *Gruppenanalyse – Zeitschrift für gruppenanalytische Psychotherapie, Beratung und Supervision,* 2 (1): 1–20

Köhncke, D. (1997). Die Gruppe als Möglichkeitsraum. Gedanken zur Kreativität des therapeutischen Prozesses. *Gruppenanalyse – Zeitschrift für gruppenanalytische Psychotherapie, Beratung und Supervision,* 7 (2): 103–127

Lehle, H. G. (2018). *Freiräume des Spiels. Psychoanalytische Gruppentherapie mit Kindern und Jugendlichen.* Frankfurt/M.: Brandes & Apsel

Martens, G. (1989). *Auch Eltern waren Kinder. Ursache und Lösungen von Konflikten in der Familie.* Frankfurt/M.: Kösel

Schneider, T. (2021). Wurzeln der Kinder- und Jugendlichengruppenanalyse. *Gruppenanalyse – Zeitschrift für gruppenanalytische Psychotherapie, Beratung und Supervision,* 21 (1): 61–83

Schon, L. (1995). *Entwicklung des Beziehungsdreiecks Vater-Mutter-Kind. Triangulierung als lebenslanger Prozess.* Stuttgart: Kohlhammer

Stumptner, K. (2019). Ohne Verbindung keine Entwicklung. Gruppenanalyse mit Kindern, Jugendlichen und Bezugspersonen – Ein institutsübergreifender und transgenerationaler Entwicklungsprozess. In C. Seidler, K. Albert, K. Husemann, K. Stumptner (Hrsg.), *Berliner Gruppenanalyse. Geschichte – Theorie –Praxis* (S. 231–46). Gießen: Psychosozial

Waldenfels, B. (1997). *Studien zur Phänomenologie des Fremden. Teil I. Topographie des Fremden.* Frankfurt/M.: Suhrkamp

Watzlawick, P. (2021). *100 Jahre Paul Watzlawick.* Compiled by J. Röhner and A. Schütz. Bern: Hogrefe

WHO (2019). Faktenblatt – Psychische Gesundheit. https://www.euro.who.int/de/media-centre/sections/fact-sheets/2019/fact-sheet-mental-health-2019 (last accessed March 29, 2022)

WHO (2020). *Eine kindergerechte Zukunft – Veröffentlichung eines neuen Berichts der WHO-UNICEF-Lancet-Kommission.* https://www.euro.who.int/de/health-topics/Life-stages/child-and-adolescent-health/news/news/2020/2/a-future-fit-for-children-whouniceflancet-commission-launches-new-report (last accessed March 29, 2022)

Winnicott, D. W. (1989). *Playing and Reality.* London: Routledge

Conceptual Developments and Vocational Policy Trends in Group Analysis for Children and Young People in Germany, Austria, and Switzerland

Group-analytical Work with Children and Adolescents: Insights into an Unusual Kind of Advanced Training

Birgitt Ballhausen-Scharf, Christoph F. Müller,
Hans Georg Lehle, Dietrich Winzer

1 Preliminary remarks

As the group of authors of the revised new edition[1], we would like to provide insights into unusual forms of advanced training for group-analytical work with children and adolescents. The concept for this was developed by the Working Group for Group Analysis with Children and Adolescents (*Arbeitsgemeinschaft Gruppenanalyse mit Kindern und Jugendlichen e.V.,* GaKiJu) and has now been presented in a revised version. So what is unusual about this training? It is the way it was developed and the way it can be acquired, namely in a communicative and constantly reflected group process.

With our contribution, we would like to arouse interest in group-analytical work with children and adolescents, in its potential and in the variety of possible applications it has in pedagogical, preventive, and therapeutic professional fields. And we would like to get you excited about acquiring the necessary competencies for this demanding and complex task within a group training course based on our guide.

In the new edition of the "guide" (Arbeitsgemeinschaft Gruppenanalyse mit Kindern und Jugendlichen, 2021), we have dispensed with the misleading designation "curriculum" of the first edition of 2014. This is because we do not see our "guide" as a textbook, but rather as a jointly written "cookbook" that can arouse curiosity about experiences of "cooking" and "eating" together. For us, the team of authors, it has been both an individual and a shared experience as a group, about which we have had a constant and lively exchange. The form and essence of this exchange are essential elements of our guidelines.

---

1 Arbeitsgemeinschaft Gruppenanalyse mit Kindern und Jugendlichen (Hrsg.) (2021). Gruppenanalyse mit Kindern und Jugendlichen. Ein Leitfaden zur Kompetenzentwicklung. (Group analysis with children and adolescents. A guide to competence development.) Göttingen: Vandenhoeck & Ruprecht.

In the first part, we would like to give an insight into the formation process of turning the "guide" into the workshop, so to speak. To begin with, we will explain what motivated the first group of authors to develop the "curriculum", what findings and questions we started from at that time, and how we as a group arrived at our findings. We will then take a look at the workshop process whereby the group of authors completely revised the "curriculum", which was intended as a "work in progress" for the new edition now available.

In the second part, we would like to take a closer look at the third main chapter of our "guide": the chapter in which we describe and explain special competencies which, based on our experience, are essential for group-analytical work with children and adolescents.

In the final section, we revisit the didactic tips for teaching theory presented in a condensed form in the "guide" and elaborate on them a little further for this article.

2   Development process of the guide

At the outset, we came together as group analysts with a wide range of experience in leading children and adolescent groups. From November 2006 onwards we met regularly, initially in a kind of pathfinding group with changing compositions, until finally 13 colleagues agreed on the setting of a closed working group.

Our working group included members of six German-speaking group-analytical institutes, which at that time offered advanced training for adult group therapy only. The special nature of leading group analysis for children and adolescent groups in the pedagogical and therapeutic field was not represented there.[2] At the same time, we identified a great need to acquire leadership skills for

---

2   This finding prompted us to ask: Why was there no advanced training concept for group analysis with children and adolescents? One reason for this might be that classic group analysis has relied too much on the spoken word and the chair circle model. Child and adolescent psychotherapists know about the importance of playful, creative, and body-related dialogues in action language when working with children and adolescents and missed this in traditional group-analytical training.
In addition, we asked ourselves: Why was group analysis, despite being partly rooted in sociology (e.g., Elias, 1976), narrowed in the German group-analytical training institutes to the field of psychotherapy? And why, for example, have (social) pedagogical perspectives been largely ignored? Our hypothesis: The German institutes for further education were oriented towards the increased demand from medical and psychological psychotherapists, since group therapy was recognised as a health insurance benefit. The inhomogeneous group of (social) educators has no common professional community of interest. Applied group analysis is not yet present there as an area with potential.

child and adolescent groups in educational and therapeutic fields of work. Fortunately, some members of our working group possessed such relevant experience.

In 1988, James H. Bamber wrote an article in "Group Analysis" about the fact that there were hardly any reports on group analysis with children and adolescents in this journal. He asked the question: Are group analysts afraid to work with groups of children and adolescents, or are they afraid to write about it? His answer was that working with children and adolescents in group analysis is by no means easy and indeed more difficult to handle than working with adults. That is why working with children and adolescents should unreservedly be part of further education programs in group analysis. There should be additional training, as those who have only gained experience with adult groups are "ill-equipped" for group-analytical work with children and adolescents.

According to the research of our working group at that time, there was no stand-alone theoretical concept and no description of the special attitudes and positions for group-analytical work with children and adolescents until then. The group analyst Malcom Pines from London, a member of the Group Analytical Society (GAS), replied to our enquiry in this regard, saying, "You are pioneers!"

The institutes in Heidelberg and Berlin were open to educators and child and adolescent psychotherapists who were interested in advanced training in group analysis, but they did not offer independent self-experience or a special theoretical program on group analysis with children and adolescents. The institutes then began to set up joint supervision groups for leaders of child and adolescent groups.

From the experiences of these supervision groups, two projects emerged: from 2005 onwards, annual workshops in which the practice of the participants was the focus; and – one year later – our working group, which aimed to distil the special features of children's group analysis work from practical experience. This group met every six months, motivated by the idea of creating specific advanced training opportunities for work with groups of children and adolescents and of developing a curriculum for child and adolescent group analysis.

2.1 Processual development

Working in a group-analytical way as a group facilitates the contribution of the individual's very own experiential knowledge into the group in a stimulating environment, while also taking in the experiences of others. And this takes place in a playful creative exchange between participants, so that something new and shared emerges, which in turn can be made available to others for their own insights or professionalization processes. Following controversial discussion but with majority agreement, audio recordings were made of our bi-annual meetings, which two of us discussed between meetings in the context of participant observation. The findings were brought back to the group for joint reflection at the next meeting, and in this way the whole working group gradually became familiar with constantly reflecting on its own dynamic communication process. We learned to perceive seemingly incidental events, atmospheric factors, tensions, and exhilarating, playful, and suddenly enlightening moments that were deemed important for our process and which had mostly not been recorded in the protocols focused on results.

First, we collected and discussed field reports from the pioneers of children's group therapy (including Samuel Slavson, 1972; E. J. Anthony, 1984; Haim G. Ginott, 1966) as well as field reports of children's groups from German group-analytical institutes, in which (socio-) pedagogical perspectives were also taken into account (e. g., Monika Moll, 1997; Holger Brandes, 2008). In an open and non-judgmental way we then began to share and tap into our own experiences and ideas about the complex, difficult to grasp, and at times even chaotic happenings in the children's groups we led ourselves. We experienced our working group process at every meeting as both stimulating and exciting. Since our administrative leadership provided only the time and space framework, we developed our own working structure in self-organization. Initially, most of us assumed that we would need much less time to achieve our goal. We therefore first developed a concept in the sense of a modular advanced training course: The child and adolescent psychotherapists were to be taught "the group-analytical", approach while the adult group analysts would learn about the conditions and needs of the different age groups of children and adolescents. We soon realized that it is not enough to add theory to the training canon of group analysis for adults in order to sufficient equip analysts to work with groups of children and adolescents.

As a working group, we then got into an emotionally much more tense, sometimes also very conflictual group process with a regressive retreat to individualized positions. We experienced polarizing processes in our group, sought to understand them, and came to the realization that we were experiencing "firsthand" the themes and dynamics of the groups of children or young people we were working with. In retrospect and on reflection we became aware of what had taken place or had been reenacted in our working group, as if in a resonance chamber. This enabled us to find our way out of a regressive process and back into a progressive working mode. What we had experienced we now tried to express in words and to transfer into a new concept of further education. In children's and adolescents' groups, communication takes place primarily – depending on the respective developmental age – on a physical-sensory level, in free play and action. With this experience, we became aware that leading these groups requires special competencies in order to keep the necessary play and development spaces open and protected. This becomes particularly clear in the case of destructively operating group communication (see Wenck and Wienberg, 2012).

In our working group process we had experiences that contributed to the development of our own professionalism. "This became not self-experience in the working group, but group experience in the service of expanding our professional selves" (Rudnitzki, 2012, p. 56). We finally formulated our experiences into a guide for the learning and competence-building process we were aiming for: Theory was to be linked to practice in such a way that both could be experienced with all the senses and thus more easily absorbed into the group-analytical stance.

Based on these experiences, we have come to the conclusion: The advanced training to lead groups of children and young people should be facilitated as an open process. This can be done by the training center providing the framework in which insights can take place through group processes. We see reflection on the experiences the participants have in the advanced training with each other as a decisive part of the professionalization process.

In revising the text of the first edition of the "curriculum", we as a group of four authors again entered into a joint playful-creative working process. What was significant about our group composition was that two of us had already experienced the first working group process, while the other two had not. This created the need to keep recalling the experiences of the previous working group process, which cannot be conveyed through reading the curriculum alone. Telling and visualizing these scenic memories opened up a new, shared space of association and thinking for us. In it, we discovered new meanings and contexts. Instead of using them hastily in a results-oriented way, we tried to understand them more deeply in a process of communication that was kept open. With a combination of playfulness and reflective amazement, curiosity, and the question "What are we actually doing right now?" emerged a process of approaching the text and its new creation.

3 Specific leadership competencies

In the second part, we would like to take a closer look at the three components of group-analytical leadership skills, which we have described in our guide as "specific extensions of group analysis when working with children and young people": play and playing, working with reference persons in a separate group, and pair leadership. Even though we can deal with each of these three components in their own sub-chapters – i.e., only separately – we experience how much the interaction of all three components expands and enriches the play and development spaces of the group and its members.

3.1 The free play in the group: playing and play ability of the group leadership

Children's groups, but also youth groups, are characterized by the fact that free play productions and action discourses dominate here compared to the verbal-linguistic communication flow of adult groups. In the group, free play enables a lively, creative, and physical-sensory togetherness, which opens up personal development opportunities for the individual as well as the group. In order to maintain a reliably protected framework, which is an indispensable condition for the possibility of free play, children are particularly dependent on a group leader who has specific competencies in understanding and dealing with developmentally appropriate play.

The theme of play runs through the development of group-analytical competence like a constantly recurring motif. We already understand the group-analytical process – as well as that of the further education group – as circular "playing" that develops the individual as well as the group as a whole, (Arbeitsgemeinschaft Gruppenanalyse mit Kindern und Jugendlichen, 2021, p. 46). In the self-experience group, additional modes of expression of the unconscious are to be experienced in the free, playful interaction with body, sound, rhythm, voice, image, language, etc. This makes it possible to "bring affective experiences on all psychophysical sensory levels 'into play' again and again" (p. 20).

> "Sensitization to one's own ability to play enables the participants in the training group not only to better perceive the needs and expressions of children and adolescents, of infants and toddlers with their parents, but also to understand them as playful group communication and to respond by playing along. Reflecting on this experience enables the group leader to comment

on the respective play processes in a development-oriented way and thus to promote the age-appropriate resources of the group" (p. 20).

In the advanced training of analytical child and adolescent psychotherapists, self-experience (which is about developing the ability to play [along] as a leadership skill), is called "profession-specific". In our "guide" we have adopted this term in the chapter "Self-experience", but we want to relate it to group-analytical work. The elements of profession-specific self-experience in children's group analysis can also enrich group work with adolescents and adults. We therefore advocate the inclusion of sensitization for one's own ability to play as well as the opening and holding of protected spaces for play as part of the self-experience within group-analytical advanced training.

3.2 Group work with parents and caregivers

We recommend – based on our experience – that work with parents and reference persons should also be organized within a group context, due to the vast potential offered by the parallel parents' group in the group-analytical work with children and young people. Parents and caregivers bring concerns about their children to the group. There, they experience compassion and sympathy on an emotional level. For the parents, who often come to the group with feelings of guilt and shame, the communicative exchange opens up new perspectives, which makes relief possible. A decisive experience for parents is to discover how important their role is for the development process of their children, how effective they are as parents, and how much the group and the group leadership support them in remaining responsible for their children and not delegating this responsibility to others.

It is always amazing to observe how much parents, once they have gained trust, benefit from the parents' group and feel encouraged to open up further developmental spaces and insights for themselves and their children. For example, a mother in a parents' group remarked that they were talking about themselves here and not at all about their children, to which the father of another child replied that the secret reason for their children's therapy was probably that they, the parents, were communicating with each other here. A further example of successful parent group work is those parents who – after many years of doing such work – "like to look at each other with pleasure again". Gerhard Rudnitzki puts it in a nutshell when he says: The more and earlier parents show their children "that they love not only them but also each other, the sooner the children learn to form themselves towards other people" (Rudnitzki, 2012).

Intensive interactions, reflections, and resonances take place between the process of the children's and adolescents' group and that of the parallel caregiver group, which can be perceived, named, and used for the developmental processes in both groups through joint leadership. Both groups thus experience an expansion of their developmental space.

For the parallel caregiver group, it is important that the group's facilitator allows it to have its own group process with a clear setting in which the participants are invited to bring in everything that is currently on their minds. The group leader therefore does not pass on information from the children's group to the caregiver group, but uses the resonance in the parent group triggered by the dynamics of the children's group for their own process; because the conflicts staged by the children are often rooted in the relationship dynamics of their families. It relieves the children when the parents recognize this and work through their conflicts in their own group, which in turn strengthens parental competence.

In order to be able to promote the processes of interaction between the two groups, a specific group-analytical attitude is needed, which is developed primarily through one's own personal experience of being held in the advanced training group and later in the supervision group. The attitude of the group leader and their special competence enables the parents to develop their own competence with the model, so to speak. Among other things, this means sensitively perceiving the unspoken signs with which their children signal needs for dependence and autonomy, but also mature abilities, and gaining confidence in their self-development potential.

3.3 Pair leadership[3]

The concept of "pair leadership" is the third distinctive feature for group-analytical work with children and adolescents. In this section we would like to take a closer look at this component of extended skills and in doing so address the advantages and challenges of pair leadership as well as possible objections.

In educational contexts, pair leadership is usually a long-established matter of course, as it is in inpatient group psychotherapy.[4] Members of the working group who developed the "curriculum" had mostly not experienced pair lead-

---

[3] We understand pair leadership as equal leadership by two people, as opposed to co-leadership, which can also be understood hierarchically.

[4] This may be due to structural reasons as well as reasons of content, because in these fields of work the management of two people is usually institutionally provided for and financed. In contrast, psychotherapists in private practice work independently in the outpatient sector,

ership in their group-analytical training, which is why they also led their own teaching groups alone. Only in a few institutes were co-led teaching groups even possible.

As a working group, we first developed the concept of pair leadership for children and youth groups. Some members started working with a colleague to pioneer pair leadership of a children's and adolescents' group and to present their experiences in our working group and in the annual workshops. In addition, they set up parent groups and also led them as a pair. Their experiences encouraged other members of our working group to lead their own children's and parents' groups in pairs as well. The enrichment for the leaders and their groups was so convincing that we have anchored pair leadership conceptually in our training. Even though many of us continued to lead our groups alone for various reasons, we were all convinced by the pair leadership model.

In our guide, we have described in detail the potential of pair leadership of the children's and parents' groups. Here we would like to highlight some aspects that are important for us once again.

Our pair leadership model is not biologically based, but corresponds to the diversity of partnership models increasingly lived today. Whether the leadership couple is same-sex, different-sex, or diverse-sex triggers different fantasies and reactions in the group that need to be reflected upon.

The transference and counter-transference events of the group are reflected in the relationship of the leader pair and can be better grasped, reflected on, and thus made usable. The possibility to perceive enactments in the groups from two perspectives, to reflect on them, to understand the corresponding emotions and contain them, is a great relief for the leaders. In addition, the leader pair can exchange experiences already during the group session as well as immediately after the group. The members of the group can deal with their particular, often intensely experienced wishes and fears with different leaders, i.e., they can divide contradictory transference aspects between two people and possibly experience that in the group the leader pair responds to this offer of a relationship differently to what they have experienced in their original family.

The complexity of the dynamic, communicative events in the groups of children, both between the group members themselves and between the children and the leader pair, is a particular challenge for the perceptual capacity of the

---

and a second leader has been difficult to finance. (This is currently changing, not least due to the professional commitment of the Working Group for Group Analysis with Children and Adolescents).

group leadership, which is regularly pushed to its limits as a result. This creates fear of not understanding, which is difficult to endure, and there is a danger that the leaders will reduce the complexity of what is happening through their unconscious defense. The presence of another leader reduces this fear or at least makes it more bearable.

Pair leadership requires the willingness to invest sufficient time for one's own relational work in the form of debriefing and joint supervision in a group. It is helpful to understand conflicts and tensions that arise in the relationship of the leader pair primarily in the context of the current transference events of the group. It is problematic when personally motivated rivalry and power conflicts become rampant in the relationship of the leader pair – despite supervision – and the leaders are therefore no longer able to contain the affects of the group as a result.

A leader pair faces the same challenges as a couple in reality: They also need to develop mutual trust, get to know each other's strengths and weaknesses by telling each other their personal stories – and, above all, they need to maintain respect for each other even under the greatest stress. Using the model of successful communication of the leader pair, group members learn respect for the otherness of the other.

4 Content and method of group-analytical theory teaching

Finally, we would like to come back to an elementary aspect of our further education concept: the linking of theory and practice in a group-analytical process. In the "guide" we write about this:

> "The teaching of theory should be understood as a group-analytical process (Hutz, 2008). In this process, the theory taught is linked to the practical experiences from the training participants' fields of work. The contents are therefore taught in a group context, if possible using case studies from the respective professional fields." (Arbeitsgemeinschaft Gruppenanalyse mit Kindern und Jugendlichen, 2021, p. 17)

We would like to take a closer look at this group-analytical process of conveying theoretical content. The group-analytical training method is one of open and equal communication between the participants in a training group and their leaders. Theoretical topics are adapted to the previous experiences of the participants from their different professional fields and thus promote their interest. The leaders offer the theoretical topics and open up a protected space of play and experience for the group to react to them with their own experiences. In this way, the topics presented can be experienced and made accessible in a stimulating way.

Against the background of one's own partly unconscious experiential knowledge, the participants experience emotional, physical, and cognitive resonances in the group that they need to perceive, name, and reflect on together. In the training group, theoretical contents are communicated in an experiential and practical way and can thus be helpful in one's own work context.

The leaders' task is to see the reference to the theme in the group's free associations, to name it, and to examine it together with the group. In doing so, the facilitator also takes into account his or her own sensitivities and resonance with the dynamics of the group and makes them available to the group selectively and in an appropriate form as belonging to the theme. In this way, the leaders' countertransference feelings become an "instrument of cognition" (Devereux, 1984).

The training group thus offers the possibility to acquire in an exemplary and experience-based way not only the theoretical content but also the method of mediation itself. In this sense, writes Pieter Hutz, we want to "use the mediation process itself for experiencing, understanding, and applying the group-analytical method" (Hutz, 2008, p. 82). The example of the mediation process is also used for direct experience of the group-analytical stance of the leadership and enables the group members to identify with this leadership model.

The facilitators bring the individual participants into conversation with each other. The tentative initial contributions are protected and promoted, thus encouraging those who have been silent hitherto to express themselves. The leader orchestrates the unfolding of the communicative development space of the group, and how he or she emphasizes some things and downplays others is significant for the quality of the polyphonic experience process (Maschwitz, Müller, and Waldhoff, 2009).

With such an interweaving of theory and practice, it is obvious that participants in further education repeatedly bring to bear personal, biographical experiences and cross the boundaries to self-experience. Group leaders should show empathy for this and at the same time point out that a specially protected space, the self-experience group, is more appropriate and more helpful. Group leaders should benevolently mark the boundary line – in the sense of providing support and protection – because a training group should not be overburdened with personal issues, especially since there are ongoing spaces for self-experience in the training.

The leadership tasks of advanced education groups are diverse and demanding and represent a real challenge. This can best be met by a pair of leaders, as favored in our leadership concept. They have an additional instrument at their disposal: their own communicative relationship! This can be reflected and maintained in the extended framework of a supervision group.

Bibliography

Anthony, E. J. (1984). Group analytical psychotherapy with children and adolescents. In S. H. Foulkes (ed.), *Group psychotherapy: The psychoanalytic approach* (pp. 186–232). London: Maresfield

Arbeitsgemeinschaft Gruppenanalyse mit Kindern und Jugendlichen (Hrsg.) (2021). *Gruppenanalyse mit Kindern und Jugendlichen. Ein Leitfaden zur Kompetenzentwicklung.* Göttingen: Vandenhoeck & Ruprecht

Bamber, J. H. (1988). Group analysis with children and adolescents. *Group Analysis,* 21 (2): 99–102

Brandes, H. (2008). Selbstbildungsprozesse von und in Kindergruppen. *Gruppenpsychotherapie und Gruppendynamik – Zeitschrift für Theorie und Praxis der Gruppenanalyse,* 44 (1): 33–51

Devereux, G. (1984). *Angst und Methode in den Verhaltenswissenschaften.* Frankfurt/M.: Suhrkamp

Elias, N. (1976). *The Civilizing Process. The Development of Manners.* Transl. by E. Jephcott. Urizen Books: New York

Ginott, H. G. (1966). *Gruppenpsychotherapie mit Kindern. Theorie und Praxis der Spieltherapie.* Weinheim: Beltz

Hutz, P. (2008). Praxis der gruppenanalytischen Theorie- und Fallarbeit im Seminar. *Gruppenanalyse – Zeitschrift für gruppenanalytische Psychotherapie, Beratung und Supervision,* 18 (1): 82–85

Maschwitz, R., Müller, C. F., Waldhoff, H.-P. (2009). *Die Kunst der Mehrstimmigkeit. Gruppenanalyse als Modell für die Zivilisierung von Konflikten.* Gießen: Psychosozial

Moll, M. (1997). Thesen zur gruppenanalytischen Arbeit mit Kindern. *Arbeitshefte Gruppenanalyse,* 2, 22–31

Rudnitzki, G. (2012). Vom Werden in Entwicklungsräumen – Über das Wachsen kinder- und jugendgruppenanalytischer Kompetenz. Unpublished co-lecture at the 8th Casuistic Workshop for Group Analysis for Children and Young People, September 2012 at the IGA Heidelberg

Slavson, S. R. (1972). *Einführung in die Gruppentherapie von Kindern und Jugendlichen* (2nd ed.). Göttingen: Vandenhoeck & Ruprecht

Wenck, M., Wienberg, U. (2012). Zerstörung tut Not?! Das Zulassen von Destruktivität in der Kindergruppe ermöglicht unverzichtbare Entwicklungsräume. Beispiele aus einer laufenden Kindergruppe mit paralleler Elterngruppe. Unpublished opening lecture at the 8th Casuistic Workshop for Group Analysis for Children and Young People, September 2012 at the IGA Heidelberg

Can Cooperation Models Help to Integrate Psychodynamic Group Therapy with Children and Adolescents into Institutional Further Training? An Experience-based Report

Thomas Schneider

1 Introduction

Before 1999, psychotherapy was considered merely an additional qualification for medical colleagues.[1] Furthermore, group psychotherapy "has still not been recognized as an independent therapeutic method under social legislation" (Küster, 2021, p. 8). We currently refer to it as psychodynamic group psychotherapy, as a distinction between depth psychology-based and group-analytical psychotherapy cannot be scientifically justified (cf. Küster, 2021, p. 8). In the Psychotherapist Act passed in 1999, group therapy was deemed dispensable because it had completely disappeared from the text of the law.[2] With the new psychotherapy degree program, future graduates will be treated similarly to medical professionals. They will join our training institutes, teaching prac-

---

[1] "The delegating physician was the contractual partner of the health insurance company and delegated, if needed, psychotherapy to a psychological psychotherapist or child and adolescent psychotherapist, who had no direct legal relationship with the statutory health insurance. The physician decided whether and how much of the fee he retained for himself." This conflicted "reimbursement process is replaced by the Psychotherapist Act of 1999" (Küster, 2021, p. 7).

[2] One year before the European Group Analytic Training Network (EGATIN) was formed, there was a significant decrease in billed services for group therapy in 1988. From 1980 to 1992, 400 group therapy studies with thirty different patient populations were published, with behavioral therapies being five times more common than others. After the reunification of Germany in 1990, members of the German working group for intended dynamic group therapy and representatives of group therapy as developed in the former GDR were discredited due to their collaboration with the GDR's State Security. The process of addressing this history could only begin with the establishment of the Berlin Institute for Group Psychotherapy (*Berliner Institut für Gruppenanalyse e.V.*, BIG), where many members of this orientation found a new home and, above all, appreciation for their experience and theory development. Only in 2011 did the promotion of group psychotherapy for improving healthcare provision and potential cost savings for health insurance companies return to health policy with the new coalition agreement. In 2017, a unique revaluation of group psychotherapy began, culminating in the new Model Specialty Training Regulations (MWBO) of 2020 (Schneider, 2020–21, p. 7).

tices, and clinics at the end of their studies as licensed colleagues, authorized to conduct psychotherapy in both individual and group settings.

In the history of group analysis, it is striking that there was an upswing in the field whenever there were more patients to be treated as a consequence of war, but practitioners were not available in greater numbers or were not to be financed by those politically responsible. For instance, in 1940 Bion began treating traumatized soldiers at the military hospital in Northfield. Foulkes also started treating soldiers and war-traumatized civilians there and in his private practice in Exeter. In West Germany, the first group treatments in an inpatient setting took place in Tiefenbrunn in 1950, and from 1960 onwards, training programs began at the Lindau Psychotherapy Weeks and the Sigmund Freud Institute in Frankfurt[3]. But it was only after the student movement in the 1970s that group analysis service, which had originated during the Third Reich, became more widely accepted. This led to a wave of group analysis training centers being founded in West Germany, Austria, Switzerland, and even in East Germany. These continue to do valuable work to this day, namely in Altaussee, Heidelberg, Göttingen, Frankfurt, Münster, and Zurich (cf. Schneider, 2020–1, pp. 3–7).

For years, due to neoliberal dissolution of boundaries coupled with isolation and violence, there has been increasing distress in families, schools, education, and society, with a lack of preventive concepts spanning all stages of life. This situation is further exacerbated by the consequences of the COVID-19 pandemic, climate change, and the war in Ukraine. Demand for psychotherapy services will push providers to the limits of their capacity. My focus is on the care of children and adolescents or young adults. Many child and adolescent therapist colleagues no longer maintain waiting lists, as it would only reinforce the illusion that every person in need could receive therapy. During the pandemic, inpatient facilities for child psychiatry were only admitting patients who were acutely suicidal or in other extreme crises and discharged them back to the outpatient sector after stabilization.

The diffuse fear of working with children and adolescents in groups has always triggered apprehension and resistance in society, especially when the group is not to be "treated" as a whole, but rather, as with Foulkes, psychoanalysis is to be practiced in and with the group. This evokes the old revolutionary approaches of psychoanalytic pedagogy in our imagination, which also elicit

---

3   In Lindau, the models of the two emigrants S. H. Foulkes ("Psychoanalysis through the Group") and Walter Schindler ("Individual Analysis in Groups") were presented and disseminated. In Frankfurt, Argelander taught based on the concept of Bion ("Psychoanalysis of the Group") (Schneider, 2020–21, p. 9).

similar counter-reactions as experienced and published by S. Bernfeld. His polemic treatise "Sisyphus: Or, the Limits of Education" (Bernfeld, 2006) ironically questions: For what purpose and for whom is education carried out? For him, the limits of education are not so much in the educability of the child or in the person of the educator, but rather in the function that education serves within the capitalist societal system. It serves the power tendencies of the educating group. Perhaps, however, in our profession of psychodynamic child and adolescent group therapy, in view of the immense demand we can succeed not only in remaining part of the care system but also in expanding our contribution through education and training in child and adolescent group analysis and, above all, in becoming more involved in the public discourse on socio-political issues.

In contrast to psychodynamic group therapy with adults, psychodynamic group therapy with children and adolescents is a very young profession, albeit with quite old roots (cf. Schneider, 2021, p. 61ff). Recently, the changes implemented by lawmakers have presented us with significant challenges but also opportunities that we should seize. Worldwide, there is no health care system in which therapy for mental illness is offered as comprehensively within the framework of statutory health insurance as it is in Germany. With the new psychotherapy degree program, two professions are finally coming together on an equal footing after a long process of emancipation.

The new Psychotherapist Act will bring about unprecedented changes in the training landscape for psychodynamic approaches, posing significant challenges, particularly for psychoanalysis and psychodynamic group therapy. Will psychodynamic psychotherapists be able to step down from the ivory tower of isolated and competing small institutes, often kept running by voluntary organizations with ageing members, and face this transformation? Will they together have the will and the strength to train the new generation, which is necessary if we are to provide psychodynamic psychotherapy in its diversity in the care system of statutory and private health insurance? Will we, as an analytical society, learn to utilize market requirements and legal regulations in a way that prevents competing methods – which have already demonstrated their ability to dominate the market in the past – from completely displacing us? I am convinced that this can only be achieved if we advance these concerns through intensive cooperation, sustainable solidarity, and a new unity among psychodynamic professional associations. I regret that graduates in the social sciences will no longer be admitted to the child and adolescent training pathway in the future. I fear the development of a behavioral-dominant study program focused on symptom reduction and reintegration into the school and work environment, which will produce graduates who are too young and thus immature. I am concerned about the development in the federal and state chambers of psychotherapists that does not focus first and foremost on the care of mentally ill people, but rather primarily pursues narcissistic-seeming ambitions and power interests in order to be able to play on an equal footing with the federal and state medical associations.

I will begin my contribution with reflections on the new Model Specialty Training Regulations (*Musterweiterbildungsordnung*, MWBO), since they form the basis for future training that presents a historic opportunity for group therapy as a whole.

Subsequently, I will present the key findings of the BARGRU study into barriers to group psychotherapists (cf. GBA and BAG, 2020), which have also been partly reflected in the new MWBO. Overall, psychodynamic group therapy owes many improvements and facilitations to this study: a basic provision of group psychotherapy, the possibility to conduct explorative sessions in a group setting, and the elimination of the evaluation requirement for group therapy or combination treatment predominantly involving group therapy. The flexibilization of group therapy now allows for fifty-minute sessions in all approaches, the joint conducting of therapy groups by two therapists for groups of six or more patients, and the provision of group therapy services outside of one's own practice setting (cf. Kassenärztliche Bundesvereinigung, 2021). The study has provided policymakers with crucial results. Unfortunately, the low number of child and adolescent psychotherapists participating in the study did not allow for a detailed differentiation of data for these professional groups. As a result, core components of professional psychodynamic group therapy for children and adolescents have not yet been implemented. Furthermore, the language barriers in the therapy of (unaccompanied) refugees have not yet been adequately addressed after 2015, particularly regarding child and adolescent therapy.[4] There are therefore several tasks that we need to tackle to ensure high-quality care for our young patients and their caregivers and encourage more colleagues to not only acquire competence in group therapy but also offer group therapy in their practices.

---

4   It is not uncommon for children and adolescents to become completely overwhelmed or retraumatized when they act as interpreters for their often-traumatized parents at authorities and (therapeutic) practices, which they often do because they have better language skills due to their schooling.

After discussing the framework of future training and education, I will briefly describe how I personally developed a focus on child group analysis and why I continue to be passionately involved in psychodynamic group therapy with children and adolescents.

These experiences and knowledge have influenced the concepts described above. I have had the opportunity to participate in and learn from those concepts, which aim to convey self-experience, practice, theory, and supervision as fundamental building blocks for acquiring a group-analytical identity.

I would be delighted if this contribution stimulated further impulses and conceptual considerations, leading to increased exchange.

2 The Model Specialty Training Regulations – tasks, opportunities, and risks

Tasks: The years-long struggle to finalize the MWBO has ensured that group therapy, including psychodynamic group therapy with children and adolescents, is no longer solely a voluntary service provided by idealistic individuals.[5] It has become an integral part of the curriculum, with the development of competence in group therapy now a mandatory requirement in the training and education of psychotherapists. The implementation and adherence to these guidelines are the responsibility of the psychotherapist chambers.

However, previous marginalization has had a significant impact. Group analysis was primarily taught in the form of group analysis for adults. There are many approaches to group analysis with children and adolescents, but it is only in recent years that the profession of child and adolescent group psychoanalysis has been institutionalized and made visible through the establishment of an international Working Group for Group Analysis with Children and Adolescents (*Arbeitsgemeinschaft Gruppenanalyse mit Kindern und Jugendlichen e.V.*, known by its German abbreviation "GaKiJu").[6] Traditional training institutions and institutes for group analysis generally do not have their own

---

5 When I started offering group analysis for children and adolescents, I had to write a continuation report for each patient before starting and after sixty sessions. The combination of individual and group therapy was prohibited in the outpatient sector. The earning potential per group under joint leadership was much lower than that of an individual session, considering the organizational time, material, cleaning, and personnel costs. Additionally, a minimum group occupancy of seven participants was required.

6 Cf.: "Die Geschichte des Arbeitskreises zur Förderung der Gruppenanalyse mit KiJu, die Entwicklung eines Curriculums und die Gründung eines eingetragenen Vereins" (Schneider, 2021, pp. 63–70).

outpatient clinics through which their trainees can bill for their training groups. Consequently, the number of training institutions recognized by the German Society for Group Analysis and Group Psychotherapy (*Deutsche Gesellschaft für Gruppenanalyse und Gruppenpsychotherapie,* D3G) with outpatient clinics is very limited. Conversely, institutes affiliated with the Association of Analytical Child and Adolescent Psychotherapists (*Vereinigung für analytische und tiefenpsychologisch fundierte Kinder- und Jugendlichen-Psychotherapie in Deutschland e. V.,* VAKJP) usually have limited expertise in group analysis with children and adolescents among their teaching staff, and there is currently no established curriculum in this area. They are dependent on establishing this competence in their training and education programs, and if they fail to do so in a timely manner, they may not be attractive to potential candidates for training and education, and the financial imbalance will worsen even faster.[7] In the future, only a few study slots will be available – currently planned at 2,500 (Küster, 2021, p. 11) – which, due to lack of financial resources and unclear regulations, have so far been offered even more sparsely in some federal states. Private universities, such as the IPU in Berlin, cannot compensate for this shortage of places. Study places will only be available at very few locations in Germany and the institutes will remain scattered throughout the country. The situation is further exacerbated by the "bottleneck", i. e., how many individuals who complete their studies will actually begin their further training in institutes. This is because other training opportunities, such as at hospitals, teaching practices, and especially university outpatient clinics, are starting to establish themselves. Even though, according to the MWBO, all approaches must be taught, the question still remains: How will psychoanalysis and group analysis find their place in universities? Who will teach them there? Currently, there are already very few professors left who have a background in psychoanalysis. It is only when psychoanalysis and group analysis are taught and made experiential by instructors who are authentic, experienced in practice, and well founded in theory, that young students can become passionate about those approaches. How can we as psychoanalysts break down the prejudice among students that psychoanal-

---

7   At the Würzburg Institute for Psychoanalysis and Psychotherapy (*Würzburger Institut für Psychoanalyse und Psychotherapie,* WIPP), we have observed that students, following the Bologna study reform, increasingly make pragmatic decisions and focus on fulfilling state regulations to obtain their qualifications quickly. Even the clinics we cooperate with have started to offer comprehensive in-house training to remain attractive to applicants. This generation of trainees is somewhat reluctant to meet additional requirements, such as those imposed by professional societies, and can only be convinced of the value of such measures through their practical training experiences.

ysis in both individual and group settings is unscientific? Especially when the German Research Foundation (*Deutsche Forschungsgemeinschaft,* DFG) continues to withhold funding for studies in this field, contributing to the risk of a growing monoculture at the expense of diversity (Bühring, 2018). The scandal of having to finance research ourselves through "private research contributions" to our professional associations (e. g., D3G, VAKJP), while other schools of thought receive public funding for their studies, is worth mentioning here.

Opportunities: It will be a few more years before the first graduates of the new program continue their education at the training centers. Until then, applicants who wish to pursue their training alongside their professional work and finance it themselves can still join our training and education institutions. According to the current procedure, this postgraduate training must be completed by September 1, 2032 (cf. Küster, 2021, p. 10). In addition, there will be approved graduates who will pursue further training as full-time employees. How will our institutes, which are primarily supported by volunteers, manage this balancing act? On the one hand, the institutes are traditionally supposed to provide teaching mainly in the evenings and on weekends, which allows their lecturers to conduct their practice during the day and enables the trainees to pursue gainful employment in order to finance their training. On the other hand, training and treatment at the institute's outpatient clinics is supposed to be provided during regular working hours for future graduates of the new degree program who are employed on a permanent basis. So far, the only thing that is certain is that current voluntary structures are not sufficient to handle this situation. In my view, many institutes have only realized the extent of the psychotherapy training reform too late or have not fully grasped it yet. Others have been engaged in intensive discussions and planning for this future training program for several years.

As an example, I will present the considerations and plans of the Würzburg Institute for Psychoanalysis and Psychotherapy (*Würzburger Institut für Psychoanalyse und Psychotherapie e. V.,* WIPP) so far. For the past two years, we have been in discussions with the Psychodynamic Institute Nuremberg (*Institut für Psychodynamische Psychotherapie Nürnberg e. V.,* PIN), the Institute for Psychoanalysis and Psychotherapy with Children and Adolescents in Nuremberg (*Institut für Psychoanalyse und Psychotherapie von Kindern und Jugendlichen Nürnberg e. V.,* KIP), and the Institute for Psychoanalysis Nuremberg/Regensburg (*Institut für Psychoanalyse Nürnberg-Regensburg e. V.,* IPNR). As a first step, we intend to establish a non-profit limited liability company (gGmbH). This gGmbH will have a management team and will be financed proportionally by all the associations that support the institutes, based on their size. The aim is for this office to take over the organizational and personnel services for the cooperating institutes with their outpatient departments. In a further step, we plan to consolidate the outpatient clinics into a medical care center and continue operating the outpatient clinics as branch offices. This is based on professional policy considerations: The medical care center would be authorized to purchase existing licenses to practice from members and maintain them in order to ensure the provision of psychoanalytic procedures and make them available again to future graduates. We have already held discussions with specialized lawyers and the Bavarian Association of Statutory Health Insurance Physicians (*Kassenärztliche Vereinigung Bayerns,* KVB) to explore the feasibility, the costs of which we have shared. There are still many detailed questions to be clarified. Above all, it is important to build trust among the boards of the institutes through the work to set up the gGmbH. Also, the members of the respective institutes still need to be convinced of this approach. In the KIP, a complete generational change in the board has led to a more open approach to cooperation and psychodynamic group psychotherapy with children and adolescents. The PIN and WIPP have lecturers for psychodynamic group psychotherapy, but only the WIPP (since 2020) is recognized by the D3G as a training institute for psychodynamic group psychotherapy with children, adolescents, and adults. Our discussions and the psychodynamics within the committees reflect, to some extent, old discrepancies among different professional societies and also their unresolved ambivalences, including the acceptance of group analysis. In the case of the WIPP's cooperative negotiations, the perspectives of the German Psychological Society (*Deutsche Gesellschaft für Psychotherapie,* DGP), the German Psychoanalytical Association (*Deutsche Psychoanalytische Vereinigung,* DPV), and the German Society for Psychoanalysis, Psychotherapy, Psychosomatics and Psychology (*Deutsche Gesellschaft für Psychoanalyse, Psychotherapie, Psychosomatik und Tiefenpsychologie, e.V.,* DGPT) clash. The state requirements for continuing education and the requirements for billing approval on the part of the respective Association of Statutory Health Insurance Physicians fall significantly short of the expectations of these associations, and the ongoing disputes within these associations make it even more challenging for psychoanalysis and group analysis to remain within the healthcare system in the future. The results of the BARGRU study (see point 3) clearly demonstrate the limited contribution we make within the overall healthcare system.

The ambiguity of the actors means that we repeatedly find ourselves making extreme demands or lapsing into a state of resigned indifference.

The scope of skills and expertise to be taught according to the new MBWO cannot be covered by the staff of the institutes at present, independent of psychodynamic group psychotherapy. Most of the institutes – including the WIPP –

already have great problems finding the functionaries for their current tasks and future challenges among their ageing members. There is a lack of young doctors and insufficient numbers of trainer-analysts. The decision of the VAKJP to allow its training institutes to appoint child and adolescent psychotherapists as trainer-analysts is a relief, but the implementation and acceptance in the respective institutes that train in child and adolescent as well as in adult psychoanalysis will still require many discussions.

In short, institutes must make these competencies available to each other through cooperation or "buy them in", so that they can offer the comprehensive range of courses and thus fulfill the state requirements for a further education institution as well as the expectations of the training and further education participants. As a first step, we have entered into a cooperation agreement between the WIPP, KIP, PIN, and IPNR, which stipulates that the courses of the respective other institute are freely accessible to the students and that the lecturers and trainer-analysts are mutually recognized. The distance between the institutes is sometimes more than 100 km, so students seldom attend the courses in person. Only a few lecturers are willing to offer courses at another institute. The COVID-19 pandemic has taught us that many face-to-face events are indispensable for the quality of continuing education and that a number of theoretical seminars can be offered online. There are already examples of offering certain topics (e.g., data protection, documentation requirements) as videos that can be viewed at any time, for example during working hours when a patient is unexpectedly unavailable. In this way, students from several institutes can attend such a seminar at the same time and the lecturer saves travel and (multiple) time expenditures. Through Dipl. Psych. Martin Schimkus from PIN, who has been a long-time member of the Berlin Institute for Group Analysis (*Berliner Institut für Gruppeanalyse e.V.*, BIG), the wealth of experience of this training and further education institute is also available to our "think tank".

Another burden hanging over from the past is that inpatient group psychotherapy has been offered compulsorily alongside one-on-one therapy, but it has only been possible to offer this in parallel in the outpatient sector for a few years (cf. GBA, 2017, p. 16).

Cooperation with the clinics, which has so far proved to be very difficult especially for child and adolescent psychotherapy training, has been given a new chance with the MWBO. Until now, students of child and adolescent psychotherapy have mainly come from (social) pedagogical programs. Thus, they were not billable for the clinics and therefore not very attractive. Consequently, our students often had to accept unpaid or very poorly paid internships and/or unattractive positions in marginal areas of clinical care. In the future, as approbated psychotherapists, they will be on an equal footing with medical psychotherapists and fully billable to the payers. They will also not have to carry out group psychotherapy without any preparation, as has been the case up to now, but will go to the clinics equipped with basic knowledge about the subject.

The common ground that characterizes most synoptic institutes[8] that are members of the DGPT is that over a long period of training and further education, analysis with adults and with children and adolescents is taught in joint courses. It is only relatively late in the course of study that specialization for the respective target group takes place. This should apply analogously to the teaching of competences in psychodynamic group psychotherapy at our institute. Greater influence from the D3G on the professional associations is urgently necessary with corresponding initiatives in this regard.

As treasurer of the WIPP, I view group psychotherapy as an important source of income for our outpatient clinic in the future. According to the current uniform value scale (*Einheitliche Bewertungsmaßstab,* EBM), psychodynamic group therapy can generate a significantly higher income per hour than individual therapy.[9] However, there are still many unanswered questions regarding the financing of future further training. Since future training participants would be permanently employed, their employing institutes would have to earn the equivalent of a salary regulated by collective labor agreements with the associated social security contributions, vacation, and time bonuses. In addition, the institutes would have to offer training participants theory, practice, self-experience, and supervision within their working hours without receiving any form of compensation from them as was previously the case. The institute outpatient clinic of the WIPP is therefore obliged to acquire enough patients. The founding of a medical care center is also being considered, because this would ensure the recruitment of patients from a significantly larger area. This all means that financing of the new training program is anything but clear and cannot be covered by the income from the institute outpatient clinic alone. To use the funds of the previous course to cover the deficits of the future course would, in my opinion, be unethical towards the students who have had to finance their studies themselves until now and who have not received any state subsidies.

---

8 This is the name given to training or further education institutes that have teaching staff composed of various psychodynamic schools and professional societies, offering equal and parallel education in each of these approaches. At the Würzburg Institute for Psychoanalysis and Psychotherapy (WIPP), students have the option to study depth-psychology psychotherapy, analytical psychotherapy, and classic psychoanalysis. Medical professionals can obtain specialization in various fields such as "Psychotherapy", "Psychoanalysis", and "Psychosomatic Medicine and Psychotherapy".

9 With group therapy, it is currently possible to earn, depending on participants, between EUR 305.70 and EUR 532.62 in 90 minutes (excluding structural or short-term therapy surcharges).

Since 2021, it has been permissible for two licensed group therapists to offer a group together with at least six participants and a maximum of 14 group participants. In this case, each therapist bills his/her patients via his/her own group license (cf. G-BA, 2017, p. 16). Thus, experienced group analysis trainers could offer group psychotherapy in our institutional outpatient clinics in which a training participant joins as a co-therapist over a certain period of time, gathers experience, and later offers his or her own teaching group under supervision in the institutional outpatient clinic. In order to do this, our institute outpatient clinics first need to be aware of how to establish the diagnostic need for group therapy and have the appropriate personnel and space. Such an offering could also take the strain off our members, who may make such a diagnosis during psychotherapeutic consultation hours but cannot offer a corresponding service in their own practices. In return, the institute's outpatient clinic could, for example, rent group therapy rooms for training groups from them. In this way, costly, non-permanently used rooms for group psychotherapy would be better utilized and refinanced. They would also be more easily accessible for the target groups as they would be more spread out across different places.

Ever since its founding, the D3G has already been appointing child and adolescent group analysts as group analysis trainers. Thus, appropriately trained teaching staff from the child and adolescent field could qualify for this in a timely manner. However, many institutes are too small to guarantee that training participants can take part in self-experience groups or lead them without there being conflicts of interest. This already poses a difficulty in one-on-one analysis. One solution could be to offer self-experience groups to another cooperating institute for their training participants by means of pair leadership – ideally one colleague from the child and adolescent area and one from the adult area. In addition, the proven tradition of trainees participa7ting in patient groups run by resident institute members should be continued.

Risks: Together with the D3G, the Professional Association of Licensed Group Psychotherapists (*Berufsverband der approbierten Gruppenpsychotherapeuten,* BAG), and the Advisory Board for Science and Research (BWF), dedicated efforts to influence the reform of the MWBO must continue. With the elimination of the obligation for expert evaluations, there is currently a risk of recoupments for group therapies that have already been conducted. The question of how quality assurance[10] and the examination of economic viability are

---

10 "Overall, there is a concern that the current development of quality assurance aims to establish a comparative quality competition with the goal of benchmarking psychotherapeutic practices" (Moors, 2021, p. 10).

to be carried out in the run-up to group psychotherapy in the future remains unanswered. Ideally, regular reflection on ongoing groups in the form of supervision or intervision should be established as a mandatory quality assurance instrument, because the essence of the group can only be experienced, learned, and developed within the group. Another – less satisfactory – solution would be to introduce one expert assessment per group and year. Questionnaires or phone calls carried out by health insurance employees during and after therapy are by no means a sensible solution and would be particularly absurd in the field of children and adolescents. How are infants, toddlers, or school-age children supposed to provide feedback on their own therapy process? Apart from that, destructive actions on the part of patients and their caregivers would be facilitated in certain phases of therapy.

In the BARGRU study (see point 3), it was already evident that many colleagues do not offer groups even though they could bill for them. My experience as a supervisor is that those who wait too long to start their training group after completing their education as group analysts often end up not starting one at all. The momentum that has built up within the learning community (see point 5) has dissipated by then. Often, the "fear of the group," the "chaos within the group," and the "expectation of powerlessness", with the group turning against the leader, act as barriers. Colleagues should receive more support in practice and supervision regardless of where and how they have acquired the prerequisites for billing approval in theory and self-experience (see point 5). All outpatient clinics authorized to bill for psychodynamic group psychotherapy have the responsibility to promptly assign patients to graduates, bill for their groups through the outpatient clinic, and provide supervision for them.

Many institutes currently lack billing approval for group therapy in their outpatient clinics as well as experienced supervisors. The greatest need for this is among colleagues working with children and adolescents, which is why, for example, GaKiJu decided in its general assembly in May 2020 to offer an online intervision program starting in October 2021. Every member, as well as interested individuals, whether working with training, applied, or therapeutic groups, can participate in this program. Depending on demand, regional virtual spaces could be opened. It is hoped that this networking will lead to the emergence of regional hybrid or in-person groups in the future. The significance of such meetings for identity and (further) concept development has been demonstrated by the workshops on group analysis with children and adolescents over the past 16 years.[11]

---

11 The diversity of topics and application areas can be found on www.kindergruppenanalyse.de under "Workshop-Chronik".

The exchange of experiences regarding difficult processes in participants' own analytical groups for children and adolescents, with various forms of application, has shaped a training program characterized by a special atmosphere of openness and collegiality. It has attracted regular participants and has brought together professionals from Germany, Austria, and Switzerland for an exchange of experiences and professional networking. At the first international workshop in Berlin in September 2021, speakers from England, Israel, Spain, and Turkey took to the stage.

3 Thoughts on the results of the BARGRU study

I have selected the results of the BARGRU study (cf. G-BA and BAG, 2020) in such a way that I omit many successfully implemented points and focus on the tasks for the present and future – especially for the importance of further training in psychodynamic group psychotherapy for children and adolescents.

As per the German Psychotherapy Guideline, group therapy is a recognized and, given the relevant diagnosis, accepted as an equivalent method to one-on-one therapy. Nevertheless, changes such as the significant increase in remuneration in 2005 and 2017 have not contributed to group therapy becoming more widespread and used in the outpatient sector. The study investigated, among other things, "barriers that complicate or even prevent outpatient group therapy or discourage private-practice group therapists from offering group therapy in their practices" (G-BA and BAG, 2020, p. 3). It also identified facilitating factors that could increase the availability of group therapy in the outpatient sector "to improve the healthcare situation for mentally ill patients and simplify procedures for practicing psychotherapists" (G-BA and BAG, 2020, p. 3). Analysis of the KBV's health care data showed a stagnation in the frequency of invoiced group psychotherapy services. "From the perspective of practitioners, numerous barriers continue to hinder the decision to offer outpatient group therapy and make its implementation difficult" (G-BA and BAG, 2020, p. 3). Despite the high socio-medical consequences, "even after establishing the relevant diagnosis(es) and medical indications, months still pass before adequate psychotherapy can be started because of supply bottlenecks" (G-BA and BAG, 2020, p. 4). In addition to broader options for medical and psychological psychotherapists to open branches for outpatient care, there should be efforts to expand group offerings that could provide indication-related care for three to nine patients – considerably more than in individual settings. "Apart from that, there are specific indications for group psychotherapy that, beyond economic aspects, suggest treating affected patients in groups" (G-BA and BAG, 2020, p. 4). Particularly concerning is the inadequate provision of outpatient group psychotherapy for children and adolescents,[12] who, based on their developmental age, benefit significantly from their peer group and utilize their resources. Especially during the COVID-19 pandemic, therapy groups for children and adolescents often served as the only reliable and continuous in-person option where they could play and interact with peers. Group psychotherapists are still prohibited from continuing their therapy groups online, despite conceptual work having been done during the COVID-19 pandemic. This forced some colleagues to abandon their patients, as it was impossible to offer individual sessions to all participants, especially considering that one group – and many therapists offer more than one group – with nine participants would have required an additional working day. Others, out of idealism and responsibility, offered their groups online but did not bill for them. Overall, only 5 % of the approved group psychotherapists[13] provided group psychotherapy for patients with the relevant medical indications (cf. G-BA and BAG, 2020, p. 5). The number of patients in group analysis under the terms of the Guideline was minimal compared to the numbers in other forms of therapy.[14] Of particular importance is also the group size, which unfortunately was not differentiated for adult, child, and adolescent group therapy. For child and adolescent group analysis, knowing the group size is crucial due to supervisory responsibilities. For certain conditions, if the group size exceeds three participants, supervision can no longer be performed by a single leader and requires co-leadership or a lead pair. The permissive attitude would also have to give way to a rigid leadership style. The study's findings show that in behavioral group therapy, the most common constellation consists of three to four participants per group, while in groups that centered on a psychodynamic approach, group sizes of eight to nine participants

---

12 The number of physicians/psychotherapists for group therapy, differentiated between adult versus child and adolescent psychotherapy, was as follows: In 2018, only 133 colleagues offering group therapy were licensed to provide both adult and child and adolescent psychotherapy. Only 289 psychotherapists offered exclusively child and adolescent group therapy, while for adult group therapy the number was 2,291 (cf. G-BA and BAG, 2020, p. 23).

13 In 2018, differentiated by guideline procedures, 1,246 psychotherapists offered behavioral group therapy, 1,192 offered psychodynamic group therapy, and only 484 offered analytical group therapy and billed for it (cf. G-BA and BAG, 2020, p. 22).

14 In 2018, 22,990 patients were in behavioral group therapy, 19,365 psychoanalytical-psychological group therapy, and only 7,251 with group analytical therapy, with the sessions being invoiced (cf. G-BA and BAG, 2020, p. 18). The reality of care becomes even more evident in a comparison with the number of patients in one-on-one therapy. In 2018, a total of 1,374,811 patients received one-on-one therapy. 24,471 patients received a combination of personal and group therapy, and 24,793 patients received pure group therapy (cf. G-BA and BAG, 2020, p. 19).

predominate (cf. G-BA and BAG, 2020, p. 28). For training purposes, it is necessary to work on specific competence building involving case work at further education centers for psychodynamic group therapy in order to learn how to deal constructively with the organizational barriers that continue to exist. The difficult time coordination (59.1%), the greater organizational effort (54.3%), the problem of vacancy fees in the case of patient cancellations (46.6%), and especially the lack of a billing option for conducting groups with a pair of leaders or with co-therapists (43.5%), as well as the insufficient hour contingent for outpatient psychotherapeutic groups (25.3%) and the refinancing of facilities (20.5%) are still unsolved or not refinanced. This applies especially in the case of child and adolescent psychotherapists who want to offer groups for different ages and parallel parent groups (cf. G-BA and BAG, 2020, p. 35). Some ideas would be establishing group indications at the institute outpatient clinics and referring patients to members with group offerings, jointly using group rooms collegially, co-leading groups with two practice owners, and co-leading with non-therapeutic practice staff (e.g., trainees, students at universities). Furthermore, institute clinics could list registered patients who can only attend therapy at specific times and match them with a database containing available group therapy slots among institute members with various days and times of group offerings. Group therapy options within institute outpatient clinics could already be initiated during ongoing training operations.

As for content-related barriers, the study identified the following: lack of motivation and willingness to participate among patients (37.2%), difficulties in acquiring patients (36.9%), lack of collegial networking (14.9%), own uncertainty in conducting outpatient group psychotherapy (14.1%), and insufficient opportunities for intervision and supervision (9.1%) (cf. G-BA and BAG, 2020, p. 37). Possible solutions could include presenting concepts based on group session protocols or video recordings (similar to the annual workshops for child and adolescent group analysis), sharing experiential knowledge, and practicing through role-playing. In these role-play scenarios, training participants could alternately take turns experiencing themselves in a group setting as potential patients or as therapists, as this would help them to understand the fears and challenges that arise in different developmental stages with regard to group therapy. Participants in the training groups described in point 5 found such role-plays particularly helpful for dealing with difficult group situations. In addition to addressing fears of group therapy, training participants, as group leaders, could engage in experiential exploration of the handling of specific group events (e.g., contact outside the group and the use of electronic media, love within the group, acting in/acting out, arriving late, sporadic attendance, dropouts) or learn different approaches and leadership styles in the model of course instructors. They could also empathize with real patients in a group setting through identification processes.

In the courses, changes in indications and contra-indications during the development of one's own group competence are also discussed, and guidance is provided for putting together a first group. Practical examples of documenting group sessions, such as keeping group diaries in child and adolescent therapy groups, completed templates of documented group sessions, and handling situations when a group leader becomes ill with or without co- or pair leadership, were demonstrated.

The handling of (group) dreams can also be conveyed most clearly through practical examples, whether through verbatim protocols or by means of real (group) dreams of participants during the training. The same applies to fears of destructive processes (e.g., scapegoating, hatred and destructiveness, dealing with therapy termination, psychotic decompensation, named or completed suicide). Such topics could be given more time with curricular teaching spread over several semesters.

Open questions, such as the regulation of vacancy or stand-by fees for patient cancellations (61.8%), can only be constructively resolved through further dedicated professional representation. The current private contractual arrangement between therapist and patient often leads to significant frustration, complaints to the respective Chamber of Psychotherapists (*Psychotherapeutenkammer,* PTK), or negative reviews on rating portals. The most urgent issue for us child and adolescent psychotherapists is the appropriate compensation of co-therapists or pair leaders (54 %) with an appropriate group size of between three and nine participants. In some regions, particularly in rural areas, potential colleagues are scarce, and legal considerations quickly lead us to challenging situations due to the duty of supervision. Moreover, the space requirements in child and adolescent therapy are higher, especially when there are groups for different developmental ages, and the equipment and operating costs go far beyond those of adult groups in a circle of chairs. The higher hourly quota for individual outpatient psychotherapeutic services (47.1%) is highly unsatisfactory, as it continues to discriminate against psychodynamic group therapy as a follow-up treatment after individual therapy or as a supplementary procedure. It may even raise notions among health ministers to temporarily place patients in groups until they are offered an individual therapy place. However, psychodynamic group therapy is an independent procedure and requires a flexible hourly quota appropriate to the disorder and processes for its process and outcome quality.

4 Where does the passion for group therapy come from, and why will I continue to be professionally committed to it?

While writing this article, I often felt pressure and wondered how I could fulfill my tasks as a member of the board, speaker of a professional group, and lecturer in different educational contexts, and at the same time sufficiently maintain personal relationships. The painful experience of the COVID-19 pandemic, having to do without many meetings in person, has made me aware of how many genuine friendships have developed during my career in the respective projects (see point 5). It was nice to be able to spend more time in the family environment during the lockdowns, but this also led to a reflection on whether, why, and under which conditions I want to continue my professional engagement. The tasks ahead, particularly those related to the MWBO at WIPP, are extensive and, despite all my optimism, could overwhelm me. I recognize that only with a full-time management team with a background in business administration, which can only be financed in partnership with other institutes, could many pressing issues be efficiently addressed through synergy effects. This also requires the willingness of young colleagues to take on voluntary roles within the institutes in the future.

I remember my training at the Alfred Adler Institute in Munich, where for many years participants training to work with children, adolescents, and adults all did their training together. This mutual enrichment, gaining a better understanding of the development and course of psychological disorders, insights into methods and techniques, and their creative implementation across different age groups and settings, is something I wish to preserve for psychodynamic approaches. I also have fond memories of the obligation within individual psychology to complete a part of the self-experience in a group at the respective Alfred Adler Institute.

During my studies in social pedagogy at the Catholic University of Applied Sciences in Munich, Benediktbeuern campus (*Katholische Stiftungshochschule München,* KSH), I had the opportunity to learn and appreciate the method of social therapeutic role-play at the Adelheid Stein Institute in Munich during the basic and advanced courses, and through several years of self-experience. I continue to utilize this method in a modified form in my therapy groups for children and adolescents, as well as in parallel parent groups (cf. Stein, 1983). Thomas Stadler integrated this method into his supervision during the training to become an analytical child and adolescent psychotherapist and adapted it for the concepts of the training analysis in our profession (cf. Stadler, 2019, p. 8 ff.).

In addition to this method, the practice of experiential and environmental education[15] had a significant impact on the development of my playful expressive abilities. Later, while working in youth welfare with behaviorally challenging children and adolescents, I had the opportunity to implement projects such as multi-week sailing trips or an alpine triathlon (cf. Schneider, 2002). These moments of self-experience were invaluable for the development of my containment in group processes. It therefore fills me with concern and, above all, sadness, that in the future, the social and pedagogical fields in child and adolescent psychotherapy will be dropped, and there will no longer be a requirement for several years of professional experience in other areas between studies and further training.

Shortly after setting up practice as a child and adolescent psychotherapist in 2002, I began my training as a group analyst. I quickly felt a sense of "loneliness". After spending 17 years in residential youth welfare as an educational and therapeutic professional, and eventually as the overall leader of a youth welfare center, and also being involved in the youth pastoral center at the Catholic University for Philosophy and Theology of the Salesians of Don Bosco in Benediktbeuern, I missed the interaction within a multidisciplinary team. In one-on-one sessions, I often felt disempowered, and I lacked the developmental space that group therapy could offer my patients. That's how I found my way to the Institute for Group Analysis in Heidelberg (*Institut für Gruppenanalyse Heidelberg e.V.,* IGAH). During my first journey to the self-experience group, I wondered what I would possibly have to work on during another four years of training analysis, this time in a group, after having just completed six years of individual analysis. I was amazed at how quickly this question became irrelevant and how inner themes and conflicts appeared in a different light or became consciously present during this analytical group self-experience. However, one annoyance remained: I had financed a comprehensive five-year training course and obtained authorization to bill for child and adolescent therapy groups, but still lacked a conceptual idea for my analytical groups or even an identity as a child and adolescent group analyst. I am therefore pleased that the new Psychotherapist Act and the MWBO make it possible that "in the future, parts of psychotherapy training can also take place in institutions of child and youth welfare" (PTK-Bayern, 2021). But I also remember why I left this field of work and turned to psychotherapy: The "cap clause" made it increasingly difficult for

---

15 The KSFH was the first university of applied sciences to offer such a study program. The high moors around the university and the mountain and river landscapes made it a paradisiacal study location.

me to reconcile my view of humanity, my educational and therapeutic thinking, and I did not want to merely manage the suffering of the children and adolescents entrusted to me. It would be a true enrichment if not only behavioral therapy and systemic therapy but also psychoanalytic pedagogy and therapy found their way back into this field of work.

All this searching led me to the working group for a curriculum on group analysis with children and adolescents, which later became the association GaKiJu. I remember our contentious meetings where we wrestled with every word while creating the curriculum text, the shared laughter, meals, and writing (see GaKiJu, no date). Without this association dedicated to promoting group analysis with children and adolescents, and without its members, our profession would never have gained so much recognition in the D3G, BAG, and VAKJP, or received as much attention in the professional community through publications. Without the workshops, this fruitful networking would not have been possible.

A still recent memory is from the first working conference in 2019 organized by the VAKJP in Düsseldorf: "New Approaches in Self-Experience for Child and Adolescent Therapists" (VAKJP, 2019), where, in addition to fascinating presentations, I could attend several practical seminars. I immediately connected with my own playfulness and play-ability, which should distinguish us as psychotherapists for children and adolescents. It is essential to continually rediscover and further develop this inner space for play. My colleague Doris Wirth-Limmer and I were so enthusiastic that we decided to document our experience in writing for the conference proceedings. We also planned to establish profession-specific self-experience at the WIPP, but unfortunately, due to the COVID-19 pandemic, it has not been possible to realize this plan so far.

Just in time for the first International Workshop on Group Analysis with Children and Adolescents held in Berlin in 2021 (see GaKiJu, no date), a new editorial group came together to completely revise the curriculum and initiate its translation into English and French. With this fully revised version titled "Guide to Competence Development," the GaKiJu association once again fulfills its goal of raising awareness about the method of group analysis for children and encouraging and promoting its further development in educational, therapeutic, and other fields (GaKiJu, 2021, back cover). These words written by Dr. med. G. Rudnitzki for the blurb bring back memories of the numerous meetings of the working group in his Heidelberg practice, my training analysis with him, and our collaborative work in education and further training. Since its initial publication in 2014, this curriculum has been incorporated into numerous training and continuing education institutions in Germany, Austria, and Switzerland. Our wish has come true: "The training and further education institutes can adopt this curriculum as a working document and adapt it to the specific conditions of their own institutions. The authors [...] are available as speakers [...]" (GaKiJu, 2014, p. 8). "We are confident that this work with children and adolescents will be appreciated and integrated into various continuing education institutions" (GaKiJu, 2014, p. 9).

In a bottom-up initiative in the fall of 2017, students from various universities and colleges in Würzburg joined forces with psychologists and psychotherapists from different theoretical orientations. This team now, among others, includes educators from various Würzburg training and further education institutions, such as the Working Group for Behavior Modification (*Arbeitsgemeinschaft für Verhaltensmodifikation,* AVM, dealing with behavioral therapy), WIPP (psychoanalysis, depth-psychology-based psychotherapy), and the Würzburg Institute for Systemic Thinking and Action (*Würzburger Institut für Systemisches Denken und Handeln,* WISDH, dealing with systemic therapy). The students felt that the education within academic psychology was too one-sided. As a result, interested individuals can now attend large events where they can listen to theory lectures from different therapeutic approaches, participate in panel discussions with representatives from various schools of thought about a specific case, and engage in three days of self-experience in the respective therapeutic approaches.[16] We are delighted with the positive response from students, some of whom now travel from across the country to participate, and they express a desire to have a similar information platform at their study locations.

All these initiatives and projects have time and again inspired me to continue advocating for psychodynamic group therapy with children and adolescents. They have also sparked interest among young students and led to valuable friendships. Through these experiences, I have gained numerous impulses that have enriched my work in therapy groups and, in essence, have contributed to the development of my identity as a child and adolescent group analyst.

5 Models of competence transfer

The open and professional exchange of experiences among otherwise competing institutes is anything but a matter of course. But affiliation to different teams of group analysts and therapists, as presented in the following, has proven suc-

---

16 "The Psychotherapy Forum Würzburg promotes discourse between different schools of thought and orientations in the field of psychotherapy, as well as related research and application fields in the social and human sciences, such as counseling and pedagogy, etc." (cf. www.psychotherapieforum-wuerzburg.de, no date).

cessful for many years. This is thanks, I believe, to our understanding of groups and our knowledge of group and organizational processes, and especially to our shared passion for psychodynamic group therapy.

5.1 The "Basic Annual DGIP Conference Curriculum" model

Within the German Society for Individual Psychology (*Deutsche Gesellschaft für Individualpsychologie,* DGIP) there is a long tradition of psychodynamic group therapy. For many years, the Working Group for Group Psychotherapy (*Arbeitsgemeinschaft für Gruppenpsychotherapie,* AGG) at the Alfred Adler Institute organized a training program under the leadership of Günther Vogel. In 1999, Robert Mathia took over chairmanship, but the psychotherapy reform meant that interest in group therapy rapidly declined. In the institutes, the valuable tradition of self-experience in groups faded and the working group disbanded. Gerd Lehmkuhl and colleagues were determined to keep the idea of group-therapy training within the DGIP alive, however, and together with Hanna Marx they developed a concept for offering the theory of psychodynamic group therapy as an "additional module" over the course of three to four annual conferences. In 2012, the first training course with 35 participants took place in Cologne. In 2013, Gerd Lehmkuhl left, and I joined as a lecturer in the ongoing course for child and adolescent therapists during the annual conference.[17] Since then, there has been a basic course for child and adolescent psychotherapists, as well as for adult psychotherapists, covering the theoretical and methodological foundations of psychoanalytic group therapy. This curriculum is highly experience-oriented, consisting of short theory inputs from the lecturers, fishbowls on specific topics, and most importantly, role-playing exercises. Participants have the opportunity to observe the lecturers in their daily practice through video sequences. In addition to selected basic literature, participants receive all materials, including sample applications, forms for record-keeping, and more, on a CD. Critical group phenomena are experienced through role-playing exercises, and "patients" with different developmental stages and levels of disturbance are briefed and assigned fictitious names for the groups. Groups are playfully examined for peculiarities at the beginning, middle, and end of therapy. The different leadership styles of the lecturers are also to be experi-

---

17 Currently consisting of: Dipl.-Psych. Gabriele Oelmann, Dipl.-Psych. Robert Mathia, Dipl.-Psych. Johannes Brachthäuser, Dipl.-Sozialpäd., Bacc. Phil./Theol. Thomas Schneider. Dr. med. Hanna Marx took a break during her term as DGIP chair and will return to participate in 2025.

enced by the participants. Throughout the course, all participants can take on the role of a patient in a group but also act as a group leader.

The disadvantage of this training program is the lack of a self-experiential group option and the limited active support from some Alfred Adler Institutes regarding the composition, supervision, and billing of training groups. This is often due to existing resentments against the method, or the additional organizational effort required. In general, participants are responsible for seeking opportunities for self-experience between the annual conferences. They may choose to participate in experiential groups offered by other providers or engage in self-experience within patient groups led by individual lecturers. Finding supervisors for child and adolescent therapy groups is particularly challenging since only a few within the DGIP have this qualification. As a result, participants often have to travel long distances to access suitable supervision opportunities.

The advantage of this program is that it has reignited interest in group therapy within the DGIP, and at least seventeen participants have attended every course so far. The integration of an advanced training course into a conference has proven to be highly beneficial. Changing the conference locations allowed many participants to experience the program by attending at different locations. The program was designed to be interdisciplinary from the beginning, and the participation of colleagues from social sciences has enriched the medical and therapeutic perspectives.

We take pride in having supported the graduates in such a way that they are now actively contributing to the provision of their own group therapies.

5.2 Multiplier training and implementation at the Alfred Adler Institute Cologne

Stefan Nauenheim became acquainted with the concept at the annual conferences. Later, when he became the first psychotherapist for children and adolescents to chair the Alfred Adler Institute in Cologne, he wanted to offer this program there. Twelve lecturers from two local training institutes came together as multipliers to receive training in a closed group. The goal was to be able to teach psychodynamic group therapy with children, adolescents, and adults when the MWBO came into force. After completing the course, seven lecturers for psychodynamic group therapy with children and adolescents formed a supervision group on site, which I was leading online during the pandemic. During this process, specific conflicts emerged, such as clarification of private interests among practice owners and the institute's objectives of having qualified instructors in the near future. The colleagues had to decide for themselves, starting already with the training group, whether they wanted to lead individually or as a pair, whether they wanted to find suitable spaces for themselves or share them with others, and whether they would offer only one group with a pair leadership or multiple groups. From the beginning, the recruitment of patients during the pandemic was very difficult. Additionally, questions about billing were complicated due to the role confusion between being an instructor and a trainee at the institute, especially when the co-leaders belonged to different institutes. Thus, there were grievances to work through, arising from the time involved, the financial cost of qualification, and the relatively high, yet varying, institute fees for billing. This is because, in addition to the participants' benefit of being able to offer groups in their practices in the future, it is their institutes that will benefit in the long term by offering this service as a complete package themselves. This would require the participants' willingness to meet the D3G standards for trainer-analysts.

Since the multiplier course in 2018/19, we, the lecturers, have been conducting the modules on site with the institute providing the premises and organizing the framework. The modules have been open to all interested individuals since then, are conducted as block events on weekends, and are completed within 12 months. In 2021, Robert Mayerle joined the team of lecturers, and now there are two lecturers for child and adolescent group psychotherapy. Currently, other colleagues have shown interest in participating, which is very encouraging. At the Alfred Adler Institute in Cologne, we have received inquiries from many professionals working in the inpatient setting, but unfortunately, we do not have a specific offering available for them.

5.3 The "Heidelberg Regional Group" and implementation in the IGA

This further training program for child and adolescent group analysis in the Rhine-Neckar region[18] was planned for 2016 and realized for the first time in 2017. It was important to us that the participants' previous experience and competence in group work from their voluntary, part-time, or full-time professional activities could directly influence the theory conveyed in the training. We had a well-rounded team to achieve this, consisting of two psychiatrists[19], a pediatrician specializing in child and adolescent medicine[20], and the rest of the team members[21], all of whom were group analysts or even lecturers for chil-

---

18 Further information: www.kindergruppen-weiterbildung.de
19 Dr. med. Gerhard Rudnitzki (Heidelberg), Dr. med. Christoph F. Müller (Zurich, Heidelberg)
20 Dr. med. Furi Khabirpour (Speyer)
21 Robert Mayerle (Schwetzingen), Gerhild Ohrnberger (Frankfurt)

dren and adolescents. Two of the team members[22] brought their expertise in applied psychodynamic group therapy within inpatient and outpatient youth welfare settings.

We, as members of GaKiJu, wanted to contribute with our own training course to the increased offering of child and adolescent group analysis. Our aim was to expand the application of this approach not only in traditional therapeutic settings but also in what we refer to as "applied groups", which encompasses (social) pedagogical fields. However, our enthusiasm was put to a test as we already faced challenges in assembling the first course. Most of the interested individuals who came forward were from therapeutic fields. We had to acknowledge that the target group of "pedagogues" was rather skeptical or even opposed to psychodynamic group therapy, preferring systemic training options for which they receive financial support or leave from their employers.

Finally, six participants met in a closed group over five weekends. Each weekend block began on Friday and concluded on Sunday with a self-experience session. The theoretical part, consisting of theoretical inputs and case work, took place on Saturdays. The self-experience group and all seminars were led by pairs of lecturers, allowing participants to experience different leadership styles. However, after the course, the participants had significant problems in forming a training group. None of them were affiliated with an institute that had approval for group therapy billing. The participants therefore switched to psychiatric practices, for example, or gave up.

After the course failed to meet the minimum number of participants in 2018, we as GaKiJu realized that we did not have the necessary structure to provide such a training program. All of the lecturers were members or felt connected to the IGA Heidelberg as their training institute for group therapy. Thus, we initiated cooperation talks with the IGA board, which showed openness to our proposal. We delivered individual lectures and started clarifying mutual conditions, such as membership of function holders in the IGA, a unified external appearance, accounting, and tax transparency. However, some points remained unresolved for an extended period of time (deficit risk, administrative costs, and representation of regional associations in the board). We were not yet ready to give up our autonomy, and the extent to which the IGA wanted the collaboration in terms of content as an institutional community was also unclear. The pandemic prevented us from announcing any further courses. Instead, we focused extensively on the question of how we can reach potential participants interested in applied psychodynamic group therapy in the future, and whether

---

22 Tilmann Sprondel (Müllheim) and Sylvia Stumpf (Heidelberg)

there are other cooperation partners besides the IGA in the region. We found that the interest from other regional institutes in our offering was low, and they had yet to fully comprehend the consequences of the MWBO. In 2021, the IGA board changed entirely, and a representative from our regional group was appointed as a co-opted member of the board. The IGA now intends to expand its educational offerings to include psychodynamic group therapy with children and adolescents and, in return, provides us with its structures (admissions committee, training regulations, state-approved final certificate). We, as a regional group, give up our independence in return. The problem of not being able to offer participants an institute outpatient clinic, which has existed since the founding of the IGA, now also affects the training participants in psychodynamic child and adolescent group therapy. To resolve this, we are currently engaged in cooperation talks with institutes that have institute outpatient clinics with group therapy approval. These institutes would benefit by gaining a pool of experienced lecturers. For this reason, we have hope that the 2022 training and further education at the IGA will be jointly offered in collaboration with GaKiJu and other institutes, transforming a challenging path into a fruitful one.

5.4 Modular training at WIPP – training center of the D3G

The WIPP already had a handful of experienced group analysts, some of whom were still on the path to becoming group teaching analysts with the D3G. It took years of persuasion before the desire among some members to offer group analysis was genuinely taken up and implemented. The discussions about the MWBO accelerated the decision-making process.

We have now successfully completed two courses for psychodynamic group therapy for children, adolescents, and adults, and the third one is currently ongoing. The number of participants is limited to twelve. Following the Heidelberg concept, we structured the theory sessions on Saturdays, with a self-experience block on Friday afternoons and Sunday mornings. In the first two courses, most participants were external, many from clinical settings. In the third course, for the first time we have many participants from our own institute. The extension from six to seven weekends was necessary because a single absence would prevent participants from fulfilling the required number of hours for reimbursement approval from the National Association of Statutory Health Insurance Physicians.

In 2020, we were well-prepared both in terms of personnel and structure (concept, training regulations, training committee for group therapy) to successfully submit an application to the D3G for recognition as a training and further education institute. Our institute's outpatient clinic was already authorized to bill for psychodynamic group therapy for children, adolescents, and adults. Additionally, we had sufficient supervisors available for the teaching groups.

However, we continue to be concerned with important issues: How can we maintain abstinence with so few group teaching analysts, especially when an increasing number of students from our own institute want to pursue this training? Who will supervise the growing number of teaching groups? We believe that we can only succeed by reaching an agreement with PIN as a first step to offer mutual self-experience opportunities for each other's institute. Already, one of our instructors from KIP decided to participate in our course. The first online theory seminars for all three institutes were well-received, but we are aware that this basic qualification is not sufficient to competently lead groups, so we are developing an advanced course that will be offered after the third basic course for the first time. We hope to find enough internal and external training participants. The goal is to gain expertise in the D3G's professional standards through theory-guided case work, using examples from our own (training) groups, and we see continuous participation in group supervision as a crucial element. Perhaps an intervision group of group analysts from the cooperating institutes could be re-established. Last time, WIPP instructors would take turns meeting in the group rooms of their colleagues. Currently, there are only two group analysis trainers for psychodynamic group therapy with children and adolescents, with one of them involved in the co-leadership of the self-experience group. We may be able to alleviate this staffing shortage through a cooperation between IGA and the GaKiJu regional group, where, in return, graduates of IGA could bill for services at the WIPP institute outpatient clinic.

In the last Group Training and Continuing Education Committee meeting, we discussed how to incorporate psychodynamic group therapy training continuously into the semester offerings. Initial discussions were held in the extended board about the extent of group self-experience in the training analysis and how to offer it during the transitional phase for postgraduate students. Currently, we are in the process of integrating profession-specific self-experience into our educational offerings. We see this group offering as an ideal interface for introducing parallel instruction in psychoanalysis, psychotherapy, and psychodynamic group therapy.

6   Final thoughts

I have tried to present my experiences in a condensed and yet comprehensible way and to let the joy of psychodynamic group therapy with children and adolescents become tangible. In case the challenges in the implementation of the MWBO weaken your optimism, or institute-internal discussions about it become very tedious, then let us, as psychodynamic educational communities, remember Seneca's wisdom: "Non quia difficilia sunt non audemus, sed quia non audemus difficilia sunt" (Sen., ep. mor. 104, 26).[23]

> **At a glance:**
> Group analysis for children and adolescents requires:
> - passion for the group and dedication in professional politics as well as close collaboration with all professional associations of psychodynamic child and adolescent psychotherapy in individual and group settings.
> - a solid place within the healthcare system with well-trained therapists from (social) pedagogical fields, as it is not only a therapy within the healthcare sector but also a form of applied group work in educational counseling and residential and remedial education.
> - not to be reinvented. Its implementation in education and training can draw on diverse experiences in various education and training contexts.
> - experienced multipliers, a location and a framework for teaching and research at universities and psychodynamic institutes and their education and training facilities.
> - a critical examination and a creative and hands-on implementation of the continuing education regulations with their opportunities and risks, because every reform is a transitional space with opportunities for shaping it.
> - a new edition of the BARGRU study with a specific focus on the needs of child and adolescent group psychotherapy, including the different settings for each age group, the requirements of co-leadership in small groups, and the implementation of caregiver groups.

---

[23] "It is not because things are difficult that we do not dare, it is because we do not dare that they are difficult."

Bibliography

Bernfeld, S. (2019). *Sisyphos oder die Grenzen der Erziehung.* Berlin: Suhrkamp

Bühring, P. (2018). Interview with Prof. Dr. rer. nat. Falk Leichsenring: "Wir brauchen eine Vielfalt evidenzbasierter Psychotherapieverfahren". *Deutsches Ärzteblatt,* Oct. 2018: 449ff

Deutsche Psychotherapeuten Vereinigung (2019). *Resolution der Psychotherapieverbände – Gesprächskreis II: "Die Potentiale psychotherapeutischer Expertise und verbandlicher Aktivität bei der Bewältigung der Klimakrise",* November 12, 2019

GaKiJu: Arbeitsgemeinschaft Gruppenanalyse mit Kindern und Jugendlichen e.V. (no date). *Geschichte der Arbeitsgemeinschaft.* https://www.kindergruppenanalyse.de/Arbeitsgemeinschaft/GaKiJu-Geschichte (last accessed March 30, 2022)

GaKiJu: Arbeitsgemeinschaft Gruppenanalyse mit Kindern und Jugendlichen e.V. (no date). *Geschichte der Workshops.* https://www.kindergruppenanalyse.de/Workshop/Workshop-Geschichte (last accessed March 30, 2022)

GaKiJu: Arbeitsgemeinschaft Gruppenanalyse mit Kindern und Jugendlichen (Hrsg.) (2014). *Curriculum für Kinder- und Jugendlichengruppenanalyse.* Darmstadt: Reyhani Druck & Verlag

GaKiJu: Arbeitsgemeinschaft Gruppenanalyse mit Kindern und Jugendlichen (Hrsg.) (2021). *Gruppenanalyse mit Kindern und Jugendlichen – Ein Leitfaden zur Kompetenzentwicklung.* Göttingen: Vandenhoeck & Ruprecht

Gemeinsamer Bewertungsausschuss (G-BA) (2017). *"Richtlinie des G-BA über die Durchführung von Psychotherapie",* resolution of February 16, 2017

Gemeinsamer Bewertungsausschuss (G-BA) (2021). *"Richtlinie des G-BA über die Durchführung von Psychotherapie",* resolution of February 18, 2021

Gemeinsamer Bundesausschuss – Innovationsausschuss (G-BA) and Berufsverband der approbierten Gruppenpsychotherapeuten (BAG) (2020). *Barrieren bei GruppenpsychotherapeutInnen gegenüber der ambulanten Gruppenpsychotherapie zu Lasten der GKV,* BARGGRU study, 2020

Kassenärztliche Bundesvereinigung (2021). *Veränderungen im Gutachterverfahren – Hinweise zur geänderten Psychotherapie-Richtlinie,* July 15, 2021

Küster, H. (2021). Die Zukunft der Psychodynamischen Gruppentherapien – Psychotherapeutenausbildungsreformgesetz und Musterweiterbildungsordnung für Psychologen. Was kommt auf uns zu? *GA – Die Zukunft der Gruppenanalyse hat bereits begonnen,* double issue 1/2 2021: 6ff

Moors, B. (2021). Qualitätssicherung in der ambulanten Psychotherapie – Was kommt auf die Profession zu? *VAKJP members' circular letter* no. 1/2021: p. 8 ff.

Psychotherapieforum Würzburg (no date). www.psychotherapieforum-wuerzburg.de

PTK-Bayern, Online-Diskussion zur Zukunft der Psychotherapie in der Kinder- und Jugendhilfe, report from July 13, 2021

Schneider, T. (2020–21). *"'Menschen sind soziale, auf Gemeinschaft angelegte und Gemeinschaft bildende Lebewesen' (Plato) – Die Geschichte der Gruppentherapie und Gruppenanalyse".* Unpublished manuscript

Schneider, T. (2002). Mit Muskelkraft von Pfaffendorf nach Venedig. Alpentriathlon des Jugendhilfezentrums Dominikus Savio. *Erleben und Lernen,* 2/2002: 21 ff.

Schneider, T. (2021). Wurzeln der Kinder- und Jugendlichengruppenanalyse. Historische Entwicklung einer Profession und ihre Institutionalisierung in der GaKiJu (Arbeitskreis zur Förderung der Kinder- und Jugendlichengruppenanalyse e.V.). *Gruppenanalyse – Die Zukunft der GA hat bereits begonnen,* double issue 1/2 2021: 61 ff.

Stadler, T. (2019). Erweiterte Selbsterfahrung in der AKJP-Ausbildung. In VAKJP (Hrsg.), *Neue Wege in der Selbsterfahrung für Kinder- und Jugendlichentherapeut*innen. Konzepte, Austausch und Ausprobieren. Überregionale Tagung in Düsseldorf,* conference documentation, May 3–5, 2019: 8 ff.

Stein, A. (1983). *Sozialtherapeutisches Rollenspiel, Erfahrungen mit einer Methode der psychosozialen Behandlung im Rahmen der Sozialarbeit/Sozialpädagogik*. Braunschweig. Moritz Diesterweg.

Vereinigung analytischer Kinder- und Jugendlichenpsychotherapeuten (VAKJP) (201). *"Neue Wege in der Selbsterfahrung für Kinder- und Jugendlichentherapeut*innen. Konzepte, Austausch und Ausprobieren. Überregionale Tagung in Düsseldorf"*, conference documentation, May 3–5, 2019

Interdisciplinary Groups with Children and Young People

Parent-child Groups with Children under Six Years Old

Anke Mühle[1]

1   Initial situation

Children often find themselves entangled in the complexities of their parents' illnesses and the manifold stresses that accompany them. These risks are not mere isolated incidents; rather, they accumulate almost exponentially. When parents are unwell or grappling with overwhelming stressors, their child or children may unwittingly suffer from the repercussions. Within those family dynamics, a profound absence emerges – the child's lack of the vital impulses and essential feedback they require to regulate their states of arousal. The extensive research on attachment and mentalization underlines a fundamental truth: From birth, children depend on caregivers, most notably their parents, to act as vigilant guardians of their development. Even if those parents are under internal or external pressure, they must remain attuned to their child's evolving needs. However, many families find themselves struggling to fulfil this critical role without external support.

---

1   I would like to thank all those who have contributed to the success of the parent-child group work in the family center at Potsdam University of Applied Sciences and to the creation of this article over the past eight years: Prof. Dr. med. Hermann Staats, under whose leadership I was able to establish the parent-child groups during the group therapy training, Prof. Dr. rer. nat. Karsten Krauskopf, currently director of the family center, who succeeded in making the groups permanent in 2021, Dr. Ulrike Diem, who gave me valuable advice on the content of the article, the psychologists Bärbel Derksen and Astrid Kunze from our team, and finally the editor Katrin Stumptner, who made it possible and accelerated the completion of the article with her enquiries and her friendly persistence, specific questions, and thoughts. Without all of them, the groups and the article would not have been possible in this quality. I would also like to thank the many interns who have been involved over the past few years. I would like to mention Elisa Rode, Anja Kosmider-Maas, and Gorden Barsch as representatives of all of them.

2 Four parent-child groups with children between four months and six years old

2.1 Institutional framework

The family center at the Potsdam University of Applied Sciences (Fachhochschule Potsdam, FHP) has been operating as one of the pioneering counselling and training institutions in the field of early intervention since 1997. Its range of services includes not only early counselling for parents with infants and toddlers who are facing significant challenges, but also assistance in parenting called Help for Upbringing *(Hilfen zur Erziehung)*, in line with the Social Security Code VIII *(Sozialgesetzbuch VIII)*. Over the past 20 years, the institute has designed and conducted 10–15 one- to three-day specialist Early Aid seminars annually to train professionals in the field of early prevention. An experienced team of psychologists, educators, and therapists, under the direction of professors from the FHP, facilitates continuous quality development and combines research, teaching, and practical application. The primary focus of these services is on parents with newborns, infants, and toddlers up to the age of three, as well as older children.

The unique connection to the Potsdam University of Applied Sciences enables a close integration of primary and secondary counselling work with new scientific research findings and the dissemination of their results.

This link to teaching fosters a strong bridge between education and professional practice in the realms of family and social work. Since 2013, a part of the family center has received funding as a Competence Center for Early Intervention from the German Federal Foundation for Early Intervention (Bundesstiftung Frühe Hilfen). In 2021, the Interdisciplinary Consultation Hour (Interdisziplinäre Sprechstunde) was established as a collaborative project between Potsdam University of Applied Sciences and the family center. On a monthly basis, professionals present challenging and complex counselling cases involving parents and their children. Initially, the case leader presents the recent cases alongside the involved professionals, then there is a collaborative discussion involving multiple professionals and various branches of psychology. All professions working with parents, children, and families, encompassing psychiatry, therapy, child protection, and family support, are invited to contribute their expertise during these case presentations.

2.2 Emergence of the groups

Parent-child groups were initially developed in the 1940s at the Anna Freud Centre in London. The psychoanalytically informed model initially served as a model for all other group contexts and was adapted to various populations and cultures (Woods and Pretorius, 2013). As a group leader, the author has been working with parent-child groups in the family center at Potsdam University of Applied Sciences for ten years. The first group started with two mothers and their babies, who would gather on the carpet once a week in the family center's room and use the time to reflect on their new roles as mothers. What may have initially seemed a relaxed gathering gradually revealed itself to be a profound, complex, and intense experience. The participants were burdened by lack of sleep, exhaustion, fears associated with sudden changes, and the great responsibility that comes with caring for a child. These parents openly discussed their concerns. They wondered if their children's healthy development might be compromised due to their own struggles, and if their children might have developmental disabilities or mental disorders as a result. Consequently, issues related to the parent-child relationship became evident early on.

In the meantime, before the COVID-19 pandemic, there were four semi-open groups, each with up to ten families per group, meeting weekly for one and a half hours. Three of these groups were homogeneous in age, while one group included siblings. This offering served as a low-threshold pilot program at the family center, aimed at identifying and reducing risks to the well-being and development of children at an early stage. Over an extended period, the development of these groups helped raise awareness of the needs within families that required focused support from available family support services. Conversely, families already receiving Help for Upbringing through the responsible youth welfare office or simultaneously undergoing outpatient therapy had the opportunity to apply the new insights gained from individual counselling sessions within the group setting. This also allowed the group experience to complement individual assistance. Unfortunately, due to COVID-19 restrictions, in-person groups were not possible for two years. During this period, there was an online parent-child group that four mothers with babies regularly attended once a week for over a year. Since April 2022, four in-person groups have resumed, meeting once a week in the group room.

2.3 Conceptional framework of the groups

The program was governed by both fixed and negotiable rules to provide a secure framework. There were no requirements or time limits for participation. Parents in Potsdam with children between four months and three years old, seeking a sense of community or wanting their child to interact with other children in preparation for kindergarten, found themselves in a group alongside mothers and fathers dealing with various burdens and mental illnesses. Some of the latter group members stayed for several years, beginning in the baby group and later transitioning to older age groups. New challenges and further needs for assistance arose in each subsequent age group, in addition to individual counselling or outpatient therapy. Before a family, which could conclude a mother, father, or both, could join the group, an introductory interview with an anamnesis was conducted. This interview was always facilitated by the group leader, with interns also present. During this process, parents were informed about the group's content, boundaries, agreements, and unique customs, and they heard brief anecdotes from the group experiences as part of an introductory overview. This helped alleviate any fears that stressed parents may have had. Each family had the option of additional individual counselling from the group leader or her well-respected colleague. Some parents were participating in the group through Help for Upbringing in compliance with the Social Security Code. For these families, a progress report had to be submitted to the commissioning youth welfare office every six months, outlining the jointly developed goals and action steps. During the COVID-19 restrictions, live group sessions did not take place for one and a half years. Instead, the infant group met online, and everyone was pleasantly surprised by this new format, although they all were eagerly anticipating returning to in-person sessions in the group room. In all groups, interns from the bachelor's degree program Early Childhood Education *(Bildung und Erziehung in der Kindheit)* at Potsdam University of Applied Sciences participated periodically. Additionally, there was a group observation seminar with students, and any absence or lateness was communicated in advance. Each session began and ended with a gong and a singing bowl, gathering everyone in a circle for the welcoming song, which mentioned each child by name, and there was a farewell song at the end. Initially, there were no predefined plans for parents or children to leave the parent-child group prematurely. If any parents or children expressed a desire to leave early, the group leader took this as an opportunity to discuss this choice in detail. The rules and routines of group life could always be discussed and negotiated by all participants, including the group leader. On the table beneath the window, coffee, tea, water, pastries, and fruit were provided. This was either set up by the family center or brought by the parents for everyone's enjoyment. After each group session, once everyone had said their goodbyes there was an opportunity for the interns to engage in follow-up discussions together with the group leader.

3 Methods and theoretical aspects

3.1 The "Watch, Wait, and Wonder" interaction method

"Watch, Wait, and Wonder" is an intervention method developed in Australia and researched in Toronto for parents with infants and toddlers experiencing multiple mental stressors and mental illnesses. This method is based on fostering relationships and interactions that allow children to develop autonomously, express themselves, and explore and adapt to the world around them, thus cultivating their own initiative. The primary emphasis is placed on the child's active role. During free play, the child's self-esteem and self-efficacy are nurtured, and their emotional regulation and attachment relationships are enhanced. Any relationship challenges are intended to be experienced, molded, and developed through play and in interaction with the parents. Independent play in proximity to the parents enables children to explore their relationships with their parents and other individuals in the group in an unhindered way (Cohen, Muir, and Lojkasek, 2003). Throughout this process, parents assume a receptive and patient stance. They observe (watch) and wait (wait) for relational cues from their children, which they then follow, and marvel (wonder) at the unfolding developments. Central to this approach is the parents' active engagement in reflecting on their child's inner world while distinguishing it from their own emotions, desires, and thoughts.

3.2 Psychoanalytical-interactional oriented group work

The Psychoanalytical-interactional Method (PiM) is an established psychodynamic approach for treating individuals with severe personality disorders or structural and ego deficits (Heigl-Evers and Heigl, 1973). Initially, it was designed for patients for whom interpretations of their behavior in relationships did not result in an improvement in their clinical syndrome. Engaging in and shaping relational spaces within the group, along with having interpersonal experiences and experimenting with behaviors and skills, can enhance one's self-confidence in engaging with others and mastering group situations

(Strauß and Weber, 2014). Recognizing various types of relationships with other children and with oneself within a community offers numerous opportunities for a child's approach to relationships. Negotiation plays a central role in fostering behavioral changes: the ability to collaborate with others in an ongoing process of negotiation that involves regulating emotions and managing relationships. "In Germany, in the form of psychoanalytical-interactional methods, initially concepts were developed in groups in which the focus was on the shape given to the interactions. Here, a relationship-oriented intersubjective approach for therapy work is conceptualized. Changes in interpersonal behavior then lead to changes in internal patterns and representations" (Staats, 2021, vol. 1, p. 31 f.).

3.3 Aspects of developmental psychology in parent-child groups

Social relationships represent a fundamental element of child development. Certain aspects of age-appropriate developmental tasks can therefore only be meaningfully observed, accompanied, tried out, and supported in guided group activities. In the case of problems and conspicuities, there are several ways to exert influence, which, in addition to direct interventions, include the particularly important social learning that occurs in groups. Children aged zero to one year old react with regulatory disorders to unfavorable relationship patterns. If efforts to communicate with the parents through smiling or laughing, or to signal their own elementary needs through dissatisfaction, crying, or noticeable issues related to sleeping, e.g., bedwetting, breastfeeding, bottle-feeding, or eating, are in vain, or if they are responded to incorrectly by the parents, this can lead to passivity or resignation in the child. This impairs not only physical but also emotional, social, and linguistic development processes. With two- to three-year-olds, the development of autonomy comes into focus, which can trigger contradictory emotions in both parents and children. Misunderstandings, helplessness, or excessive demands in relationships confront parents and their children with great challenges during this time. Additionally, there is an almost insatiable thirst for discovery that draws children away from their parents while simultaneously causing fears of venturing too far. For three- to four-year-olds, the further development of the child's self and self-efficacy are a priority. Cognitive and affective changes in perspective and skill acquisition in peer groups become more important. As for four- to five-year-olds, their parents face challenges, such as their growing ability to accept other perspectives, the development of moral values, competition with others, and the invention of creative strategies for victory. Parents and professionals alike know that there are no clear answers to the mysteries that children present during their preschool age. There are no general guidelines or instruction manuals for supporting a child's development or for raising a child (Fraiberg, 1984, p. 7 ff.).

3.4 Group matrix

The concept of the matrix becomes evident in the interactions among individual group members. It is reflected in various aspects, including differential awareness of norms within groups, the formation of psychosocial compromises, group cohesion, the level of regression at which the group operates, and roles and relationship patterns enacted by group participants. "The matrix cannot be observed directly. It can be accessed via its efficacy, similar to accessing the unconscious" (Staats, 2014, p. 101 ff.). The collective unconscious, which Foulkes and Bion posit in their theories, appears to be constituted through sensory-symbolic forms of interaction. In the case of children, for example, this may occur through play. Foulkes defined the concept of the matrix as the "hypothetical fabric of communication and relationships in a given group. It is the basis which ultimately determines the meaning and significance of all events" (Foulkes, 1974, p. 33). In the group matrix, there are numerous opportunities for changes in the child and parental relational elements (Staats, 2017, p. 101). In the controlled context of the group, children have many opportunities to develop skills and abilities, the effects of which will become apparent in their family, kindergarten, school, club, and profession experiences. Similarly, parents can accomplish tasks and achieve results within the protective environment of the group that they might not be aware of in every situation that arises during the process. These benefits include:
- the development of a sense of security,
- increased self-assurance for both children and parents,
- the development of communicative skills, and
- enhanced mentalization skills.

The "Watch, Wait, and Wonder" intervention method outlines specific tasks for this purpose:
- ensuring that the child engages in independent play and explores the environment in the presence of the caregiver,
- allowing the child to navigate and explore the relationship with the mother, father, other children in the group, and group leaders freely, and
- encouraging the child to test and develop a sense of self in relation to others.

4 Goals

4.1 Target groups

The primary focus is on children with regulatory disorders related to crying and sleeping, abnormalities in breastfeeding, feeding, and eating, as well as children facing difficulties in self-regulation, attachment, autonomy, and other aspects of social-emotional development. These challenges manifest differently depending on the child's age phase. The plan included describing possible abnormalities and disorders based on international standards, utilizing standardized criteria from DC: 0–5, a diagnostic instrument for children and infants.

4.2 Goals for the groups

In addition to addressing the physical needs of a human being and providing quality childhood education and upbringing, the focus is on managing relationships between children and their parents, emphasizing psychological, emotional, and social development. What occurs in these interactions? What developmental opportunities do groups offer to individuals? Between self-assertion and adaptation, retreat, and communicative exchange, participants learn to integrate experiences, engage in interactive processes, and explore boundary situations. Groups offer a space where children can explore "relationship struggles" through play and interaction with others, fostering experience, shaping, and development. Other goals for group work include:
- encouraging the group to be a familiar space for exploring parent-child dynamics together (developing a mindset of understanding, sharing ideas, collective thinking),
- focusing on the development of psychological, emotional, and social relationship-building skills for both children and parents,
- enhancing understanding of relationships within relationships,
- strengthening integration and a sense of belonging, and
- promoting interactive exchanges between group leaders and members (Staats, Bolm, and Dally, 2014, p. 21 ff., 47 ff., 256 ff.).

4.3 Goals for the parents

Many parents in parent-child groups did not have the opportunity as children to establish trust with their own parents or other adults. Recurring themes in the biographies of adult group participants guide their tasks as they navigate the challenges of parenthood. Quick relief in crisis, such as exhaustion and anxiety, is a top priority for them. Alleviating feelings of fear, insecurity, and self-doubt related to parenthood is addressed through shared observations, clarification, and exchanges within the group. Over time, parents receive help and support related to psychological issues, illnesses, and educational difficulties. The goal of parent-child groups also includes strengthening the parent-child relationship, promoting parental perception, increasing sensitivity, regulating emotions, and fostering conscious changes in perspective. With social support, successful coping strategies, and effective communication skills, parents develop a stable self-concept and positive self-assessment skills. Past influences – referred to as "ghosts in the nursery", as described by Selma Fraiberg – can be challenging or impossible for parents to recognize, address, and classify, especially where these influences have persisted over two or three generations (Fraiberg, 2011, p. 227). Identifying and raising awareness of these influences, and subsequently coping with them, are important objectives in parent-child-groups, often requiring ongoing clinical services.

4.4 Goals for the children

"Watch, Wait, and Wonder" is a psychotherapeutic approach that places the child at the center of parent-child work, emphasizing psychoanalytical-interactional orientations in interpersonal relationships. In group settings, children find a secure environment for undisturbed exploration alongside peers and adults, addressing issues related to social-emotional development, crying, sleeping, feeding, and eating. This process also involves acquiring and strengthening triangulation skills, enabling children to navigate different relationships within the group context. In the controlled and manageable setting of fixed groups, developmental delays can be prevented or mitigated through regular guidance and support.

"The happiness of even small children when they meet other children in the group is clear to see. They actively seek out these relationship experiences, few of which they as a rule have at home. Integration into a community – and later into more of them – is elementary for the development of identity (Staats, 2021, vol. 1, p. 163).

4.5 Goals for families

Parents are encouraged to develop the capacity to withstand uncertainties that arise in dealing with individuality and differences within the family. The aim is to foster stable individual autonomy for both parents and children while adhering to uniform group rules. Promoting and consolidating triangulation skills, which aid in handling competition, envy, and jealousy, is another important objective for parents and children, as these skills can be effectively tested and mastered in parent-child groups (Staats et al., 2014, p. 21 ff., 47 ff., 256 ff.).

4.6 Tasks according to "Watch, Wait, and Wonder"

A challenge in the psychological treatment of very young children and infants is that although the child is the central focus of treatment, the emphasis is often on the parents (Cohen, Muir, and Lojkasek, 2003). Thus, a central question arises: How can the child be directly involved in the development of the parent-child dyad, and later the triad, through their own activity. Specific tasks have been developed for this purpose, including:
- providing space for the child's initiative, curiosity, and self-expression,
- allowing opportunities for the child to explore and master their environment,
- creating an environment where the child can engage in relational struggles through play and in interaction with parents, enabling them to experience, shape, and develop relationships, and
- offering children opportunities to discover, develop, and express their unique ways and creative ideas.

5 Five children and their siblings

5.1 Paul

Paul, three years old, joined the group with his father. During the introduction, his father mentioned that Paul's older sibling took one and a half to two hours to fall asleep in the evening. Paul, despite being very tired, struggled to rest. He was brimming with ideas and consistently tried to involve the parents in playful activities. Whenever his parents attempted to leave the room, he would start crying heartbreakingly. Gradually, the parents found it challenging to remain affectionate with him. During the day, Paul displayed disobedience, put himself in dangerous situations, and threw objects across the room, even though he knew it was not allowed and was dangerous for his three-month-old brother. While his parents tried to be patient and repeatedly explained what he could and couldn't do, their patience wore thin during evening routines. He just didn't seem to understand, looked at them mischievously, and overstepped boundaries. Both mother and father were introverted, as evident from two home visits made by the group leader early on in the counselling. The mother appreciated the father's loving and caring nature towards her and the children. She preferred a quiet and orderly environment, finding Paul's behavior "out of character". Over time, Paul, who initially sat on his father's lap without playing, became more independent and self-sufficient. He started defending his play area against other children and became more assertive in confronting overly dominant playmates. He developed strategies to initiate contact but still made efforts to please his father.

Father and child attended the group 18 times. Towards the end, the father reported that Paul would say "good night" at bedtime, roll over, and no longer expect his parents to be present. He showed a cautious interest in his baby brother but initially struggled to play with him in an age-appropriate manner. His parents were better at helping him manage his emotions, but he still couldn't refrain from throwing objects.

5.2 Cosima

Cosima was nearly three years old when her parents sought early counselling. She had watchful eyes, played imaginatively, and was friendly. The parents attended counselling due to conflicting views on parenting, which caused frustration for their daughter. The father was strict and often overly controlling, while the mother wanted to grant her daughter more freedom with appropriate support. The father's fear of something going wrong often prevented this. Cosima, being particularly adventurous, resisted obeying her parents and often disregarded their expectations. The mother attended most of the twelve appointments, but occasionally both parents participated. They were able to identify and address changes positively, finding ways to work together. The combination of support in regulating emotions and maintaining boundaries within the parent-child relationship led to progress in both parent-child and social relationships. The father observed how his daughter cheerfully and confidently learned to assess risks during group sessions. Gradually, his excessive caution diminished, leading to a more relaxed family life where he trusted the mother's child-oriented parenting skills more, and this made her feel like a good mother.

5.3 Melia

Melia was four years old and her brother Nelson two months old when their mother contacted the counselling center. According to the mother, the infant was uncomplicated, slept well, and breastfed regularly. However, Melia reacted to disagreements with her parents by refusing to listen, crying, and throwing tantrums. She couldn't be calmed down through well-intentioned words, gestures, or reconciliation attempts.

Getting her ready for kindergarten each morning was a daily struggle. She refused to get dressed, eat breakfast, or go with her mother. After a recent visit to her grandparents, Melia began refusing to eat almost entirely, becoming disgusted by many foods and watching others eat. She ate a maximum of two yoghurts a day and drank one or two cups of juice. At kindergarten, she didn't eat anything for days. The parents were unable to exert significant influence on her behavior, and her pediatrician even considered sending her to the clinic for parenteral nutrition.

Thankfully, Melia received outpatient therapy three times a week with a psychoanalytical child and youth therapist. Initially, Melia refused to attend, and her mother had to carry her into the therapy room for the first three sessions. Over time though, Melia began to enjoy therapy and made progress in group sessions. However, she did not succeed in playing with other children. She claimed all the toys for herself alone, reacted with anger and became abusive. The other children were irritated and turned away. With both therapies, she could express anger in a more age-appropriate way, and was gradually able to stay in contact with her mother, the group leader, and later finally with the children. Her difficulties in playing with others lessened, and she was able to get in touch more benevolently. In the final session, she initiated a group game involving two children. She sat with another girl in a small wooden boat while a boy pulled the two of them "through the storm". All three visibly enjoyed it. In the past, Melia always wanted to play alone with the boat, but now she could celebrate it joyfully together with the other children.

5.4   Sophia

Sophia, aged four, and Glenda, nine months, came with their considerably exhausted mother and father. Sophia was remarkably shy and never spoke a word to strangers, while Glenda demanded breastfeeding frequently, cried, and whined throughout the day. The parents didn't seek individual counselling but consistently attended group sessions for two years. At the same time, Sophia was seeing a therapist once a week. With the third child, a son, the mother stayed at home and the father continued to attend the group with his daughters. Due to the pandemic, the groups ended, although the families wanted to continue. The mother's exhaustion was addressed during the pandemic with weekly home visits, as she had decided to attend therapy. Glenda gradually improved her communication skills in the group, transitioning from whining to age-appropriate forms of communication. Sophia became more open during the group sessions, engaging actively with the group leader and displaying creativity. She occasionally succeeded in connecting with other children, especially when she used humor to defuse tense situations. Once, when Arko, another child from the group, shouted for a long time, she imitated the group leader, held her ears, closed her eyes, and shouted: "It's too loud for me, oh dear, so loud, I have to cover my poor ears!" Arko then immediately stopped his crying. Apparently, he could relate better to the seemingly fragile girl than to an adult. The group leader was impressed. In that session, no one screamed anymore.

5.5 Arko

Arko's mother sought counselling and described everyday situations involving her five-year-old son. Arko lived with his father after his parents' separation and exhibited extreme anger, often making his mother and twelve-year-old sister fearful. He would scream loudly, hit his mother, kick her, throw objects randomly around the room, destroy household items, and damage furniture. He also demonstrated auto-aggression in various situations.

Despite his mother's attempts to discipline him, Arko continued to defy boundaries. She believed her mothering skills were very good, but she said: "My child does not obey. My child cannot accept boundaries." He displayed fears alongside his autonomy, anger, and sadness: "Does mummy not love me?", "But I want to be in charge", "She should always do what I say", "I'm angry and sad when I don't win", and "I tell my dad everything!" are some examples of Arko expressing his doubts about his mother's love and his desired control over her. However, he behaved differently with his father and at preschool. Sometimes he was inconsiderate towards younger children, especially girls.

His father refused to attend the group sessions, viewing the problem as primarily between mother and child. Mother and Arko attended ten sessions, and other children often discussed Arko at home. They found him cheerful and wild but occasionally intimidating. They were afraid of him, yet they always looked forward to seeing him again. They also enquired about him when he was absent. During those group sessions without Arko, they tried to assume a leadership role, and even several of his childish cheeky traits.

6 The group as psychoanalytically maternal object

6.1 Group sessions

In the group, there were constant triggers for the transference of relational experiences with parents. Each participant was part of the group and at the same time dependent on others for play, in scuffles, in struggles, in fights, in observing, and in being observed. These experiences could be repeated as needed. The parent-child groups aimed to provide parents and children with stabilizing experiences such as acceptance, emotional support, care, guidance, connectedness, attention, goodwill, sensitivity, emotional protection, inclusion, and belonging, as well as feeling and showing trust, finding a play partner, being allowed to be a play partner, receiving sympathy and comfort, being admired, and trying out new things in the protection of the group and parents. Besides that, they also enabled them to suffer failures and to learn to cope with failure, to be given limits, to experience different emotions interactionally, to get to know new sides of others, to develop a culture of conflict, and to learn to cope with conflicts.

6.2 The session begins

Often, disputes arose among the children over the singing bowl and the wooden stick at the beginning of the group. Every child wanted to have them. If they could not have them, they would try to steal them. The group leader chased the thief through the whole room. "You would like to keep the singing bowl, but I would like to have it too." The group leader grabbed the singing bowl, held it tightly, and they both pulled on it. While she laughingly reported back to the child how strong they were, the children were able to engage in this game to varying degrees. The friendly setting of boundaries, support for emotion regulation, relationship work, and humor alternated again and again in the scene. Sometimes the parents urged their children to let go of the singing bowl. This led to child insecurity and was worked through with the parents. For example, one child said: "As a child, I would be a bit annoyed if my mum didn't stand by me." Another added: "As a child, I would now ask myself whether my wish is wrong, or whether I am not allowed to show what I want." Children learn abstract concepts such as convictions, even false ones, which they quickly infer from parental reactions and reactions in their social environment (Fonagy et al., 2008, p. 37, 211). Their perception of the self can, because of others' influence, become a representation of the child's experience. If they do not succeed in representing an intentional self, they are likely to integrate the representation of others into their self-image, resulting in a false self (Fonagy et al., 2008, p. 204). "All three of you would like to strike the gong. Melia, Paul, and Cosima want to ring the gong so much," said the group leader, slowly and clearly. Everyone looked at her expectantly, as if she had the solution. "Watch, Wait, and Wonder"; first "watch": Three children addressed by name expressed the same wish. Then "wait": All were still looking with a wait-and-see attitude, alternating their gaze between the group leader, their mother, or father. They waited. And now? "Wonder": No one shouted, cried, or reached for the singing bowl or the wooden stick. Everyone saw their wish taken seriously. No one intended to give up their desire. Everyone seemed to be thinking about how to make it happen. It was difficult for the parents to remain silent. After a few moments of silence, the child with the wooden stick in their hand rang it first and passed it on to the next child. The idea caught on, and all the children took turns ringing the gong. Their wish came true without intervention from parents or the group leader, without regulation or determination. "Wonder": These were the ideas from creative children in a group situation. During the song in the circle, some children did not sing along but were already playing or hid in the tent. They still needed time.

6.3 Snack together in the group

During each group session, parents gathered around the table for a set time to enjoy tea and biscuits while engaging in conversation. The children could choose to participate or go and play. The atmosphere at the table ranged from relaxed and cheerful to thoughtful, informative, and often quite personal. Sometimes, disagreements arose when it came to feeding the children. Some parents preferred not to give their children food at this time of day, as high tea was already over, and dinner would be served later at home. The situation required some common ground to be reached. In many cases, eating was viewed by infants and toddlers in the context of regulation disorders or social-emotional problems. Observations of eating situations provided insight into the parent-child relationship or the causes of noticeable behavior. The children engaged in activities related to physical well-being not just when they were hungry. Childlike curiosity, the urge to explore, communal play, or the desire to have a drink were observed. They had fun with food, enjoyed it together, or tried new and unfamiliar things with an open mind, whereby the new and unfamiliar things were the greater focus for the children. For children aged one to two, this was their first experience playing together. For instance, they scattered blueberries on the carpet and joyfully ate them together, often sharing generously with other children despite their parents' reservations. In most cases, children between the ages of two and four preferred to decide for themselves what and when to eat, and sharing was challenging due to the dominant nature of self-assertion at this age. This often left parents perplexed. Additionally, focusing on food as a social experience and implementing age-appropriate eating requirements within a shared setting proved to be a challenge for them. In these families, fixed mealtimes, the choice of food ingredients, and table manners held high importance. Excessive demands on both sides, mutual misunderstandings between parents and children, and disruptions in eating and feeding were common issues in the groups.

6.4 The session ends – cleaning up and saying goodbye

In the midst of the most beautiful game, it would be time to say goodbye, and the process of cleaning up also formed part of the routine. It wasn't always popular with the children and parents, who complied with it but preferred to skip the task. Interestingly, a strong aversion to cleaning up often persisted into adulthood. From an early age, the grandparents had made sure that the parents kept order and tidied up as a matter of course, but it seems that the plans of the earlier generation did not work out. From a developmental psychological perspective, children under twelve months typically enjoy taking items out of the cupboards, but putting things away or tidying were not yet concerns for them. They needed play partners who enjoyed tidying up so they could express their joy in taking toys out. Children between 15 and 20 months, on the other hand, were more inclined to put things back, although they might take them out again right away. Here, a quick reaction is needed to items being put back in the box with friendly praise once it is just full. Children between 18 and 36 months would occasionally tidy up if they felt like it at that moment. Otherwise, they clearly demonstrated their resistance to their parents' desire for tidiness, which left parents unsure how to handle the situation. For children aged four and older, it was sometimes possible to persuade them to tidy up by turning it into a game, like a target-throwing competition with toy bricks, where whoever landed the most hits was the winner.

Initially, the group leader took on the responsibility of tidying up for efficiency reasons, ensuring that all toys were returned to their designated places to maintain order. This was essential, as it allowed children to always find their toys in the same place, which was crucial for highly irritated children. Any deviation in toy placement could lead to additional restlessness and stress. Some group rooms had an abundance of toys, making tidying up a challenging task for small children. The group leader took photos before the first group meeting to maintain order at the end. Families weren't involved in the clean-up process. Instead, parents were tasked with preventing their children from taking out more toys if they wanted to continue playing. This led to interesting observations of parent-child interactions during the farewell to the toys. Gradually, the children developed a desire to help clean up, but they were not yet allowed to do so. Children would not be children if they did not single-mindedly try negotiating and pushing boundaries, and their persistence succeeded. When their parents came with the toys and wanted to put them away, their children took pride in knowing where each toy belonged, and tidying up became quick and less burdensome. After two or three pieces, the youngest children felt that they had tidied up everything – how nice! – and it didn't hurt at all. At the end of the group session, the group would gather around a gong and participate in a group farewell song, while negotiating about saying goodbye. In case of strained parent-child relationships, dressing, saying goodbye, and leaving were often challenging. Various children's experiments, such as hiding in the tent, attempting to run away, signaling hunger and thirst, or resisting when parents tried to dress them, prolonged the process. The resigned empty promise of the mother, "Then mummy will go without you", was addressed by the group leader. Such promises give the impression that the mother was indifferent to whether their child comes along or not. This can potentially have devastating effects on the mother-child relationship and the development of the child's self-esteem. A maternally sensitive, but consistent demarcation of boundaries, in conjunction with an offer of a relationship, is usually a better approach. The group leader acknowledged the child's wishes: "You would like to stay here and continue playing." "Yes," the child answered. The next step involves giving the child an authentic presented boundary. At the same time, the boundary is repeated to the child once again to make it clear: "Hm, but I would like to go home. You don't want to at all." "No." Finally, in addition to the loving words, she offers a relationship: "If I leave now, I'd like to take you with me." This approach generally made the children happier and better equipped to handle the process of saying goodbye. If the mother was still unsuccessful, the process was repeated with sensitivity, loving, clear boundaries, and the offers of a relationship.

6.5 The group as a whole

An individual's ability to think within a group setting is influenced by their personal development. However, this ability depends on how their parents have been informed about children's behavior in groups, which begins in places like kindergarten, at school, among friends, associations, and later in university and at work settings. Unfortunately, these group experiences are often not reflected upon, and it's only within a group that one can truly understand what it's like to be part of a group.

The ability to think as a group involves both linguistic and non-linguistic communication during ongoing interactions within a specific context. At the same time, groups also function as public social situations where all utterances are understood contextually (Dally, 2014, p. 391).

For the group leader, managing the complex processes within different groups and ensuring they are helpful and transformative for the participants is demanding. In the early years, she was less successful in considering the group as a whole, since individual parent-child units often dominated the group's attention. For example, when a child like Arko got into a violent rage against the group leader because she blocked the door when he wanted to escape, the participants often focused on resolving the situation, waiting to see how the group leader would handle it. This sometimes overshadowed the broader group process. In cases like Arko's, it was essential to prevent him from running out into the cold alone without proper clothing or his mother, setting clear boundaries while supporting the regulation of his emotions and offering opportunities for building relationships. These steps were often addressed within the group setting, where everyone could witness the dynamics and the roles of each group member, along with the group's norms and rules. It wasn't sufficient for the group leader to listen to group members and deduce their thoughts and inner conflicts and structural limitations; she had to act in a way that others could see and hear, as expressions within a group are not only heard but also evaluated and judged by others (Dally, 2014, p. 391).

7   Interferences

At the Family and Competence Center on the campus of Potsdam University of Applied Sciences, significant interferences occasionally arose for the groups. For instance, the sound of students moving chairs from the seminar room above was quite audible in the group room. Some of the children were curious about these noises and their origin, prompting the adventurous ones to investigate with their parents, while other children remained fearful of the unfamiliar sounds. On one occasion, an employee emerged from his office to address a boy who was shouting loudly in the hallway, asking him to lower his volume due to the disturbance. He explained that the noise was making it difficult for him to work. The hallway, known for its remarkable noise resonance, often tempted children to explore and experiment with this phenomenon. Reactions among the children varied; some were impressed by the request for quiet, while others were not. Some children needed to grasp the concept of changing perspectives and the consequences thereof. On another occasion, a staff member became distressed upon hearing a child crying loudly and repeatedly in the group room, expressing a strong desire to leave: "I want to get out of here! The colleague could not imagine why the child was not allowed to leave when it seemed to be so important to him and was causing apparent distress. She contemplated entering the room – should she enter? But she ultimately decided against it. In a subsequent team meeting, she raised the issue, and the group leader provided a more detailed explanation of the situation.

8   Cooperation ideas

Opportunities for collaboration exist primarily with Potsdam University of Applied Sciences, facilitated by the leadership positions of Prof. Christiane Ludwig-Körner, Prof. Hermann Staats, and Prof. Karsten Krauskopf. These positions have established close ties between teaching, research, and practice. The group leader of the parent-child groups has been conducting professional seminars for students for several years, covering topics such as "The basics of conversation" and "Observation of the parent-child group". Additionally, she and two other staff members have served as lecturers at Potsdam University of Applied Sciences. Over the years, interns have worked at the family center for weeks or even months, taking on various roles, including organizing the parent-child groups. Notably, they focused on observing the parent-child relationships and children's play behavior within the groups. They familiarized themselves with the concept and methods through practical experience. After each group session, the group leader and all the trainees discussed the relationships, the children's interactions, developmental milestones, and challenges. Consequently, students deepened their theoretical understanding of early childhood development, attachment theory, and childhood abnormalities in the development of relationships through practical group experience. This systematic inclusion of students as future professionals is valuable.

9   Final thoughts

Group analysis can be used in various fields of work, including psychotherapy, education, social work, and organizational development (Staats et al., 2014, p. 17). Specifically, parent-child groups focusing on children between the ages of four months and six years prioritize relationship work. Simultaneously, they aim to identify and address unfavorable patterns and Selma Fraiberg's "ghosts in the nursery" to prevent their perpetuation. Group analysis is increasingly important for infancy and toddlerhood, with continuous parental involvement, as early childhood relationships are considered crucial. Methodologically, these specially guided parent-child groups incorporate the child-centered intervention method "Watch, Wait and Wonder", along with psychoanalytical-interactional principles including the group matrix, without neglecting developmental psychological aspects. The extension enables parents to actively participate in group processes, supporting their children's development and addressing psychological aspects throughout their lives. This makes parents more receptive and sensitive to additional pedagogical or therapeutic measures. However, the complexity of the group necessitates conceptualizations to assist the group leader in accomplishing their tasks within these methodologies and achieving participant objectives. The described methodology for infant and toddler groups can also benefit older children and adolescents facing corresponding challenges. The networking of health care, early intervention, and youth welfare can identify early difficulties and prevent them before they become deeply entrenched.

10   Outlook

One notable challenge is that parents, especially those facing sickness or significant burdens, may resist recommended measures for their infants and toddlers due to concerns. This resistance can extend to refusing inpatient psychiatric treatment or prematurely discontinuing treatment due to inadequate family support. Addressing this requires outpatient assistance that can prevent or abbreviate clinical measures while facilitating parental acceptance for specialized support. This can be achieved very well in a combination of individual and group settings. A regular, guided interaction group involving infants, toddlers, and their parents offers ongoing support for mental health issues, including personality disorders, addictions, and depression, often spanning several years. Psychosocial stress factors such as a strained parent-child relationship, lack of emotional availability for children, and low family cohesion, combined with unstable living conditions due to illness, pose a high risk for behavioral and developmental abnormalities of children. Attachment and mentalization research highlight the need for caregivers (parents) who can attentively monitor a child's developmental phases from birth, even when facing their own challenges. Encouraging these parents to participate in the interactive group concept presented here is crucial. Group encounters and play are elementary for the formation and development of relationships. These settings provide opportunities for sharing experiences and ideas related to stress and enhancing parental self-efficacy through social learning, alongside psychoeducational elements. Engaging in play within these interaction groups fosters joyful self-discovery, which can provide valuable services on the way to the liberation of the subject, autonomy, and the development of creativity (Pflichthofer, 2015). In essence, neither psychoanalysis nor play are devoid of joy.

At a glance:
Consequences of group-analytically oriented work in supervised parent-child interaction groups include:
- opening and expanding the patient's space for thought and experience,
- increasing awareness of each other and experiencing the weaknesses and strengths of each group member, allowing oneself to relate to the experiences of others,
- strengthening individuality and the development of one's own ego strength, and
- learning to navigate different relationships.

Parent-child interactional groups
The effectiveness of group analysis in a psychiatric context is evident through the visible and perceptible positive development of patients within the broader group context, beyond individual or group therapy. Depending on the age, structure, and context, the following methodological considerations are suitable for this field of work:
- the intervention program "Watch, Wait, and Wonder" (Cohen et al., 2003),
- relationship- and psychoanalytical-interactional oriented groups with parents and children, and
- recognizing play as an expression of health, a means of communication, and a form of expression on the path to maturation (Winnicott, 1997).

Bibliography

Cohen, N., Muir, E., Lojkasek, M. (2003). "Watch, Wait, and Wonder". Ein kindzentriertes Psychotherapieprogramm zur Behandlung gestörter Mutter-Kind-Beziehungen. *Kinderanalyse*, 11 (1): 58–79

Dally, A. (2014). *Gruppen leiten lernen. In H. Staats, A. Dally, T. Bolm (Hrsg.), Gruppenpsychotherapie und Gruppenanalyse. Ein Lehr- und Lernbuch für Klinik und Praxis:* 390–399. Göttingen: Vandenhoeck & Ruprecht

Fonagy, P., Gergely, G., Jurist, E. L., Target, M. (2008). *Affektregulierung, Mentalisierung und die Entwicklung des Selbst.* Stuttgart: Klett-Cotta

Foulkes, S. H. (1974). *Gruppenanalytische Psychotherapie. Der Begründer der Gruppentherapie über die Entwicklungsstationen seiner Methode in Theorie und Praxis.* München: Kindler.

Fraiberg, S. (1984). *Die magischen Jahre in der Persönlichkeitsentwicklung des Vorschulkindes. Psychoanalytische Erziehungsberatung.* Reinbek: Rowohlt

Fraiberg, S. (2011). *Seelische Gesundheit in den ersten Lebensjahren. Studien aus einer psycho-analytischen Klinik für Babys und ihre Eltern.* Gießen: Psychosozial

Heigl-Evers, A., Heigl, F. (1973). *Die psychoanalytisch-interaktionelle Methode. Theorie und Praxis.* Göttingen: Vandenhoeck & Ruprecht

Pflichthofer, D. (2015). *Spiel und Magie in der Psychoanalyse.* Wiesbaden: Springer Fachmedien

Staats, H. (2014). *Feinfühlig arbeiten mit Kindern. Psychoanalytische Konzepte für die Praxis in Kita und Grundschule.* Göttingen: Vandenhoeck & Ruprecht

Staats, H. (2017). *Die therapeutische Beziehung. Spielarten und verwandte Konzepte.* Göttingen: Vandenhoeck & Ruprecht

Staats, H. (2021). *Entwicklungspsychologische Grundlagen der Psychoanalyse.* vol. 1: *Schwangerschaft, Geburt und Kindheit.* Stuttgart: Kohlhammer

Staats, H., Bolm, T., Dally, A. (2014). Das Göttinger Modell der Gruppenpsychotherapie. In H. Staats, A. Dally, T. Bolm (Hrsg.), *Gruppenpsychotherapie und Gruppenanalyse. Ein Lehr- und Lernbuch für Klinik und Praxis:* 47–56. Göttingen: Vandenhoeck & Ruprecht

Strauß, B., Weber, R. (2014). Allgemeine und spezielle Wirkfaktoren in Gruppen. Theoretische Konzepte und empirische Ergebnisse. In H. Staats, A. Dally, and T. Bolm (Hrsg.), *Gruppenpsychotherapie und Gruppenanalyse. Ein Lehr- und Lernbuch für Klinik und Praxis:* 72–79. Göttingen: Vandenhoeck & Ruprecht

Winnicott, D. (1989). Playing and Reality. London: Routledge

Woods, M. Z., Pretorius, I.-M. (Hrsg.) (2013). *Eltern-Kind-Gruppen. Psychoanalytische Entwicklungsforschung und Praxisbeispiele. Schriften zur Psychotherapie und Psychoanalyse von Kindern und Jugendlichen.* Frankfurt/M.: Brandes & Apsel

ZERO TO THREE (2019). *DC: 0–5, Diagnostische Klassifikation seelischer Gesundheit und Entwicklungsstörungen der frühen Kindheit.* Stuttgart: Kohlhammer

From Holocaust Denial to a Personal Family Tableau: "Narrative Group Work" – How to Apply Group Analysis in Schools to Support Democratic Skills Europe-wide[1]

Harald Weilnböck

1 Social impact of group analysis

Group analysis was always intended be more than just therapy. Indeed, it was meant to have a societal impact, helping to promote liberal, democratic societies and support their resilience. In today's world, where democracies have come under enormous pressure from polarization, group-based hostility, conspiracy narratives, and violent extremism, and are also being undermined by parts of their own economic and political elites, group analysis can be applied as a much-needed form of "intensified civic education" for the younger generations (Weilnböck, 2019). A practical implementation to serve the goal of group analysis, namely, to have a sustainable social and educational impact, is now available in a pedagogical method – narrative group work. This was developed as a means of non-formal civic education in schools and youth institutions (Weilnböck, 2019; Cultures Interactive e. V., 2020). The current project focuses on rural and small-town settings, with the intention also being to prevent young people from slipping into right-wing extremist social milieus.

2 Application in schools and civic education

In discussions with teachers and colleagues in civic education, it is actually not that difficult to explain the goals and principles of process-open group work as opposed to those of "group analysis", as they happen to coincide with many of the educational objectives laid down in most schools' basic curricula. Hence, for example, narrative group work can promote important social and emotional

---

[1] The narrative group work approach is currently being further developed in the Horizon Europe project "OppAttune", coordinated by The Open University (cf. bibliography). This article is an English translation of Weilnböck 2021.

competencies among students, whereby their language education likewise benefits. After all, group work is dedicated to the essential psychosocial – and indeed pre-political – skill of having an engaged interpersonal conversation in the first place. This means actively listening to one another and paying as much unbiased attention as possible – and doing so with different people or in situations of equal diversity and open group conversation.

What is also immediately convincing for experienced educators and teachers is the fact that in this kind of group conversation, narrative skills, above all, can and should be developed. This is achieved by encouraging and enabling students to talk about greater or lesser personal experiences, i.e., to share their own experiences and listen to those of others. For these experiences and subjective perceptions are the experiential background of our views and opinions, which, taken on their own, often lead us very quickly into heated arguments and escalate fruitlessly, especially when so-called extremist views are held. If, however, students are given a space in which they can calmly be aware of each other's experiences, views, and circumstances, they will also learn to be more honest with each other and with themselves. They will learn to be better connected to their own feelings, experiences, and also to their insecurities – and to negotiate disagreements without developing personal resentment or denigrating others. These skills will effectively prepare students to reach across rifts of personal tension and social polarization to engage in conversation even with those who seem furthest removed from their own social milieu and opinion. Narrative skills and social-emotional agency in a diverse, democratic society are mutually dependent.

It is, however, indispensable that the students find and develop the issues covered in their conversations completely independently – and that no agenda and no thematic controls or taboos, no matter how subtle, are able to affect them. Furthermore, they should be accompanied by facilitators from outside the school who can guarantee confidentiality because they are not otherwise involved in the students' school matters. These facilitators deliberately limit the opening of the group conversation to a cordial "So, how's it going?", "What's going on with you, here at school or beyond?", or "What would you like to talk about here?"; or otherwise, "We are here to provide you with an open space, so you can talk among yourselves within the school!" Experience has shown that despite the complete thematic openness, or precisely because of it, students naturally end up talking about experiences and issues which touch upon current socio-political topics and questions of social interaction (e.g., prejudice, homophobia/sexism, bullying/hate speech, regional right-wing populism/extremism, etc.). Optionally, these topics can then also be taken up by teachers in related classes, while the specifically personal contexts of how the topics came up in the group remain anonymous, as a matter of course. In this way, the basic social and communicational skills among students are strengthened, as are their democratic convictions – and their passion to talk, share, and connect socially. At the same time, this also helps with prevention and intervention against anti-democratic and anti-human rights attitudes in and around the school.

3 Setting and methodology

In practice, narrative group work, which takes place over the course of one to two school semesters in sessions of one hour per week, works well with an existing class from which two groups of about nine to thirteen students are formed spontaneously. The schools make time available for this during regular school hours in different ways, e.g., utilizing the hours of social, language, or creative school subjects. Each group of students has a separate room and is accompanied by two group facilitators. These are preferably of mixed gender and socio-culturally diverse make-up (e.g., with regard to a migration background), so that temporarily dividing the group into two smaller sub-groups can be used all the more effectively. These sub-groups can be formed spontaneously for a variety of reasons, whereby the dividing line may be based on gender, other social criteria, or tension lines that have arisen in the group dynamic. As an additional setting variable, a time-out room with a fifth facilitator is provided, to which individual students can temporarily withdraw if necessary or to which they can be temporarily invited if the protection and support of the group conversation require it.

Given the circumstances of the project, the group facilitators are recruited on a rather ad-hoc basis from the ranks of civic educators and social workers. They can only be trained to a comparatively limited extent, learning a few techniques of narrative dialogue facilitation, active listening, and the very basics of dealing with group dynamics. On a more technical level, the participants then practice, for example, how to effectively ask narrative questions such as "how" questions: "How was the situation exactly?", "How exactly did it come about that …?", "Can you remember another experience that was similar/very different? How was it?" – while steering clear of "why" questions. The most important overarching element of this training, however, is that it supports the future facilitators of narrative group work in schools in putting aside the usual patterns of (counter-)arguing and discussing, which we have internalized from our omnipresent culture of debate and from civic education, and in cultivating an attitude that favors establishing relationships and joint narrative exploration.

Those schools that are interested are usually found through school social work and committed school heads, or through knowledgeable persons in the state ministries of education and schooling, with whom we have contact as a framework partner NGO within the federal program "Live Democracy!", aimed at strengthening democracy. Cultures Interactive is a non-profit association that has been active for 20 years in so-called model projects for the prevention of right-wing extremism, primarily in eastern Germany and eastern Europe, utilizing youth culture workshops, civic education, and group work in varying innovative combinations. The colleagues in our field are predominantly civic educators and social workers, and more recently they are increasingly also (systemic) counsellors. Only the project lead is trained in group analysis.

We offer the teaching staff of the schools an information event and, if they are interested and if the project budget allows, advanced training in using our methodology. The setting of the narrative conversation groups[2] described above has three important interfaces, with the first being subject teaching in the classroom (as already mentioned). The second is municipal youth and family welfare services, which may also provide targeted measures of so-called deradicalization or other forms of psychosocial interventions (e.g., mental health, prevention of suicide, violence/sexual assault, drug abuse, etc.), since the need for these may become evident during group work with the students. The third interface is school counselling in the event that systemic issues emerge in the particular school in the form of systemic bullying and so-called extremism, or otherwise inappropriate behavior among teachers.

This interagency cooperation along certain interfaces of the group work setting aims to further the lasting impact, especially in rural schools with high needs for prevention of right-wing extremism and group-focused hatred (cf. "Group-Focused Enmity"). In the medium term, the objective is to inspire ministry-level education policies to the effect that narrative group work, serviced by independent NGO practitioners, can become a standard element in the state school education system and potentially a special focus of European education policies.

---

2 For further explanation of the setting, see the "Evaluation Report", available in German on the project page (cf. Weilnböck, 2019).

4 Reconstruction of consecutive group work sessions with students

4.1 Saying the unspeakable I – Holocaust denial

The dynamics of a particularly impressive sequence of two sessions with such a narrative conversation group may well illustrate the potential inherent in this method of intensified civic education. In a group at a rural high school in eastern Germany, close to the Polish border, participants interacted in a comparatively prosocial, open-hearted, and consensual manner. The 15-year-old students opened up personally so quickly and to such an extent that, as early as the third session, they also made some hints and statements about their political attitudes and those of their families and village communities. This was probably not easy for them, as in some of their communities the extreme right-wing populist party AfD (Alternative for Germany) enjoys an approval rating of more than two-thirds of the population. Furthermore, in some of the groups in this school there were indications of connections to right-wing extremist and vigilante milieus ("Reichsbürger"), some students carried concealed iron swastikas, and questions of illegal gun ownership in the families became a topic. The group facilitators (from an independent NGO external to the school) had previously assured the students in their groups on various occasions of the fundamental confidentiality of everything that is said in the group. In the course of the continual relationship-building process, the students developed increasing confidence in the open and unbiased space of group work, the reliability of the facilitators, and also among the students of their own group (which comprises half of their class).

One 15-year-old, for example, took advantage of the third weekly session to provocatively relativize the Holocaust with a tone of conviction and without any apparent immediate reason. He stated very emphatically that "the Holocaust wasn't that bad after all"; that "there weren't that many by far", and that "the Jews had always been persecuted". He went on to say that "Germany was so technically advanced"; "... We had the gas chambers ... and someone had to do it anyway", but "now it's just Germany carrying the can for it" and "forever being reproached". "And besides, what about the German prisoners of war in Russia? There were 270,000 of them, and only 5,000–6,000 came back. Ask yourself why that was! ... But you're not allowed to talk about such things at school anyway." The young man then got ready to show the group on his cell phone where all this and much more that could be read on "forbidden websites".

This relatively abrupt, drastic statement was certainly to be understood in this group partly as an attempt by the 15-year-old to underpin his social status and to continue to test the group facilitators' trustworthiness and composure. However, the views expressed were recognizably also what the young man and a significant part of his family-like village environment authentically believed and voiced. In any case, this gave the group facilitators a welcome opportunity to enter into direct personal conversations and relationships by means of narrative dialogue questions about an issue that is also a central topic of historical and civic education – and thus to further deepen their previous work with the group. They therefore refrained from contradicting or rebuking the young man at this point, nor did they present the historical facts or take a specific position, as is usually the impulse and procedure of civic education in such situations. The fact that the boy's assertions are factually wrong and also punishable by law in Germany, and that they themselves do not, of course, hold this view, was mentioned by the group facilitators here rather in a by-the-way fashion, depending on the personal style and need for clarification on the side of the respective facilitator. Nor did this group have the slightest doubt as to what attitude the team, which had come from a metropolitan – supposedly leftist – area, would have on questions of German history.

Instead, the group facilitators firstly expressed their fundamental respect and appreciation for the openness with which the boy expressed himself – and then successively and carefully made an effort to explore the individual and social background of this statement, together with the group. Young people usually find such exploration very exciting and like to actively engage in it. An initial question as to whether he often confronts those around him with this or similar statements signaled the facilitators' intent to build closer contact with him – but at this point in time only led to the boy underlining the factual seriousness of his statement. This was perhaps because he was not yet able to understand the question as an invitation to narrative personal storytelling. The group facilitators' way of moderating the conversation then followed the guideline: "By the way, I don't agree with you about the Holocaust (which you probably already guessed yourself), but tell me how you arrived at this conclusion – and also, more broadly, who you actually are as a person? … Do you often have conversations about these topics? … What moves you on this? … Tell us a little bit about the people you mix with – and also those who tell you these things. … What else do you experience with them? Do you ever argue with them? Do you sometimes have questions? What do you usually experience when you say things like that in school?", along with other narrative dialogue questions. This attitude of narrative interaction follows the basic pattern of "No!-But-yes,-do-tell-me-more-about-it!"; that is, it leads away from the level of opinions, views, arguments, and also facts, and tries to approach the level of individual experience, memory, biography, also personal emotions and motivations.

In this session, however, the young man did not seem to want to get involved yet – and with this behavior proved to be similar to other students at the school in another group. They also showed similar right-wing extremist attitudes (carrying concealed iron swastikas with them) and displayed rather obstructive and oppressive behavior (cf. Weilnböck, 2020). For this reason, the facilitators took measures as early as possible to involve the group as a whole, to pick up on the polarization and emotionalization that was caused – and most likely intended – by the boy's provocative statement and led the group conversation in a direction that allowed for the narrative dialogue and sharing of personal experiences. This proved to be hardly necessary, as this comparatively trusting group became engaged quite quickly and was supported by the facilitators with appropriate questions: "What can the rest of you say about this?", whereby the focus is on the level of personal experience and observation rather than that of opinion and arguments: "How do the rest of you feel about these statements? Have you had personal experiences where you could relate to this? Where else do you encounter such situations/topics? What happens in these situations? How do they unfold? Which people are involved? What do you experience with them?", etc.

In this, a series of short, often simultaneously and overlappingly spoken contributions took place, which offered various possibilities for further deepening through narrative inquiries. Two students demarcated themselves immediately, naming the technical term "Holocaust denial" themselves, thus indicating a certain adeptness in discourses of civic education. Another boy seemed to want to partly distance himself from the 15-year-old's statement, but explicitly concurred that "you can't talk about all this in school." Another told the facilitators that such statements were often heard in the area, which provided further opportunities to garner new experiences relating to the views as reported from the community. Two other students attempted to mediate on behalf of the boy, commenting on what "he was like" and that this should be understood on a personal level ("that's just his thing"). The boy himself then responded intermittently and affirmed some assessments, which indicated the relatively high degree of personal relating, understanding, and communality in this group/class across different fractions. In fact, one or two similar situations when the boy had acted out in this way were specifically alluded to, which offered further opportunities for experiential deepening – especially since one situation had implied a public display of the Hitler salute, which then had serious consequences for the young man.

The group engaged in this self-motivated, group-dynamic conversation with the help of the external facilitators in a confidential space, addressing this politically explosive topic and their confrontational classmate – and this alone may already be deemed immensely valuable from a pedagogical perspective. Such conversational space will easily evolve into exploring other experiences, memories, and reflections relating to local right-wing extremist subcultures, which could then be built on pedagogically in various ways and on different levels of schooling. Furthermore, such sequences of a narratively oriented group conversation support the students' conversational, social, and reflective skills as well as their skills of interacting in groups and their level of emotional intelligence. Consequently, in this and later sessions with this group, the topic of right-wing extremism in the region and in some of the students' families was addressed from an increasingly personal perspective. This is only possible in a safe and confidential space in which this historical topic is not brought to the students top-down through a planned teaching unit as part of an educational agenda.

4.2 How to save and strengthen future civic education

To begin with, it is important to underline what the narrative group work setting achieved here, already in one of the first sessions of this group: It succeeded in avoiding a frequently occurring and tragic failure of civic education. Because this shocking – and of course condemnable – statement from the young man is generally viewed as the worst-case scenario of civic education; which it is really not, depending on how you look at it and which setting you have put in place. However, the general view of civic education is that here absolutely unacceptable and unspeakable things were said; and the ethos of the profession thus demands that this must be avoided and refuted by all means. The young man must therefore be corrected, even sanctioned and "put in his place"; civic education, as it were, needs to crack down on this – and the statement must be entirely annulled at all costs.

Some civic educators even feel anxious that if they do not intervene restrictively and with maximum impact, they may violate the unalienable standards of pedagogical practice under penalty of professional excommunication. In fact, the fear of being bitterly reproached about not being strict enough with such youngsters and their statements seems to be quite widespread in the professional community in Germany due to a somewhat polarized, decade-long controversy about the so-called "accepting approach" in youth work ("akzeptierender Ansatz"). Moreover, it is thought that if such a statement is not immediately confronted and revoked, this would unfailingly result in strengthening right-wing extremist propaganda – hence the view of a presumptive worst-case scenario: civic education being turned into its opposite, i.e., into extremist propaganda. This fear is understandable in various respects; after all, the young man even goes on to share "forbidden web pages" in the group (which, however, he has probably been doing all the time in his class, school, and beyond anyway).

But in what sense may this stringent crack-down on the unacceptable, right-wing extremist statement be a tragic and frequently occurring failure of civic education, as has been claimed above? By strictly correcting the statement at all costs and sanctioning the 15-year old boy by "putting him in his place", the group work practitioners would instantly and inevitably lose the trust of and contact with precisely those young people with whom we most urgently need to stay in personal and pedagogical contact – because we are about to lose them as future citizens of our liberal and human-rights-based, democratic society.[3] In fact, they would not only risk losing the 15-year-old boy in question but to a certain extent also put at risk the trust, respect, and openness of the entire group. Because some of the group understandably say "that's just his thing", and they actually like their fellow student more or less, which is in and of itself not a bad thing within a diverse and dynamic group. Also, another young man who distanced himself from the statement said, "but at school you're not allowed to talk about that kind of thing anyway."

Hence, in this particular situation and through the setting of narrative group work, the team succeeded in avoiding this tragic and frequently occurring breakdown of civic education – and, in fact, it became possible to turn the situation around quite positively in the end without strict corrections, sanctions etc., but rather by viewing what at first may have seemed to be a worst-case scenario of civic education as quite the contrary – a most promising opportunity. How was this possible?

During the first sessions, the group, with the help of the external facilitators, has effectively elicited their status quo in terms of Holocaust awareness as well as associated topics and personal experiences. These were all addressed with surprising openness. This already constituted a significant success in the work, especially since experience shows that it is in such early moments that the first processes of psycho-emotional reflection and a change of attitude begin to set in with the students in an imperceptible manner. A further intensification of

---

3   This is not to say that in conventional settings of civic education and, above all, in semi-public situations of teaching/education it would not be at least partly necessary to clearly refute such statements. Also, one key concern of narrative group work, of course, is always to first check with and take care of those who may suffer and/or have been victimized by any such inappropriate and provocative statements in the group.

these processes can now be initiated in many ways through the above-mentioned techniques of asking narrative dialogue questions (see above: "Are there comparable situations/experiences?", "Who is involved?", "What else do you experience in them?", "What do the teachers say?", etc.). For each of these questions would lead to an exchange of personal experiences, observations, and reflections on this highly relevant issue of community life and democratic politics that is otherwise unlikely to occur in school, either in class or in informal student conversations.

Towards the end of this session, however, one of the facilitators decides to go one step further and ask a different kind of narrative dialogue question, which addresses the young man more directly and personally: "I am very interested in what you said about the Holocaust. However, when I listen to how you talk about this topic, I wonder first and foremost whether you are possibly a cruel person. What do you think? Is that so? ... Can you maybe describe a situation from your life to me where you would say, yes, that's where I was cruel – and sometimes I am a cruel person?" And because the end of the hour was already near, the facilitators opened up this question to the entire group, presenting it as homework for the week: "Why don't you all think about this before next week, ... i. e., whether you have ever said things similarly to your classmate about the time of National Socialism or similar issues ... or heard them – and also, regardless of this, whether you think you are sometimes cruel and what related situations there might be to talk about."

4.3 Saying the unspeakable II – the family tableau behind Holocaust denial

In the follow-up session, it became apparent that some of the students had actually taken the weekly task seriously, which is not always a given. There were also indications that the students had since talked about the issues from the group session in their informal contact (at recess, between lessons, or outside of school) and had also discussed the week's homework. In any case, the 15-year-old and two classmates reported at the beginning of the session that they had thought about it and had come to the conclusion that they were not cruel. They could not remember any such situations. What struck them, however, was that they probably did not have "many strong feelings anyway" and were sometimes rather "callous".

Moreover, there was a very big shift in the general quality of the group conversation, both thematically and in terms of mood and atmosphere, compared to the last session. The latter had a predominantly provocative and boisterous character – up to the point that the 15-year-old wanted to show the "forbidden websites" (which, of course, was prevented with the clarification that anything could be said in narrative conversation groups, but nothing illegal should be done). In contrast, the follow-up session, in which the young people came back with observations about the topic of cruelty, was rather contemplative. To the facilitators' surprise, much was said about death and dying – and also some things about being sad – without it being initially apparent how these topics had come up in the group (which, however, did unconsciously correspond to the topics of the Holocaust and cruelty, especially since they were what had triggered the homework). Thus, the group talked about various experiences of death within families, but also about the death of animals, whether on the farms or of pets. It was apparent that meaningful informal conversations among the students had preceded the group session.

This course of open conversation, mainly taking place within a self-determined group dynamic, then suddenly arrived at a very remarkable statement. The statement came from the same 15-year-old who had previously denied the Holocaust in an evidently right-wing extremist manner, and had thus given rise to the question about cruelty to begin with. After the group had grasped and adopted the mode of narrative, storytelling communication surprisingly quickly (which is often the case with young people) and the group conversation had evolved to speaking about death and sadness, the 15-year-old now talked about what it was like when his paternal grandmother died, who had lived with the family in his parents' farmhouse in the local village. His father had "not even winced" and had "gone about his duties quite normally the following day and swept the yard." The boy mentioned this in relation to the topic of insensitivity/callousness, which was introduced by him and two classmates, and thus in response to the weekly homework (which had originated from his Holocaust denial). From this narrative, however, he moved on to a very sober, yet shattering observation: He said that he was "deeply convinced that his parents would not be sad if he died".

In this moment of the group process and surrounded by half of his classmates, the young man came to the point where, in an outwardly relatively unaffected but very serious manner, he presented a personal assessment that was actually unbelievably sad: He assumed that his parents would probably not be sad about his death. These are thoughts that the teenager had presumably never testified to before and possibly had not even been aware of with any great clarity. Hence, this personal observation had been enabled and facilitated by a group process that had developed over just three sessions (but also the numerous informal intermittent moments the classmates spend together on a daily basis). The first culmination of this process was the striking denial of the Holocaust, which the facilitators made space for in an entirely unagitated and self-assured manner and with which the boy probably also tested the trustworthiness of a setting that was completely unknown to him. This led to an engaged and sincere group conversation about the topic of the Holocaust – and to the question of possible personal cruelty on the part of the young man as well as of other students, then on to the weekly task of reflecting on cruelty. Some students' observations about moments of their own emotional insensitivity followed, bringing to light memories of moments of callousness on the part of parents, especially in relation to the topics of death and dying. A general conversation about death, dying, and callousness ensued within the group at this point, leading the young man to assume his parents would not regret his death. The starting point was, as said, a moment of Holocaust denial.

The fact that it was possible to talk openly and confidently about all these thoughts, experiences, feelings, and views (especially in an institution where, the students said, people are "not allowed to talk about such things here anyway") was of great value for the personality and skills development of each and every young individual in the group. Furthermore, the school's curriculum objectives regarding intellectual, emotional, and social competence were fulfilled to the utmost here, while the issues touched upon are also relevant to the specific curricular content of subjects such as history and civic education. Hence specialized lessons dealing with the Holocaust and Holocaust denial or a regional history project can easily be linked thematically.

Also in the group work setting itself in which historical teaching should not take place, the pedagogical effect of this situation can be deepened in many ways by the facilitators. For one, facilitators will certainly use the opportunity to signal their empathetic presence as attentive and solidary human beings: "Oh, I'm sorry about your parents. That certainly wouldn't feel good to have those thoughts." This may be followed by further questions or comments and experiences from the young man or the other young people in the group. More detailed reflections may be prompted by remarks such as, "somehow, I'm not so surprised now that you sometimes say things that are so cruel and don't seem to notice."

Of course, an authentic civic educator and group facilitator can also just say more directly what he or she might spontaneously think: "I just had the idea that maybe you say all these rather right-wing extremist and cruel things because there is this thing of 'insensitivity' with you, some of your classmates, and with your parents. Has anyone else here experienced anything similar or had related thoughts?" Further: "And as far as cruelty and right-wing extremism are concerned, there is quite a bit of it at this school and here in the region, which we have been hearing about in the meantime. Do you want to tell us more about it?"

The group or individuals may intuitively succeed in recognizing some of the psychological connections between cruelty, "insensitivity", Holocaust denial, certain family dynamics, and political issues of the region and regional history (as regional right-wing extremism, assaults by cruel fathers, emotional under-provision for children/sons, etc.). Where this is the case – and one should never underestimate students in their intuitive psychological intelligence, after all! – then the pedagogical effectiveness of this series of weekly group conversations is optimally enhanced.

In any case, it hardly comes as a surprise that the topic of cruelty came up again and again later on in group sessions – and also in cautious conversations about some fathers "who are right-wing" and occasionally also cruel.

5 Advocating for narrative group work in school to be included in governmental education policies

From the perspective of civic education and the prevention of so-called extremism, it can be assumed that the greatest possible impact was achieved with this group, which was made up of young people from a right-wing extremist milieu and family environment. This may be especially true for the 15-year-old who, one may justifiably hope, might no longer resort to patterns of Holocaust denial so easily or at all in the future despite his environment. In any event he, along with the group of classmates around him, will presumably always remember the conversations about cruelty, Holocaust denial, insensitivity, and his presumption about his parents and family.

In the overall group-analytical view of these two sessions, one might reasonably claim that one moment of saying the presumably unspeakable seemed to have led to something else – i.e., Holocaust denial on the one hand, and the recognition of insensitivity and callousness in one's own family and oneself on the other. This resulted in a highly effective pedagogical process, which in principle also holds the potential for bringing a psycho-social impulse to the community and the region as such. But one would not have been possible without the other. With regard to the methodology of civic education, one may conclude: Those not willing to allow the unspeakable to be spoken because of political considerations and fears must know that they will have to sacrifice the possibility of any such profound social-therapeutic effect.

Furthermore, we can draw the important conclusion that in our responsibility towards young people, the generation to come and the school education put in place to raise them, we are well advised to provide these kinds of safe spaces of maximum expressiveness, free talk, impartiality, and openness to diverse (group) relationships, in which young people can express and explore everything that affects them. This seems especially relevant for regions and social milieus burdened with (right-wing) extremists and similarly anti-democratic and anti-human-rights attitudes. For in each case, the unspeakable obviously always wants and needs to be said – be it the unspeakable in the sense of being brazen, provocative, and politically shocking, or in the sense of being not entirely conscious or personally-not-yet-sayable. If, however, there is no space provided for exploring and saying the unspeakable, education and personality development will tend to falter, and things may easily move towards the "cruel" and extremist.

The intensified pedagogical method of narrative group work is one possible way to make things sayable and thus support education and public schooling. What has yet to happen though, on national and European scales, is that state education ministries adopt such methods of intensified civic education, provided by independent NGO practitioners, into the standard curriculum of schooling as a successful combination of formal and non-formal education. The NGOs providing the non-formal education element should therefore work in cooperation with a university of applied sciences for education and social work that could provide the framework for facilitator training and quality management. This would result in a sustainable framework of civic education in schools – which would be able and effective in safeguarding liberal and resilient democracies in times of increasing polarization and loss of political trust.

> **At a glance:**
> School education systems need a fundamentally new pedagogical element to support students from all social milieus in developing their capacity of "doing democracy" and practicing human rights. Current anti-democratic and so-called "extremist" subcultures among young people underscore this necessity.
>
> A group-analytically oriented setting – such as the "narrative group work in schools" setting – can serve as this new, intensive-pedagogical element. It is here that young people can be trained in the often underestimated basic relational and democratic skills ...
>
> ... to lead a respectful, engaged, and trusting conversation with each other,
> ... to share, communicate, listen to, and process personal experiences,
> ... to do this in group situations that are completely open in their topics and results, together with various other young people,
> ... to become fully attentive to each other and themselves in the group and to enter into a dynamic group relationship,
> ... to practice honesty with each other and with themselves,
> ... to better deal with their own feelings and insecurities as well as with the feelings and insecurities of others,

> ... to navigate conflicts and negotiate disagreements free of bias, resentment, and devaluation of others.
>
> A vibrant and resilient democratic society needs these skills in order for its citizens to remain in contact and keep up the social discourse across all divides and polarization.

Bibliography

Cultures Interactive e. V. (2020). *Good practices in preventing intolerance, discrimination, and group hatred in Central and Eastern Europe.* https://www.ceepreventnet.eu/publications.html (last accessed September 28, 2023)

The Open University (OU), Cultures Interactive e. V. (CI) et al. (2023). The OppAttune project (CI project subtitle: *"Attuning Oppositional Extremism through Social Dialogue. Recognize, Attune, Limit";* OU project subtitle: "Countering Oppositional Political Extremism through Attuned Dialogue: Track, Attune, Limit" (last accessed September 28, 2023)

Weilnböck, H. (2019). *Intensivpädagogische politische Bildung – Narrative Gesprächsgruppen an Schulen im ländlichen und kleinstädtischen Raum.* Ergebnisse der qualitativen Selbstevaluation von Gesprächsgruppen. (Engl.: Intensive-pedagogical civic education – Narrative group work in rural and small-town schools. An evaluation report.). https://cultures-interactive.de/de/das-projekt-narrative-gespraechsgruppen.html (last accessed September 28, 2023)

Weilnböck, H. (2020). *Rekonstruktive Fallbeschreibung des Verlaufs der Gruppensitzungen der "Alpha"-Gruppe – Phänomene und Bearbeitung von Herrschafts- und Verhinderungsdynamiken sowie von Rechtsextremismus unter Schüler*innen einer neunten Klasse.* (Engl.: Reconstructive case analysis of group sessions of the "Alpha" group. Phenomena and processing of dynamics of domination and oppression – and of right-wing extremism among students in a ninth-grade class). https://cultures-interactive.de/files/publikationen/Fachartikel/2020_Weilnboeck_Rekonstruktion%20Gruppenverlauf%20Alpha-Gruppe.pdf (last accessed September 28, 2023)

Weilnböck, H. (2021). Von der Holocaust-Leugnung zum persönlichen Familientableau – Kleine Verlaufsvignette zu zwei Sitzungen von Narrativen Gesprächsgruppen an Schulen. In K. Stumptner (Hrsg.), *Gruppenanalytisch arbeiten mit Kindern und Jugendlichen. Impulse für eine kreative und vielfältige Praxis?* (S. 96–109). Göttingen: Vandenhoeck & Ruprecht

Playing

On Playing

Dietlind Köhncke

Children need to play in order to develop. Play is their inherent drive, their desire and will. They play tag and other movement games, they try out and create roles, they animate objects, they test the unwritten rules of the community in the peer group. If this is interrupted for a prolonged period of time, as it was during the pandemic in 2020–21, it has an impact on their well-being, their vitality, and their social behavior.

During the 2020–21 winter lockdown, children and adolescents suffered from a lack of exercise, play, and social contact with their peer groups. Pediatricians and adolescent therapists observed an increase in behavioral problems. "No wonder," said Andreas Gassen, head of the National Association of Statutory Health Insurance Physicians (*Kassenärztliche Vereinigungen,* KBV), "if they have no other children to play with and no structured days for weeks" (from "News" on the "Tagesschau" TV program, January 30, 2021).

Child and adolescent therapists know how essential play is for the development and well-being of their clients, and they use this in their groups. They will be better able to do this the more they have their own approach/access to play (Winnicott, 1971, p. 49). This enables them to discover in themselves the resources and opportunities for change contained in play, and at the same time to empathize with the children and adolescents. The curriculum for the training of child and adolescent group therapists also states that the opening of play spaces and the ability to play are among the key qualifications. What could be more suitable for gaining access to this than one's own group self-experience?

One notion of play is part of the everyday knowledge that we have accumulated from childhood to adulthood. We know that playing is exciting and brings joy, that you can forget about time, that you need other players, that there are rules to the game and that there can also be spoilsports. But even though we know all this, it is worth taking a closer look at the game in order to understand its facets and its potential, its complexity and effectiveness, to get suggestions for one's own play behavior and to consider whether and how one could profit from it in the group self-experience. This will be attempted in the following.

1   Come dance with me! Play as movement.

The word for "play" in German is "spielen", which can be traced back to the Old High German and Middle High German "spil," meaning "dance" or "to move quickly and joyfully" (Mackensen, 1966, p. 328; Kluge, 2002, p. 865). Dancing as a rhythmic movement in joyful togetherness is thus inscribed in the word, even if we are not aware of it, as both a natural and a cultural phenomenon. The natural, innate urge to move and to experience this as pleasurable is taken along into the dance, in which the togetherness is shaped in rhythmic fellowship, the natural is combined with the cultural. And this was already the case in early times in a group in which there was a "spiliman", a lead dancer, who taught the rules of the respective dance.

It is interesting that both body-oriented psychotherapist George Downing and infant researcher Daniel Stern also characterize the early interaction between mother and child as a dance without an etymological reference. For them, play in rhythmic togetherness is a "dance of interactions" (Downing, 1996, p. 147; Stern, 1979, p. 107).

Even in the animal world, playful movement sometimes seems like a dance. For example, American game researcher Stuart Brown reports on the game of two grizzly bears in the Alaskan wilderness performing a real dance. With ears laid back, eyes dilated, mouth open, they went at each other, circling, pirouetting, leaning on each other, head to head, body to body, paw to paw (Brown, 2009, p. 28).

The deeper meaning of the connection between movement and play is taken up by the philosopher Hans-Georg Gadamer. Play as movement, he says, is a free, repetitive back and forth that pursues no other purpose than this movement itself. "The freedom of such movement [...] implies that it must have the form of self-movement. Self-movement is the fundamental nature of the living. What is alive has the drive of movement in itself, of self-movement. Play now appears as self-movement [...], which means, so to speak, a phenomenon of surplus, of the self-presentation of the living" (Gadamer, 1998, p. 30).

Infant researchers Janus and Mechthild Papoušek also emphasize the importance of self-activity. Early childhood play is seen as spontaneous, self-initiated learning that is guided by curiosity, self-activity, self-efficacy, a need for exploration, and as integrating experiences: "In self-directed play, the child is guided by the developmental dynamics of its maturing motor and integrative abilities" (Papoušek, 2003, p. 32). The related exploration, in turn, is the basis of all learning.

Play as self-movement, i.e., movement of one's own accord and free of a specific purpose, is obviously innate as something natural and is shared by humans and animals. The Canadian research group led by Jan Panksepp even counts play as one of the positive innate basic affects driven by a search-reward system, i.e., stimulating curiosity and exploration and rewarding this with pleasure (Schultz-Venrath, 2011, p. 117).

But although it is directly purposeless, play has a "higher" evolutionary meaning that the players are not aware of, in that it contributes to the development of the skills needed to adapt to the environment and to survive. By playing, young animals learn to capture prey, test rank order, and explore the limits of social compatibility of their own behavior within their own species. However, they do not capture prey, they do not defend territory, and the regulation of rank is not a motive for play. And by playing, children develop physically, mentally, and spiritually and gain experience with their own social behavior. The players themselves, however, basically do not pursue any direct purpose except that of playing itself. Humans are able to play until old age, while animals stop playing when they are adults, because animals only play under the protection of parental care, whereas humans can shape the framework for play themselves.

2   I give you both my hands. Play as interaction

Playing is a reciprocal process. Play always requires co-playing, says Gadamer; it is a "communicative act" (Gadamer, 1998, p. 31). This is also the view of Panksepp, who sees play as "dependent on responsivity" (cited in Brown, 2009, p. 62). From the perspective of attachment research, playful exploration is only possible within the framework of a secure attachment (Bowlby, 1969).

Play thus begins in earliest childhood, initially in the interaction between the first caregivers and the infant, and continues in the peer group. Today, we know from video-based interaction analyses of the early mother-infant relationship that successful dyadically structured play follows an intuitively coordinated choreography. In early body-related play, for example, there is a ritualized sequence with many repetitions, with a shared sequence of tensions that is soon anticipated by the baby, which is discharged in shared pleasure and leads into a recovery phase. Gergely speaks of "natural pedagogy" (Gergely and Csibra, 2005). It is not so important that the play always runs harmoniously. It can also be abruptly disturbed and interrupted. The only important thing is that there is then a phase of "repairing" in which the harmony is restored. In his model of reciprocal regulation, the interaction researcher Tronick describes that the caregiver-child interaction follows an oscillating interplay of mutual adaptation and missing adaption (Tronick, 2007). Here the basis for the distinction between togetherness and separateness is laid. A brief painful experience of separation is followed by reunion. Under stress – and separation is stress – the attachment system is activated, and this is precisely the basis for our learning to tolerate separation.

Studies on mother-child interaction show that depressed mothers play less with their children than healthy mothers, e.g., they are much less able to imitate the child and mark the child's expression, their interaction style is hardly stimulating and is withdrawn, intrusive, and not very sensitive or responsive (Field et al., 2000). They also have few verbal and play interactions with their children (Righetti-Veltemam, Bousquet, and Manzano, 2003).

Thus, it is possible to study at an early age what disrupts a child's ability to play and to infer that restoring playfulness is a therapeutic goal, both in child and adolescent therapy and in adult group self-awareness.

3   Play as sensory-symbolic communication

Today we know that changes are not so much initiated by awareness and cognitive understanding but by what happens and is lived through on the levels of pre-verbal communication, which simultaneously implies that not everything gets into consciousness. This preverbal communication refers, on the one hand, to the level of the procedural unconscious as body memory and, on the other hand, to sensory-symbolic communication, a term coined by Alfred Lorenzer. This refers to the level between body memory and conscious declarative knowledge (Lorenzer, 1992, p. 161). It is at this level, which includes play, that changes are initiated, according to Lorenzer's view. The cognitive, linguistically mediated insight can only consolidate what was previously triggered on the pre-linguistic level of sensory-symbolic communication, which he considers play to be part of, and often leaves us puzzled that something has changed, and we cannot say exactly why. Foulkes also attributed great importance to nonverbal communication, especially facial expressions and gestures, but did not pursue it theoretically.

What Lorenzer developed in psychoanalytical discourse is now also supported by neuroscience. In his book "Save the Game," neurobiologist Gerald Hüther reports that in MRI scans, we can see that the nerve cell clusters in the area of the amygdala, the center where fear is mobilized, show reduced activity during play. In other words, we lose fear during play. At the same time, the brain shows an increased activity for the formation of new neural connections, through which the challenges of the respective game can be mastered. This is exactly the basis for creative ideas and imagination. Creativity is nothing other than the ability to create unusual new connections or to have them created. The more complex the challenge, the more complex the new connections. At the same time, each solution also fires up the reward system, resulting in the experience of joy (Hüther, 2018, p. 19 f.). Stuart Brown also speaks of interconnections. He says that in play, the brain stem, limbic system, and cortex are networked, i.e., movement, feelings, and thoughts are connected (Brown, 2009, p. 62).

4 Group-analytical setting and play in the 'as-if' mode

Even if in group analysis play seems to have no or hardly any role, it cannot be said that it has no place at all. On the contrary, a number of playful elements can in fact be shown to have a major impact.

In order to develop the ability to play, it is important that protection and security are provided so that a space for play can develop, and trust can grow. This is guaranteed in the group-analytical setting. It is not for nothing that the framework and setting are so important in group analysis. This includes a fixed time, a place, reliable participation, confidentiality, and the renunciation of violence. Here the institution, the leadership, and the group members work together. Group analysts know, however, that this is also to be understood as a process, because trust is not established by the provision of a setting alone but is repeatedly questioned and tested by the group. Another playful element is that in the group-analytical setting no specific purpose is pursued, as, for example, in a work group, but rather everyone submits to the process within the framework of the rules. The fact that we experience this with others in the group, because play is always a shared experience, brings about what Johan Huizinga called the community-building effect of play (Huizinga, 1938/2009, p. 22). In group analysis we talk about cohesion building, which is considered one of the most important effective factors of group analysis because it triggers the feeling of belonging as an alternative experience and thus satisfies an elementary need.

By learning to participate in the group on a regular basis, to contribute their own feelings and thoughts, to refrain from violence, and to keep everything that happens in the group confidential, participants can develop a process that is detached from the everyday happenings outside the group and that enables communication in the 'as-if' mode, which must be clearly attributed to play.

In order to enable playful communication in the 'as-if' mode in the group, a secure framework is thus needed. Conversely, it is also communication in the 'as-if' mode that creates security and trust. In the animal kingdom, where young animals play under the protection of adults, we can observe the "as if" in the gestures and "play face" with which mammals initiate playful interactions: open mouth, widened eyes, no hurtful behavior. These invitations to play always mean: I'm not going to hurt you, I just want to play. By sitting face to face in a circle in the group-analytical setting, thus showing the vulnerable parts of the body, the participants also express that they are there with peaceful intentions and want to engage with each other.

By asking the group members to say everything that runs through their heads, that pops into their minds, i. e., by encouraging them to associate freely, an offer to play is made and an invitation is extended to enter the 'as-if' mode. No goal is formulated, no purpose is stated other than that of association, no task is set that is supposed to lead to a result, and no judgments are made. Everything is open and at the same time moving, because association means listening to the movement of one's own thinking and feeling, to bring what is thought and felt out of oneself and into the group. It is also important for the 'as-if' mode that, in contrast to everyday life, what the participants communicate has no consequences. The game, which is thus indirectly called upon, requires an attitude of letting things happen, of not controlling, which favors regression and gives the unconscious a space.

Winnicott speaks here of the "intermediary in-between space," a space between the inner and outer worlds that involves symbolic action, that stands outside ordinary life and yet completely engages one emotionally (Winnicott, 1971). This strong emotional involvement ensures that we perceive what is happening as real, even though our minds tell us that what is happening in the here-and-now in the group, while reminiscent of earlier situations, is not identical to what was actually experienced at the time.

However, the fact that both can exist at the same time has its developmental-psychological reason as in the course of time the child discovers how to play with symbols. The symbol stands for something else but is not the something else. A child role-playing, such as "father-mother-child" by themselves or together with friends, is fully aware of the fact that it is just a game, and yet experiences it with emotional involvement in such a way that life and thereby sensory presence is breathed into it. They find themself playing in the 'as-if' mode, which contains both: the certainty of the real, gained through a strong emotional involvement, and the knowledge of the non-real.

In the course of their mentalization research, Fonagy, Gergely, and Target have dealt extensively with the importance of the 'as-if' mode in early mother-infant interaction. Thus, they see the mother's exaggerated responses to the child in connection with the baby's ability to distinguish between its own emotions and its mother's, as well as for the difference between "it's like this" and "it's as if". This lays the foundation for the child to distinguish between play and reality (Fonagy, Gergely, Jurist, and Target, 2002, p. 295 ff.).

The special nature of the 'as-if' mode makes it possible to bring previous conflictual experiences onto the stage of the group and to play through them here. The term "play through" is deliberately chosen here, in contrast to the term "work through," which is primarily reminiscent of the seriousness of the working world and less of the playful and creative sides of the group process.

What occurs in contact with others repeatedly takes on the character of unconscious enactment. This is due to the fact that, symbolically speaking, we are on a stage where a play is being performed. J. Lichtenberg says that model scenes from one's own childhood are re-enacted as transference events (Lichtenberg, 1989), and thus earlier traumas from one's own childhood come to light through being enacted.

In group analysis, this is referred to as 'scenic understanding' (Beck, 1997; Haubl, 1999). Although we associate play with ease, it need not feel easy at first. After all, tragedies are often enacted on the group stage. But what matters is how they are transformed in the here and now of the group, as what has happened becomes what is told and shared with others.

If one considers the characteristics of play developed by Johan Huizinga in his famous book *Homo Ludens* published in the 1930s, parallels can be seen with the group-analytical process. As Huizinga puts it:

"Summing up the formal characteristics of play we might call it a free activity standing quite consciously outside "ordinary" life as being "not serious", but at the same time absorbing the player intensely and utterly. It is an activity connected with no material interest, and no profit can be gained by it. It proceeds within its own proper boundaries of time and space according to fixed rules and in an orderly manner. It promotes the formation of social groupings which tend to surround themselves with secrecy and to stress their difference from the common world by disguise or other means" (Huizinga, 1938/2009, p. 22).

The group-analytical process also shows these traits. It is a free action, participation in it is voluntary, it is limited in space and time, it follows or develops rules, it is outside of everyday life, it is exciting, it captures attention, it creates a reality of "as if," and it is community-building.

5   Play in the group self-experience of child and adolescent therapists

What has been said so far about the place of play in classic group analysis is essentially implicit; that is, it has not emerged from a concept of play. This relates to the fact that in self-experience groups, therapeutic groups, or supervision groups the emphasis is, first of all, quite different. After all, the people who seek out a group would not think that their personal and professional problems could have anything to do with a lack of play space and play experiences. Not everyone sees play in the way Schiller once put it: "Man only plays when he is in the fullest sense of the word a human being, and he is only fully a human being when he plays" (Schiller, 1795/1980, 15th Letter). This reality has to do with the widespread assumption that play and work, just as play and seriousness, contradict each other. Stuart Brown, in a lecture on the subject, says, "The antithesis of play is not work, but depression." He also recalls a painting by Breughel of a wide variety of games and people of all ages playing, and asks, "Have we lost something in our culture?" (Brown, 2008).

In the group-analytical processes of adults, therefore, there are quite a few features that are characteristic of play. However, these sublime elements of play, which are tied to language in comparison to movement play, are not as obviously play as, say, romping around in a playground, playing with objects, or role-playing.

In the setting of adult group-analytical self-awareness, playful physical movement and the inclusion of musical and pictorial elements rarely have a place. Instead, the process is facilitated by sitting in a circle of chairs and by the central importance of language, which, as in psychoanalysis, is the primary means of communication.

In view of the great effectiveness of play for mental health, the question is whether it would not make sense, especially in the group self-experience of future child and youth therapists, to integrate play more deliberately and consciously into the group-analytical context. This modification aims at direct communication on the procedural and the sensory-symbolic level and thus to initiate processes of change.

The options here depend on what group leaders can bring to the table in terms of experience and skills and whether it is conceivable for them to play a more active role. It is crucial that all modifications remain bound to a clear framework, a clear setting, in order to guarantee the necessary safety. Within this setting, however, it is conceivable, for example, to get up from the chairs, to move in the room, to consciously perceive the body. It is also conceivable that voice and other musical elements as well as pictures and creative design can be included.

6   Case study

The example of a workshop with young musicians, which I led together with Christa Franke and Katrin Stumptner in August 2017 on the sidelines of the international conference of the GASi (Group Analytic Society International), will now be used to present options for play.

These young people – around 20 years old – came from different European countries and did not know each other. They had been selected in an application process to participate in an international master class for chamber orchestra and chamber music for one week, to work on pieces that were to be presented in a public concert at the end of the group-analytical conference. Every morning, the participants of the group-analytical conference could listen to a public rehearsal of the 1908 experimental piece "The Unanswered Question" by the American Charles Ives, which lasts only six minutes. This piece placed high demands on the young musicians.

In return for their public rehearsals, they wanted a workshop on "stage fright" to work through their fears of performing. A total of 30 people signed up for this, and we had two sessions with a large group in a room where 30 chairs could be placed with great difficulty in a circle. The language was English.

We had already spent many years working on pre-verbal communication, the language of the body, music, images, and their access to the unconscious (Franke, Köhncke, Siegler-Heinz, and Stumptner, 2013, pp. 4–32), and had tested a connection with verbal language via creative writing. In light of this, we decided to directly address the sensory-symbolic level of communication in the short time available.

Unlike a minimally structured group that relies solely on words and imposes restraint on the leader, given the size of the group and the time frame of two sessions, we provided structure to the group's play space and focused on the topic of "stage fright" that the group had requested.

Each of us had our own focus to bring to the process, and each took the group lead. It was important for us to lead with a group-analytical focus, i.e., to provide a setting that built trust, to observe the process, and to relate our impulses to it. First of all, we wanted to reduce the fear that accompanies a new situation and thus, in an unspoken way, also to focus on the stage fright associated with fear.

After introducing ourselves, introducing Chatham House rules, and encouraging the group members to share the feelings they experienced when they had to show themselves on a public stage, we invited them to join us on a journey. Our intention was to allow individuals to connect with themselves and others on a basal physical level, thereby reducing fear, building trust, and opening up a space for play.

We began, therefore, with a physical exercise: Participants sat on the chairs with their eyes closed, feeling the ground under their feet, concentrating. They then stood up with their eyes closed to say aloud their own names, to give their own names a sound.

Then the group was asked to open their eyes, walk around the room, greet each other, and say their own name. At the end of this sequence, everyone was asked to find a place on the floor of the room and from there to sense how it feels to be in a group with others from this perspective. The group agreed to this and so we were able to take a step further towards the topic of "stage fright".

We spread postcards, paper, and pens on the floor, and the participants were asked to choose one to three pictures that expressed what they spontaneously associated with their own "stage fright", the fear of showing themselves in public, and to draw or write something about it, as they wished. The young people clearly enjoyed tackling such a difficult topic in a playful way. Concentrated and curious, they looked for suitable pictures, drew and wrote something. They lay or sat spread out in the room; it was very quiet, only the sound of scribbling pencils could be heard, a musical event in its own way.

After some time, the group was asked to choose a picture, a drawing, or something written from their own selection and to use it to create a group picture that clearly showed the facets of the fears. The group then stood around the group picture and looked at the result with curiosity and fascination.

Back in the chair circle, we opened a conversation with the questions: What is the same for everyone, what is different? Do I recognize myself in the pictures of the others? Is stage fright a simple or a complex problem? The group began to exchange and share their feelings. It was about very personal things, about loneliness, about shame, about the prison of fear.

At the end, we reflected together on the session: How do you feel now in the group, is it different than at the beginning? Whereas everyone had been excited before, they were now amazed at how much they had learned from the others and about themselves, and how good they felt.

The following morning in the public rehearsal, we were waved at. The young people obviously felt quite familiar with us, and we then heard that the rehearsal in the evening after the first session had been quite different from usual because they had gotten to know each other and no longer felt so isolated. Thus, they named the two phenomena that we count among the most important effective factors in group analysis, namely the sharing of experiences and the experience of belonging.

The next day we dealt with the topic in a different way. Once again in the chair circle, we asked about dreams and afterthoughts, then there was a suggestion for participants to write down in their own language everything that was most important to them personally in the first session and what they had experienced from others. With this we entered the level of communication, in which the experiences of the past were to be verbalized. The group agreed to this as well. Everyone wrote. The sensory experience of the writing sound then gave rise to the impulse to switch to the musical level and to ask the group to read their texts aloud simultaneously and to reflect on the question: How does one's own language sound, how do the other languages sound? How does it sound when they are spoken at the same time? Everyone was amazed at the effect. We thought we were listening to a large choir in which common and different sounds were heard at the same time. Only then did we turn to the content of what had been written and there followed, now in English, an exchange about situations in which one had felt ashamed. This exchange led to the realization that it was inevitable to have stage fright when they were in public as professional musicians. It was even more important to leave previous embarrassments behind and to accept a tolerable level of fear.

Next, we wanted to focus on the resources, the hopes and aspirations that were associated with the profession of being a musician, and thus put the fear into perspective. Therefore, images were now to be selected under the question: How and who do I want to be on stage and what helps me to deal with the fear?

Each individual now chose pictures that represented the desired self-image as a professional musician, as well as pictures that showed their own strategy for confronting fear. Then, again, a picture was chosen for a group design and placed in the middle. The group stood around this picture and perceived with great interest the pictures of the others.

Back in the chair circle, there was an exchange about the group picture. The high level of identification with the profession to which all aspired became visible and was shared in the group. The most important strategy for their dealing with stage fright turned out to be the wish to talk to people they trust. And that is exactly what they did in the here and now of the group.

We ended with a body-oriented exercise and with the memory of the positive images that had become visible in the group in dealing with stage fright. We then said goodbye with an African song that the group learned very quickly, adding their own improvised variations.

In the final concert, the young musicians radiated great joy and enthusiasm. We sought them out during the break and asked them how they were doing, and they said they were doing very well, that the workshop had helped them to feel connected to the others and at the same time to have confidence in their own voice.

This example shows a comparatively large group in a very short session and with a declared goal, namely to work on the topic of "stage fright". This justifies the clear structuring of the sessions and the many options for play. In this short workshop, we as leaders offered many suggestions, which the group received in a highly motivated and unbiased way and were able to use for themselves. This was possible because we were dealing with young people for whom childhood play associated with movement is a close experience. As in a time-lapse, a process can be observed here, which under other conditions, e.g., over a longer period of time and in a small group, would take place less spectacularly but would certainly lead to similar results, namely to the experience of the connection with the others and a feeling for oneself. And playing in the group and a group-analytical approach, which provides a space for playfulness, has an essential part in this.

> **At a glance**
> Play in a group promotes both personal development and belonging to a community.
> - It has an anxiety-reducing effect and allows new connections to form in the brain.
> - It is associated with movement and the feeling of joy.
> - It promotes the growth of skills and social competence.
>
> Play needs a safe and protected environment.
> - This creates a space for play.
> - Communication can take place on the sensory-symbolic level.
> - Communication can take place in the 'as-if' mode.
>
> The child and youth group analysts should experience play themselves.
> - They should be able to go beyond verbal language.
> - They should gain experience with images, musical elements, and movement.
> - They should experience how play and creativity are connected.

Bibliography

Beck, W. (1997). Szenisches Verstehen und Leiten von Gruppen. In M. E. Ardjomandi, A. Berghaus, W. Knauss (Hrsg.), Leitung und Autorität im gruppenanalytischen Prozess. *Jahrbuch für Gruppenanalyse*, 3: 65–76.

Bowlby, J. (1969). *Attachment and Loss*. New York: Basic Books

Brown, S. (2008). *Play is more than just fun*. https://www.ted.com/talks/stuart_brown_says_play_is_more_than_fun_it_s_vital (last accessed March 29, 2022)

Brown, S. (2009). *Play*. New York: Penguin Group

Downing, G. (1996). *Körper und Wort in der Psychotherapie. Leitlinien für die Praxis*. München: Kösel

Field, T. (2010). Postpartum depression effects on early interactions, parenting, and safety practices: A review. *Infant Behavior & Development*, 33 (1): 1–6. DOI: 10.1016/j.infbeh.2009.10.005

Fonagy, P., Gergely, G., Jurist, E. L., Target, M. (2002). *Affektregulierung, Mentalisierung und die Entwicklung des Selbst*. Stuttgart: Klett-Cotta

Franke, C. H., Köhncke, D., Siegler-Heinz, M., Stumptner, K. (2013). Was uns bewegt, unter die Haut geht, in den Ohren klingt, als Bild vor Augen und zwischen den Zeilen steht. Kommunikation und Symbolisierung: ein Gruppenexperiment. Gruppenanalyse. *Zeitschrift für gruppenanalytische Psychotherapie, Beratung und Supervision,* 23 (1): 4–32.

Gadamer, H. G. (1998). *Die Aktualität des Schönen.* Stuttgart: Reclam

Gergely, G., Csibra, G. (2005). The social construction of the cultural mind: Imitative learning as a mechanism of human pedagogy. *Interaction Studies,* 6 (3): 463–481

Haubl, R. (1999). Die Hermeneutik des Szenischen in der Einzel- und Gruppenanalyse, Gruppenpsychotherapie und Gruppendynamik. *Zeitschrift für Theorie und Praxis der Gruppenanalyse,* 35.1: 17–53.

Huizinga, J. (1938/2009). *Homo ludens.* London: Routledge

Hüther, G., Quarch, C. (2018). *Rettet das Spiel. Weil Leben mehr als Funktionieren ist.* München: Random House

Kluge, E. (2002). *Etymologisches Wörterbuch.* Berlin: de Gruyter

Köhncke, D., Mies, T. (2012). Der Matrixbegriff und die intersubjektive Wende. Gruppenpsychotherapie und Gruppendynamik. *Zeitschrift für Theorie und Praxis der Gruppenanalyse,* 1: 26–52

Lichtenberg, J. (1989). Modellszenen, Affekte und das Unbewusste. In E. S. Wolf, P. Ornstein, J. D. Ornstein, J. Lichtenberg, P. Kutter (Hrsg.), *Selbstpsychologie. Weiterentwicklung nach Heinz Kohut* (S. 17–53). München/Wien: Verlag Internationale Psychoanalyse

Lorenzer, A. (1992). *Das Konzil der Buchhalter. Die Zerstörung der Sinnlichkeit. Eine Religionskritik.* Frankfurt/M: Fischer

Mackensen, L. (1966). *Etymologisches Wörterbuch.* Stuttgart: Reclam

"News" on the "Tagesschau" TV program on January 30, 2021

Papoušek, H. (2003). Spiel in der Wiege der Menschheit. In M. Papoušek and A. von Gontard (Hrsg.), *Spiel und Kreativität in der frühen Kindheit* (S. 17–55). Stuttgart: Pfeiffer bei Klett-Cotta.

Righetti-Veltema, M., Bousquet, A., Manzano, J. (2003). Impact of postpartum depressive symptoms on mother and her 18-month-old infant. *European Child & Adolescent Psychiatry,* 12 (2): 75–83. DOI:10.1007/s00787-003-0311-9

Schiller, F. (1795/1980). Über die ästhetische Erziehung des Menschengeschlechtes in einer Reihe von Briefen. In F. Schiller, *Sämtliche Werke,* vol. 5. München: Reclam

Schultz-Venrath, U. (2011). Das Gehirn in der Gruppe oder die Gruppe im Gehirn. Gruppenpsychotherapie und Gruppendynamik. *Zeitschrift für Theorie und Praxis der Gruppenanalyse,* 47 (2): 111–410

Stern, D. (1979). *Mutter und Kind. Die erste Beziehung,* Stuttgart: Klett-Cotta

Tronick, E. (2007). *The neurobehavioral and social-emotional development of infants and children (Norton series on interpersonal neurobiology).* New York: W. W. Norton

Winnicott, D. W. (1971). *Playing and reality.* London: Tavistock Publications

Hansel and Gretel

Furi Khabirpour

"Human beings are body parts of each other,
In creation they are indeed of one essence.
If a body part is afflicted with pain,
Other body parts uneasy will remain.
If you have no sympathy for human pain,
The name of human you shall not retain."
(The Bani Adam from Gulistan by Saadi Shirazi)

Based on a group session, I would like to describe the impact and themes of the fairy tale "Hansel and Gretel" by the Brothers Grimm. The memory of a twist in the story was crucial for the processing of an inner conflict by two participants. The effect of the fairy tale in the parents' group and its topicality in the social context are addressed, and its connection with the matrix of the children's group is implied.

Fairy tales are part of our culture. As children we absorb them, and those tales stay with us into adulthood. Many expressions and phrases, such as "where the fox and the hare say goodnight to each other" (translator's note: The meaning of this German idiom is roughly equivalent to the English idiom "in the middle of nowhere"), "Sleeping Beauty", "the wolf in sheep's clothing", and "the princess and the pea", are heard in everyday conversations. Fairy tales convey many images, mostly colorful, but also cruel and frequently unpalatable. It is often these images, more than the language itself, that speak to children.

1   A children's group session

The following is an account from a children's group with five children (two girls, three boys) from age six to eleven. The session was conducted by me and Jessica on May 11, 2021.

Zlatan arrives five minutes after the start of the session. Bastian hides and wants to scare Zlatan. Aaron says, "Bastian doesn't like Zlatan." Bastian laughs mischievously in his hiding place. Zlatan sits down and suddenly spots Bastian behind him and laughs. "Maybe Bastian and Zlatan have more of a love-hate relationship, like brothers?", I ask Aaron. He thinks while Bastian and Zlatan laugh. Then we begin our sharing circle.

Bastian talks about good grades at school. No one responds. Aaron reports that he challenged his father and brought up his unhealthy lifestyle. Zlatan prefers not to speak. Marie, who initially just sat quietly, reports that her mother wants them to move to another village with her new boyfriend. Everyone wants to know where this place is and then they discover that it is about seventy kilometers away from the group. Marie is not happy about moving. She does not want to lose her home in the countryside and her friends. Amanda suddenly seems thoughtful and sad. I ask what is going on inside her. After some hesitation, she says that she remembers losing her family home when her parents separated. A lively conversation about divorce and family breakdown ensues. Bastian says that his parents promised him they would never separate. Aaron remarks that he and Bastian are the only ones in the group whose parents have not separated. At this point, Zlatan joins the conversation, expressing his regret at his parents' separation and how he has lost hope of them ever getting back together.

The sharing circle was over and the question "What would we like to play?" came up. Marie and Amanda did not want to play with the others. The suggestion to try the doodle game (Winnicott, 2006) with me was met with approval. Two boys played hide and seek with Jessica. Meanwhile Amanda, Marie, and I sat and played the doodle game. I started and drew a crooked line; Marie developed it into a beach chair; Amanda thought of SpongeBob in his house in the ocean. Finally, Marie completed the picture, which the girls titled "SpongeBob, the Banana, and the Sea" (see figure 1).

I am unfamiliar with the stories of SpongeBob. The picture conveys peace and security in a house deep underwater. The sea snail also rests in its house. Loving greetings are sent out into the world.

The same procedure was followed for the second picture. Marie began by drawing a rectangle, which Amanda completed by making into a house. Thinking of Marie's countryside home, I drew a stable. Marie added a door and a window to the house and said that she was thinking of Hansel and Gretel. The witch appeared in the window. To finish, Marie and Amanda together drew Hansel and Gretel and titled the picture accordingly.

Figure 1: "SpongeBob, the Banana, and the Sea"

While we sat in our room sketching, another game was going on outside. We heard screeching and laughter as the boys romped around. Then the noise level calmed down a bit, and Bastian and Aaron brought us a bowl of chips and something to drink and were of course curious to see what we were doing. They did not stay for long and went back outside to play. Zlatan stayed in his place in the group room the whole time and talked to Jessica. At this point I feel the need to point out how important it is to conduct these groups in pairs. The game with Marie and Amanda could not otherwise have taken place in this form.

After the second image was created, the two girls related the story of Hansel and Gretel (see figure 2). It was fascinating for me to experience how Amanda and Marie used this fairy tale to process their current challenges, with the conclusion being the drawing of a happy ending (see figure 3). In the fairy tale, the siblings lose their home. Due to poverty and famine, they are taken to the forest by their parents. They are dependent on each other as they struggle to survive in a hostile environment, discover food in a gingerbread house, and then must fight for their lives. By their own efforts, they free themselves from the clutches of a witch and lift their family out of poverty. I suspect the story's message of children's agency and empowerment – how the siblings work with others to successfully change things for the better – inspired Amanda and Marie and gave them confidence in their own abilities.

While the children were drawing the third picture, the mood was relaxed. There was laughter at the story of Hansel and Gretel, especially about how they outwitted the

Figure 2: Hansel and Gretel

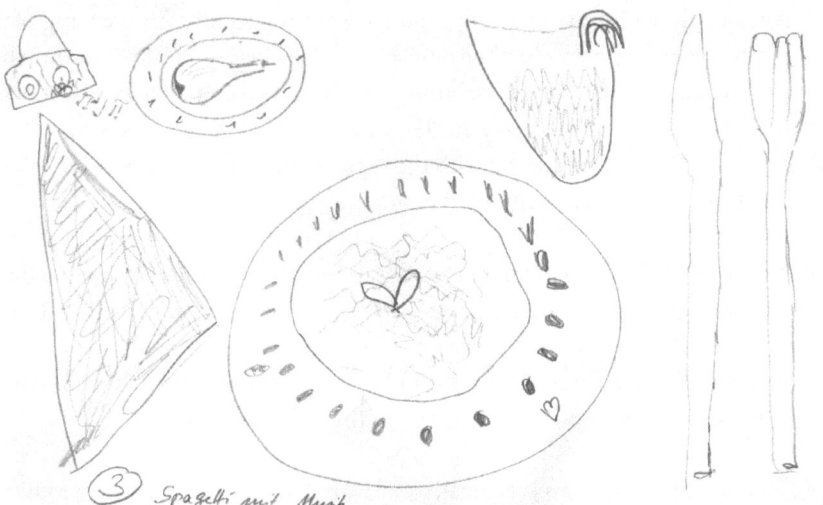

Figure 3: "Spaghetti with Music" for dinner

witch, who had poor eyesight, and how they stuck a thin stick out of the cage instead of their fingers, thus escaping death. They thought of their favorite food, and thus the third picture was created (see figure 3).

The group came together again briefly before parting. The separation of parents and its consequences was once again the topic of conversation, but the boys' unrestricted romping about was also discussed and discovered to have a deeper meaning. It highlighted the stress caused by the loss of the family's living space, which had been expressed as imagery. And, of course, Aaron asked me to bring more gummy bears for the next session ...

2 A short history of the group

The children's group was set up in November 2019 with four children: Thomas (age eleven) came because of sleep disorders, which disappeared after half a year. He left the group after one year. Anna (age ten) came to the group because of family conflicts and a seriously ill mother. Her participation was interrupted by the Corona crisis from April 2020 (concern of risk of infection to the mother). Bastian (age eight) had issues with social interaction that became a problem not only at home but increasingly at school. Zlatan (eleven years) was saddened by the separation of his parents and suffered from anxiety disorders. After Thomas left, Marie (age eight) joined the group. She was not coping at school, was increasingly withdrawn socially, and suffered repeatedly from crying fits. The group was not open to further new joiners (see below). Only after much deliberation was Aaron (age six), who suffered from tics and anxiety disorders, admitted to the group in February 2021. A little later, Amanda (age seven), who was having a difficult time coping with the separation of her parents, joined the group with the encouragement of her mother.

The children's group takes place weekly and is conducted by me and Jessica Schmeichel (aged 24), who has not yet had training in psychotherapy. Following four children's group sessions, we have one parents' group session. Although all parents are invited to attend, it is rare that both parents are able to be present. The objective of this parents' group session is to discuss the issues of the parents themselves and not to report on progress in the children's group.

The children's group session is typically structured as follows: Start with a sharing circle (lasting about 20–25 minutes), then have play time (lasting about 35 minutes), followed by refreshments, and finally a short wrap-up discussion. The parents' group session is not structured.

The group also took place regularly during the pandemic; the group's increasing coherence was noticeable, and there were no dropouts and hardly any absences. If there were any absences, they were, as in Anna's case, corona-related or due to a temporary quarantine because someone in the environment of one of the participants had fallen ill with COVID-19. Anna returned to the group in spring 2021.

3   Some thoughts on working with the children's group

School-aged children do not usually like to talk about their feelings; rather, they display them in other ways. Their posture, facial expressions, actions, and expressions during play reveal more about their inner and social conflicts than words. Occasionally, I tell a little story about another child I've met with their challenges, and a conversation ensues.

A clear structure for the group session (not enforced in a regimented way) helps to avoid chaos and uncertainty. Collectively agreed-upon rules (for example, no physical aggression) make sense, but experience shows that they are not always followed. As mentioned above, I consider conducting sessions in pairs to be very important, not least for the sake of ensuring we meet a duty of care.

My experience thus far leads me to emphasize the importance of the following two factors in determining the effectiveness of children's groups:

- The first is the realization of the universality of suffering, which Yalom has written about extensively (Yalom, 1970/2007). Indeed, the discovery that they are not alone with their challenges and conflicts brings relief to children. No sooner does one participant articulate a problem than the others express their own familiarity with it. For example, in one group session, a boy complained that it was terribly annoying to him that his mother is always on her phone and hardly finds time for him. Immediately, a girl said that she observes the same behavior in her father. In a broader sense, this is also a development in the ability to mentalize that is helpful for the children in their social environment.
- The second factor is the attitude of the group conductors. They need to concentrate on the children, allow a lot, forbid little, be open to suggestions for change, avoid judgment and criticism, try to better understand the participants, and work with them to seek solutions. This attitude opens spaces for the children to have a different experience with adults, to be seen, to express themselves creatively and effectively, and ultimately to trust.

4   The parents' group after the above session

I brought up the fairy tale of Hansel and Gretel in the parents' group. Zlatan's mother and Aaron's father were not familiar with this fairy tale. Marie's mother was absent again. Amanda's mother summarized the fairy tale for the group. Bastian's father recalled the pain of having to flee his in-laws' house in the dead of night. Aaron's father recalled the disappointment of his career aspirations because of a knee injury, which also caused a drug addiction. Zlatan's mother could not make much of the fairy tale, and Amanda's mother brought up the question of how much closeness and distance was appropriate in raising children, and this was then discussed. To put it in the language of the fairy tale: How far should children be allowed to roam away from their home and parents? How should the risks of the forest be assessed …?

When it comes to Marie's mother, who was absent, I get the impression that she is already intensely involved with the move and her new romantic relationship and has lost sight of her daughter's needs. Zlatan's mother was not satisfied with her salary as a sports lecturer in an Eastern European country and, in search of a "gingerbread house," entered a relationship with Zlatan's father, from whom she separated five years ago. She unknowingly feels abandoned and alone, clinging to Zlatan and constantly dissatisfied with his behavior. Zlatan's father has never participated in a discussion in the year and a half of group therapy …

5 Some thoughts on working with parents' groups

Since the parents' groups are held much less frequently than the children's groups, the development of coherence is delayed. In the early days, there tends to be a perception that the group would be some sort of parents' evening, like in the children's schools, and a report on the individual children is expected. After about four to five parents' group meetings, the parents, who are usually represented by only one co-parent (because the other is watching the children or is not interested) also begin to talk about their own conflicts and challenges. If this is successful, then new levels of understanding of the children's behavior emerge for the group conductors. At almost every meeting, I emphasize the important contribution that parents make to the children's group, because without them, the children's group would not be able to take place. Cultural aspects should also be taken into account, because in some places it is taboo to talk about family problems; therefore, a wait-and-see attitude is usually more promising than a provocative one.

6 The social context – back to Hansel and Gretel

Of course, no group takes place in a vacuum. It is embedded in a social context. One of the challenges of our time is the refugee crisis. Countless families have lost their homes to war and violence. Millions of parents, in the face of poverty and hunger, have sent their loved ones into the "woods" out of sheer desperation. Few have yet reached the "gingerbread house", and their entry is hampered by borders and quotas. The suffering of these displaced millions cannot be put into words and will not end as long as nationalist thinking holds sway and the world is not perceived as a collective entity. Elements of all this can be found in the matrix (Brandes, 2003) of the children's group. The "quota system" allowed Marie access to the group. In the case of Samuel and Amanda, several negotiation sessions were necessary, and resistance had to be worked through. They were grudgingly admitted, with Zlatan continuing to undermine the group decision and interrupting the "newcomers" as they spoke. One could imagine that fears of sharing the group room (the gingerbread house) and the therapists, of getting less attention and fewer gummy bears, and of not being able to cope with the strangers play a role. Encouragingly, the attitude of the second children's group that Jessica and I conduct is completely different. Here, every announcement of a newcomer has been joyfully received, and the group size was readily increased from five to seven …

At a glance:
I have drawn the following conclusions regarding group analysis with children from the above case study:
- The social context heavily impacts group dynamics.
- Conflicts are worked through in language, play, and interactions with the conductors and between the children themselves.
- Mentalization skills and a sense of agency are developed.
- Fairy tales and stories can be quite helpful in working with groups of children.
- Among other things, the parents' group raises the level of understanding of what takes place in the children's group.

Bibliography

Brandes, H. (2003). Eine Frage der Ehre. *Jahrbuch für Gruppenanalyse,* 2003 (9): 159–70

Winnicott, D. W. (2016). The Squiggle Game. In: The Collected Works of D. W. Winnicott: Vol. 8, 1967–1968. Oxford: Oxford Univ. Press

Yalom, I. D. (1970/2007). *Theorie und Praxis der Gruppenpsychotherapie. Ein Lehrbuch* (9., völlig überarb. und erw. Aufl.). Stuttgart: Klett-Cotta

When the Jubjub Bird Freezes Everything around Himself – Pain Treatment with Families in Group Psychotherapy with the Use of Digital Media

Christoph Radaj

When children and young people with pain amplification syndrome (PAS) enter treatment in a clinic or an outpatient facility they are usually dealing with considerable psychosocial stress. Physical examinations are being carried out at length in order to reach a differential diagnosis, which leaves the children and adolescents often wondering whether they have a rare disease or some kind of strange syndrome. The biopsychosocial explanatory model of disease plays a central role in understanding the pain amplification syndrome. For many years a causal stimulus-reaction time concept was assumed to be the underlying reason for existing pain (Nickel, 1999, p. 16). With the cybernetic model, this understanding has been further expanded, so that we now know that the psyche consists of subsystems which interact with each other down to the molecular level (Hoffmann, 1993, p. 2). Many of these subsystems can only be accessed and influenced by changing the way we live in order to promote mental, emotional and physical health (Mental Health Definition). As a result of more recent research, the stress regulation subsystem, responsible for the development of chronic pain, has moved more and more into focus (Dobe and Zernikow, 2019, p. 1–2). How hormonal stress regulation works, can be easily be demonstrated and explained to the patient using psycho education. Yet, the underlying "cause" is unspecific enough for the patient to be able to embark on his/her own journey of discovery and change. This process might include their day structure, lifestyle, exercise and/or nutrition.

Before beginning any treatment, psycho-education, i.e. awareness of the disease model, is particularly important in order to anchor the healing process and set the best possible foundation for the patient's compliance (Dobe and Zernikow, 2019, p. 118).

In this day and time especially young people for the most part access knowledge via digital media. However, the study by Healthcote found that most of the YouTube videos on the subject of pain were not created by a trustworthy known institution and only one of the videos contained all the central explanatory models (Heathcote et al., 2019, 7.22). It is therefore important to establish early on in the anamnesis which pain construct it is that the patient comes into the practice with. The central task of psychodynamic pain psychotherapy is to ascertain their particular construct and to sense and deconstruct it later in therapy.

In addition, group therapy, utilized as a resonance chamber, offers a therapeutic framework that is highly effective dealing with the complexity of PAS (Nickel, 2001, p. 11).

In group psychotherapy the children and young people can learn to understand and experience each other's social and psychological structure. The concurrent parent group develops practical ways to help contain the patient and to support her/him in their stress regulation. Furthermore, the parent group is not only utilized therapeutically, but also functions as a self-help group. New behavior strategies are being put into practice in the parent group and via a messenger chat group a real life support structure is being created, which then also becomes available outside of therapy. Parents are encouraged to network within their group and support one another should an acute crisis arise. The integrated model of multimodal pain psychotherapy, in addition to psychotherapy, includes cooperation with family physicians, physiotherapists and occupational therapists, thus developing and implementing a coordinated multidisciplinary treatment pathway.

This chapter's main focus will be on the use of digital media in group psychotherapy for PAS. For further in depth reading on the subject of pain psychotherapy, I recommend the literature found in the accompanying list of references.

As an example I aim to explore the treatment setting of a group of children and the concurrently running parent group. The general treatment plan will be described, as well as the digital media used and their effect on the patients, with notes on what has been observed and can be understood within a psychodynamic framework.

1 Developing a treatment plan

After the initial anamnesis, we start with psychoeducation, in which specific videos along the lines of the biopsychosocial explanatory model, neurophysiology and pain sensitization are put to use. These videos can be accessed by the patients on YouTube at any time they choose and thus achieve a high level of effectiveness (Heathcode et al., 2019, 1.22). In my own practice the systematic solution-focused Kids' Skills Manual by Ben Furman is used for the development of a therapy goal (Furman, 2004). Doing a time travel exercise with the patient helps to determine what would be different when the therapy goal will have been achieved. Great care is taken to ensure that the therapy goal is both positive and achievable. For example, in the case of a child with difficulties swallowing and the urge to throw up, this could mean, that he or she would aim to be able to and enjoy eating an ice cream.

Then we will be looking for skills that the child already has, which might come in handy in reaching their goal: for example, the ability to love ice cream in general or that the symptom does not occur when enjoying a soda. Furthermore, the goal must be achievable whether pain is felt or not. In the next step, real as well as symbolic helpers, such as a cuddly toy or an ice cube, are being drafted in to aid the patient in achieving their goal. The child will then set up a chat group for themselves and their helpers, both real and symbolic, which enables direct communication between the patient and their vital support network. The therapy plan itself is being monitored via an app which is accessible and supportive to both children and parents. The advantage of working with the manual and the app is that the awareness and imagination exercises and other methods promoting mentalizing can be integrated and coordinated effortlessly and in a playful way. This preliminary work is of great importance so that the therapy group is free to work within the context of the therapy goal.

2   Group process

Using the example of one specific childrens' psychotherapy group with a parent group running parallel (the in-person groups were scheduled as twenty-five sessions for the children and six for the parents). I will be describing the in-person group process with a close look at the parallel online contact and an evaluation of the differences between my therapeutic interventions in the in-person group and the online group, aiming to establish which methods and mentalizing processes should be worked with and through in the in-person group for the online group to build on.

For the in-person sessions I found it very important to focus on the somatosensory experiences between the children, so that inner representations can emerge which subsequently will effect and impact the online group. As the online game of choice I am using "Min(d)craft", which will be played by the children together in the group room for the duration of 25 sessions, after which the children will continue playing with each other for 10 sessions from their own individual homes, and then the children take over the game themselves.

In 2011 Dittrich described the potentials inherent in the use of digital media for creating a transitional space for anxious children which can then be used therapeutically (Dittrich, 2011, p. 262). Around the time Dittrich developed his concept, I also began looking into this phenomenon in my own childrens' groups. When the children brought their media into the therapy room, it initially seemed to me like an orphaned space, with a very notable absence of parents. The parents on the other hand were treating their childrens' chats and video playlists like diaries, precious and in need of privacy protection. When I began immersing myself in this world with the children, I was confronted, among other things, with childrens' films in which swear words, sexual violence and genitals appeared to be tightly woven into the story line, flashing up repeatedly, which led to outbursts of instinctual laughter and chuckling in the children.

After some time I began allowing the childrens' digital games in the group room, so they brought their Minecraft game along with them, a game in which landscapes are being built out of cubes, a world of mountains, lakes and forests and various animals. At first the group took care of the frame themselves. It was important to me that this world should not be infinite, but rather would be set up similar to a board game, in order to have a space that I as their therapist can overlook and protect. The fact that this digital playing field, like any other game in the therapy room, had to be in my physical therapeutic set-up in the form of a server, was self evident, due to data protection concerns and in order to keep the therapy setting safe. The children set up the server for me, so everyone was able to log in from their own device. The game was being played in "creative mode", implying that everyone has an infinite amount of resources and lives and has the ability to fly. In the age group of the 6 and 12 year olds, I decided to offer my patients an omnipotent game environment, so as to create a therapeutic frame which would facilitate unconscious access and modification of inner object representations via imaginary play (Hopkins, 2008, p. 63; Weinberg, 2019, p. 321).

In order to be able to analyze the dynamics in digital play, I utilize the "Small Table" technique, through which a felt sense of the group object can emerge in a playful way (cf. Foulkes, Antony, 1973, p. 191; Haar, Wenzel, 2019, p. 53). In this method a game board is divided into sectors, each child chooses a sector with previously prepared play material. Although transferring this exactly to the online game wasn't quite doable, it could be observed that in the as yet untouched Minecraft landscape the children were looking for their own personal space to settle and initially built their own individual base from which animated communication was initiated, eventually leading to them combining their individual game sectors into a unified whole.

In order to be able to get a sense of the group body in digital space, both the foundation matrix and the dynamic matrix need to be taken into consideration. I understand the dynamic matrix as a sensory, tactile enactment of the group members in space. "The symbolic dimension inscribed in the body, which is being enacted and thus communicated via posture, gesture and facial expression, represents, due to its proximity to the body, an immediate expression of the unconscious and thereby also of the deepest layers of the actors' personalities" (Brandes, 2005, p. 161). This dimension can of course be captured only to a very limited extent or even not at all in digital play, though it can be experienced in-person in the group room. Some children were playing by themselves in the digital game, but were sitting very close to one another in the group room, while others were moving around in the room or wriggling on their seats while gaming, some putting their voices and comments into the room, some enacting the game, while others appeared to be in a trance state, absorbed and completely focused on their online game.

This trance state is particularly important in pain therapy. To achieve a reduction of pain stimuli, in classic behavioral therapy distraction methods are being used to interrupt the pain pathway through diverting conscious attention before the "pain gate" opens, thus intercepting the pain message before it reaches the pain receptor in the thalamus.

In addition to distraction methods, awareness exercises and acceptance-based methods, computer games are particularly suitable as a distraction method which can be integrated into an imagination exercise in order to achieve defocusing. The children are already familiar with the trance state they enter when gaming: their parents call them for supper, a call which often goes completely unheeded, with parents then having to reach out and physically touch the child to get their attention because they are so engrossed in the game.

3   Group therapy

The participating children in the group were Rosa (8) Boris (12) Juri (10) Greta (13) Xaver (13) Arthur (7). Three children were presenting with migraine headaches and school absenteeism, two children were diabetics in treatment for a somatization disorder manifesting in abdominal pain. All of the children showed school avoidance behavior. ADHD, depression and, as it turned out, a post traumatic disorder all played a role as comorbidities.

The first thing Rosa made clear quite loudly was that she had no desire whatsoever to be with us, with Juri promptly hiding behind his tablet. It was touching to see Greta trying to take care of Rosa. Having watched her for quite a while, she commented on Rosa's nagging, while sitting next to me and trying to calm me down, saying I should just wait a little. After some time had passed she asked Rosa to play dolls with her and the two of them subsequently gave "the stupid boys" a hammering in the dollhouse. The boys, unfazed by what was going on in the dollhouse, were in the meantime already busy building a Minecraft world.

This brief description is quite typical. Within the room, just like in a table game, the group is fractioned and tries to create a connection among its members. A pivotal moment of this connection turned out to be a German children's film. "Bibi & Tina: Girls vs. Boys". This movie is often re-enacted, and there is a famous song in the film's soundtrack that most children are familiar with. With the motto "girls versus boys" the first group rule was drawn up and converted into a game.

Van Loh (2021) has introduced the concept of media introjects, so that this phenomenon can now be utilized in analytical work. A content-related media introject forms in the psyche through a movie or a game evoking emotions, in the absence of a physical object in real life. As these introjects are artificially generated through films, books, avatars etc, without there being a somatosensory real object reference, they tend to have a strong hypnotic impact, in that they are fragmented due to not being connected to or anchored in reality (van Loh, 2021, p. 128). This could mean that the childrens' physical, embodied reactions in the in-person space during the digital game are being enacted much closer to individual implicit behavioral knowledge than actual role play and we then need to determine whether this was caused by the projection of a transference or by a media introject.

Brandes writes: "The fantasies within a group are not the cause of the perceivable dynamics within the group and the expressions of the individual, but rather the other way round: the dynamics of the group, perceived by the senses and communicated through embodied forms of expression, are the starting point for the emergence of specific thoughts and fantasies" (Brandes, 2005, p. 164). It could often be observed that the group quarreled in the digital game, yet the group members were physically very close in the group room. In regard to the foundation matrix, such as the cultural imprint that every individual brings into the group, not much is changing. As in every role play, these boundaries are omnipotently split open enabling the children to incorporate the particular foundation matrix into the game that they are ready and willing to enact. Girls can become boys, shy children become brave, and cultural backgrounds can be hidden. The phenomenon that it is possible to invest cathexis into avatars is also being described by Haim Weinberg (2019): "This definition of presence involves the idea of transportation, whether the user is transported to another place, or another place and its objects are transported to the user, or both people in interaction are transported to another place. Consider the science fiction movie Avatar [...] Transportation to another place does not necessarily have to involve a traffic vehicle. It only requires good imagination" (Weinberg, 2019, p. 201).

When I spot a connection between a digital introject and what is happening in the group room, I try to bring this into focus, encouraging the group to transfer the emerging theme into the Minecraft game. This process was working rather well with this group, as already in the second session the children began playing girls vs boys in Minecraft.

4   The first parent group

In the first few hours the parents reported much about school and how incapable they experienced the teachers. Thus it became possible for them to express their helplessness: which mother had to pick up which child, when and why, and how the fear of the phone ringing at home made her angry, wondering if and when her child had to again be picked up during school hours. Greta's mother reported about a terribly disinterested teacher and Xaver's mother was annoyed by a "softy" teacher. The mood became quite heated and in their quest for relief the enemy tended to be located outside the gates.

Parents of pain patients often find themselves with their backs against the wall due to the lengthy medical diagnostics process and the social difficulties that arise. In group therapy I understand this as a form of massification. "This assumption is expressed in bi-polar forms of incohesion. When activated, groups and group-like social systems oscillate between aggregation and massification. In the massification polarity the group seems unified, members tend to merge with the 'mother-group'" (Scheidlinger, 1974), deny differences and an illusion of togetherness and sameness prevails. In the aggregative polarity, people feel alienated from one another and indifference, hostility and withdrawal from relationships are prevalent. In its extreme form a massive splitting mechanism is active and each subgroup is against each other subgroup (Weinberg, 2019 p. 98). The theory of the social unconscious becomes useful in this context since both school and the health care system are social phenomena with which the parents are confronted.

Aiming for cohesiveness, it is therefore important to work together with the parents in their own group towards an understanding, that these social phenomena are directly related to the interaction between parent and child.

In one of the early sessions, Rosa's mother talked about how helpless she felt with Rosa, constantly having to be after her, while being showered with the worst swear words imaginable (for example: "You stupid bitch!"). The mother would further describe, how Rosa would also escape, running all over the housing estate while she as her mother, would be left alone in her fear and helplessness.

Hearing this, Arthur's mother just grinned and dryly claimed that her son would never ever do such a thing, upon which Juri's mother suddenly burst into what appeared to be somewhat misplaced laughter. Greta's mother was shocked. The mood in the group threatened to turn destructive. It was the outside world that was supposed to be bad, yet a failing mother had just been discovered in their own midst. Drawing the emerging aggression towards myself, I ventured into saying that Juri still seemed to be so exhausting for her, even though the therapy had already begun. The mother now became really angry with me, letting her frustration run wild, which prompted Greta's mother to become protective of me, whereupon Juri's mother started sobbing and me asking Arthur's mother to reach out to comfort her.

The situation just described would certainly have turned out quite different in a purely online group, in which language is very much at the forefront and the participants' contributions usually flow rapidly one after another. In an in-person group, on the other hand, emotions and implicit memory emerge and are perceived much quicker. In an online group, the attention would have to be more on the group's tendency to be inundated by everyone's verbal expressions, as well as focusing on the development of a differentiation process in order to make sense of the contributions. In an in-person group meeting, the focus would be more on mentalizing overwhelming emotions and transforming these into language.

The opposite process of translating language into sensory perception plays an important role in pain psychotherapy, becoming possible only when the children and adolescents have learned to modulate their pain perception. Therefore, in the treatment of PAS, it is vital to initially translate implicit processes in the in-person group from sensory perception into language and then to integrate this process in the online group from the linguistic level into somatosensory perception.

The group of children, on the other hand, were living out their aggression with relish and abandon (Kernberg, 1995, p. 17; Bürgin, 2013, p. 16). In Minecraft, the children formed into boys' and girls' gangs and built fortresses for themselves. During this construction process, the in-person group was divided into girls with girls and boys with boys. After the first online battle had been carried out with the aid of lava, the children rebuilt their fortresses and managed to support each other. Within the room they each ran to the other group in order to show off their individual expertise, in the online game they remained separate. Then the first signs of a desire for more physical closeness began to emerge. I accompanied these attempts of being closer physically with my comments, focusing on body experience in the group room. On the other hand, when the children were engrossed in the online game, I tended to comment more on my countertransference feelings: "Oh, dear, it's gonna be real hot here in no time!" when the lava was about to be unleashed. When gaming, many of the children's physical senses are stimulated while they perceive the online game intensely with and through their eyes. However, their largest sensory organ, their skin, is not being put to use. While the child has an emotional experience, this emotion is not being mirrored by the avatar. Over and over I would be watching how the children suddenly were jumping up to relieve their tension or to huddle anxiously with their playmates.

Violence as a theme began to crystallize more and more in the children's group. By making sure the content of the online game would remain within the boundaries of the pre-determined frame, the game could remain a safe space, even though the children played these battles quite relentlessly over 15 hours with the "girls vs boys" media introject was dissolving over time. Slowly but surely I came to the conclusion that what I was witnessing had to be a re-enactment of their object relationships. I began to understand their play to be a "trauma game" (Kernberg, 1995, p. 17, Bürgin, 2013, p. 16), that is, the desperate attempt of the children to process the as yet unprocessed by repeating it.

The parents in their group, on the other hand, were working on their own individual life stories. It turned out that three of the parents had grown up with violent fathers and one mother had been sexually abused in her childhood. Greta's mother had died when she was born, so Greta had been taken in and raised by her grandparents. The grandmother suffered from a masked depression after the death of her daughter. From an anamnestic point of view, it can be assumed that most of the parents were themselves having difficulties with self-regulation of tension states due to the trauma they had experienced. Extensive psycho-education and stabilizing exercises helped the parents to regulate better. Additionally a supportive emergency agreement was drawn up, for the parents to get in touch with each other via messenger service in the event that one of the parents would get into difficulties with their child.

The children, on the other hand, when in distress, were switching from the "as if" mode of the computer game to the reality of their in-person group. Juri and Rosa began to attack each other physically and I, as a real object, became necessary to stop the violence. This led to the atmosphere in Minecraft calming down and the first attempts of the group to connect via in-person play in the matrix. I often observe this phenomenon in children: The attempt to process their experiences in virtual play only, in the absence of the necessary additional embodied in-person processing, usually leads to acting out and impulsive behavior in in-person groups.

In the following session Yuri continued shouting swear words, while Rosa was keeping her hands on her ears. Then Arthur joined in and I began to notice a re-enactment. I could see Rosa's mother, who was known for swearing loudly, and Juri's mother, who had previously become violent towards Juri's father. The moment before I was about to intervene, my muscles being quite tense, Arthur suddenly came up with a solution, walking over to Rosa and giving her a hug. This made Juri even more furious, leading to him developing a headache and thus forcing the group to calm down. Rosa stated, reassured by the hug, that there seemed to be a Jubjub on the move, the bird being a symbol for the pain. Greta then ventured into telling the story of the Jubjub bird from the book "Alice's Adventures in Wonderland" (Carrol, 1865) describing a loyal fighter in the service of the Queen of Hearts, loyal to the point of self-abandonment, who freezes everything around him by letting out a bloodcurdling scream. This Jubjub bird was then transferred to the Minecraft game and there showed up in the form of an Ender Dragon. I found it important to remind the children of their symbolic helpers from the "Kids' Skills" program, encouraging them to draft these helpers into the game as well. The Ender dragon was fought and finally slain by the children and their helpers, all working together towards this common goal. The transformation of pain with the help of the media introject Jubjub bird had been a success. What had transpired in the children's group made it obvious to me, that violence within the family had clearly been a fact. Like the children, I also was now set free, in my case from my dissociative frozenness, enabling me to confront this violence in the parent group.

Dobe writes in his book "Practical Treatment Options for Chronic Pain in Children and Adolescents", that 60 % of pain patients have previously experienced trauma which makes it especially important to first focus on treating and dealing with the actual (potentially ongoing) trauma as well as the accompanying symptoms before pain modulation can be successful. In the dovetailing of parent group and children's group and the different social subsystems that affect families, Dobe's assessment seems very plausible to me (Dobe, Hechler, and Zernikow, 2009 p. 306).

Further therapy for the group took place online, with the parent group meeting once a month and the children's group every other week. The parents found to more clarity in regard to their children and were able to stop symptom-reinforcing behavior, with the emergency group having an important supportive function. Through the intensive in-person group work, the parents began to recognize when a mother became overwhelmed or dissociated and were able to provide support. The children, on the other hand, devoted themselves to dealing with the Jubjub bird and continued working on symbolizing their pain symptoms. This way the online game could best develop its defocusing effectiveness, distracting from pain. The children noticed how easy it was to distract themselves and how relaxed they were when they made room for their needs through play. The children's group did not abandon the physical contact that had become so dear to them either, but continued to meet in a playground without me.

5   Conclusion

In my experience, integrating digital media into the standardized treatment of children and adolescents has brought about two important changes. Through streaming videos for psycho-education, the chat groups and the app, it became possible to sustainably expand the effect of the in-person groups. Patients are able to repeat the content on their own accord by watching videos or utilizing the app. Via the chat group, patients and parents can connect with and support each other, in case a problematic situation should arise, so as to actively and in a targeted way implement in the home environment what has been learned in clinical treatment. Furthermore, the chat group supports the parents on their own personal journey towards more independence and further development after therapy. In this way, the parent group continues to sustain and unfold its therapeutic impact long after treatment has ended.

What I have come to conclude is that online groups and digital media are experiential spaces with different boundaries and offering different possibilities. The loneliness of the patients in their physical experience within the online group, finding their environment reduced to language only or having to deal with the sudden discontinuity when the online group is shut down by going off-screen, create rich opportunities to work on transitions and boundaries in new, creative and development enhancing ways. Using computer games to have patients enter a state of reduced external perception is no more difficult than leading a fantasy journey in a group.

Media introjects, that is media avatars that the patients identify with and subsequently internalize, are of a different nature than the conventional transitional object that we have known, such as a cozy blanket. Also, both behavior and affect expressed by the children through these avatars in the game has been notably different from the observable behavior and affect of the very same children's embodied presence in the group room, thus triggering very different countertransference feelings in me, a fact that I found quite astonishing.

This expansion of experiential space, as I have described in this chapter, has encouraged me to use these treatment methods in various other contexts so as to increasingly be able to meet and support the children and adolescents in their everyday world of experience. In my opinion, no fundamentally different treatment technique is needed when working with patients using digital media, rather a common understanding within the group of the experiential space that we inhabit at any given time.

At a glance:
Media supported *integrated multimodal psychotherapy for children and adolescents*

Psychotherapy that becomes necessary in the context of pain therapy or after a secondary disease in the form of diabetes mellitus requires a special approach.

This article describes a model of a multimodal psychotherapeutic approach for children and adolescents. Three quarters of the psychotherapy was conducted online.In rural areas, media-supported therapy is a great opportunity to maintain the therapeutic framework.

The first section deals with the organization of an interdisciplinary and multidisciplinary collaboration (medical, psychological, and supporting therapeutic professional groups) in the context of integrated care, which uses analogous tools, especially those online (e. g., online specialist forum, video consultation).

The second section is divided into three subchapters: psychoeducation, children's group, and parents' group.

In the psychoeducation part of psychiatric disorders, videos, apps, and interactive charts are presented.

In the treatment section, two post-inpatient process groups are described, which were conducted through the pandemic, initially face-to-face and then online. First, there is a description of the psychotherapy process with a group of children who stabilized through video chat and video games.

A look at the accompanying parent group presents the resource-strengthening effect of messenger services, which were used by parents as infrastructure in addition to online sessions.

In the author's view, it is important to integrate media-supported forms of therapy in the training of child and adolescent psychotherapists. Patients are used to moving in a digital world. Research such as digital media and algorithms influence the group matrix is therefore an important factor that should be scientifically researched.

Finally, the interlocking of the two processes, the common matrix of the transgenerational traumas between child and parents, will be an area of focus.

Bibliography

Brandes, H. (2005). Gruppenmatrix und Theorie des Unbewussten. Über Bewegungen und Perspektiven in der gruppenanalytischen Theorie und Praxis. *Gruppenanalyse. Zeitschrift für gruppenanalytische Psychotherapie, Beratung und Supervision,* 15, 2, 151–169

Bürgin, D. (2013). Das Spiel, das spielerische und die Spielenden. *Zeitschrift für Kinder und Jugendlichenpsychotherapie,* 157, 9–28

Carrol, L. (1865). *Alice's Adventures in Wonderland.* London: Macmillan

Dittrich, K. (2011). Wir kennen uns nicht, doch will ich Dir vertrauen, ich teile mit Dir Träume von 'nem Glück frei von Zeit und Raum. Interneterfahrungen in der hochfrequenten Analyse eines schwer trennungstraumatisierten Mannes. In K. Münch, D. Munz, A. Springer (Hrsg.), *Die Fähigkeit, allein zu sein* (2. Aufl.; S. 261–276). Gießen: Psychosozial

Dobe, M., Hechler, T., Zernikow, B. (2009). The pain provocation technique as an adjunctive treatment module for inpatient pain treatment for children and adolescents with chronic pain: A case report. *Journal of Child & Adolescent Trauma,* 2, 4, 297–307

Dobe, M., Zernikow, B. (2019). *Therapie von Schmerzstörungen im Kindes- und Jugendalter* (2., vollst. aktual. Aufl.). Berlin, Heidelberg: Springer

Foulkes, S. H., Anthony, E. J. (1973). *Group Psychotherapy. The Psychoanalytic Approach* London: Penguin

Furman, B. (2004). *Kids' Skills: Playful and Practical Solution-Finding with Children.* Victoria: Innovative Resources

Haar, R., Wenzel, H. (2019). *Psychodynamische Gruppentherapie mit Kindern.* Stuttgart: Kohlhammer

Heathcote, L. C., Pate, J. W., Park, A. L., Leake, H. B., Moseley, G. L., Kronman, C. A., Fischer, M., Timmers, I., Simons, L. E. (2019). *Pain neuroscience education on YouTube.* PeerJ 7:e6603 http://doi.org/10.7717/peerj.6603

Hoffmann, S. (1993). Das bio-psycho-soziale Krankheitsmodell. In U. T. Egle, S. O. Hoffmann (Hrsg.), *Der Schmerzkranke. Grundlagen, Pathogenese, Klinik und Therapie chronischer Schmerzsyndrome aus bio-psycho-sozialer Sicht* (S. 1–17). Stuttgart/New York: Schattauer

Kernberg, P. (1995). Formen des Spielens. *Studien zur Kinderpsychoanalyse,* 9–35

Nickel, R. (1999). *Therapie somatoformer Schmerzstörungen. Manual zur psychodynamisch-interaktionellen Gruppentherapie.* Stuttgart/New York: Schattauer

Nickel, R. (2001). Manualisierte psychodynamische-interaktionelle Gruppenpsychotherapie. *Psychotherapeut,* 46, 11–19

Scheidlinger, S. (1974). On the concept of the "mother-group". International Journal of Group Psychotherapy, 24, 4, 417–428.

Weinberg, H. (2019). *The Paradox of Internet Groups: Alone in the Presence of Virtual Others.* London: Routledge

Destructive Processes in Groups –
The Stance of Group Leaders

"Must I become a Villain?" – On the Significance of Destruction in Existential Conflicts

Anja Khalil, Carla Weber

Every group of children stages existential conflicts revolving around love, hate, and knowledge. Boundary transgressions and destructive attacks are an intrinsic part of the group's enacting dialogs and its creative development process. Superficially, these destructive attacks violate central basic needs of the group, especially the needs for protection and cohesion, belonging and acceptance. They occur abruptly, usually in connection with the group's conscious or unconscious experiences of separation, and momentarily or persistently shatter the group's capacity to play creatively, dream together, and engage in fruitful communication. In our therapy groups we found them to be linked to violent assaults, destructive impulses, or scenes of domination and submission. In our reflections, we will focus not only just on risks but also on intrinsic development potential of these destructive impulses in the group process, both for the individual and the group as a whole.

1 Pressure to act and the capability for negative capability

When a father in a parent therapy group asked a simple question about what a good boundary was and how he could deal with his son crossing such boundaries, he encountered the perplexed silence of exhausted parents. Parents who knew of themselves that in such moments they tended to take physical action against their children. Parents who talked about how they rejected their children's feelings. Parents who were afraid of their children.

How could these parents who had themselves experienced physical and mental cruelty, find reliable boundaries and stability within themselves? What could they derive from their experiences in the parent therapy group that would help them provide adequate protection for themselves and their children? What did it take for them to better manage their destructive impulses without having to deny them any longer?

In our children's therapy groups, we often experience children claiming of others such things as that "You always let things escalate, you freak!", or making unforgivingly punitive statements like "You need that, otherwise you'll never learn! It's your own fault!", or the blithe brushing aside of pain "Don't make such a fuss! That was nothing!". Over time, we realized that in decisive moments of destructive aggravation our interventions were inadequate and simply petered out. The group seemed to provoke our support and intervention precisely in these moments of heightened destruction in which the children's creative games deteriorated, the intermediary space collapsed, and a total presence set in that seemed to know neither a before nor an afterwards, and yet simultaneously it was in these very moments that they rejected it most vehemently. How were we to understand this response? Some things brought us to limits of our own immunity, triggering destructive impulses in us towards the group and drowning us in a sense of helplessness, which made us less able to feel empathy. Were we still in good therapeutic contact with the group's unconscious in the face of these overwhelming feelings? Was the traumatic relational action that manifested itself in these acute moments, which we increasingly understood as a "process of post-tolerance" (Ferro, 2005, p. 102), something that could be transformed in any way within the group process? These unanswered questions led us to embark on a journey of research from which we, above all as children's group analysts, came back as different people.

2   On the necessity of destruction and survival

As early as 1912 with her paper "Die Destruktion als Ursache des Werdens" (Destruction as the Cause of Becoming), Sabina Spielrein postulated a force in human psyche that is opposed to our fundamental tendency to differentiate. Central to our search for clues is her consideration of the bi-directionality of the two forces. She attributes destruction, as a propensity towards dissolution, towards de-differentiation, to a "transformation of the ego into a we" and includes it among the instincts of species preservation (Spielrein, 1912/1986, p. 41 f.). In this context, destruction is necessary in order to dissolve or destroy the old so that something new can arise. Helpful in this context is Spielrein's insight that the stimulation of the pole seeking separation always likewise stimulates the pole seeking connection – and vice versa. She thus construes the development-promoting tension in contrast to the lack of tension that inhibits development between these two poles as being fundamental.

We find the significance of destruction relevant to development is advanced in the lectures of Donald Winnicott (1945) on "Primitive Emotional Development" and "Hate in the counter-transference" (1994), as well as in the both emancipatory and relational observation by Jessica Benjamin "Master and Servant" (2005). Both authors address the question of destruction, the creative and necessary annihilation, or rather a relevant dynamism between subjection and dominance in the struggle for mutual recognition during human individuation.

In this context, Winnicott explores the primitive feeling of hate that the mother must allow in herself in order to enable an emotional differentiation between herself and her child. He postulates that in this early time in which he places these processes, there is a primary unintegration.[1] Following Melanie Klein (1952/1999), he discerns in the emerging process of differentiation an absence of the primary object which becomes in the infant a presence that attacks him. At this juncture Winnicott (1945) locates the inseparable and palpable connection between love and hate. In this regard, unlike Benjamin, he still assumes a view of origin logic in the tradition of Freud (1915c/1946) in which hate precedes love and derives from the narcissistic ego's initial rejection of a stimulus-providing external world. However, it is his conclusion for therapeutic work that is crucial for our focus: "If the patient seeks objective or justified hate he must be able to reach it, else he cannot feel he can reach objective love" (Winnicott, 1949, p. 72). For us as children's group analysts, this means we are put to the test of whether we can hate objectively and allow love and hate to materialize in their mutual dynamics in the group, all without revenge and retribution or annihilation becoming too real or the necessary tension between the two poles being lost. "It seems that he [the individual] can only believe in being loved after reaching being hated" (Winnicott, 1949, p. 72).

Extending Winnicott, Benjamin takes her thoughts on the destruction that makes existential separateness and dependency possible in a somewhat different direction. She describes a mutual process of recognition in which subjection and domination relate to each other in a creative tension. In this perspective, hatred only arises when this relationship of tension regularly breaks down, and the mother is unable to withstand the destruction and retaliates or withdraws and remains compliant. This lack of subjectivity on the part of the mother, who makes the experience of being separated difficult or even hinders it, is the "great, of not the greatest, impediment to the experience of successful destruction and survival" (Benjamin, 1988, p. 82). The child intensifies its rage,

---

1   Here, integration is described as being distinct from the state of unintegration. The infant is disintegrated or rather unintegrated because it has not yet completed the existential separation from or sensing itself to be different to its mother, does not yet exist psychologically by and unto itself. The infant needs the mother as an all-encompassing shell with which it only exists mentally. Moreover, the infant does not yet distinguish between ego and non-ego. By contrast, we understand disintegration as the result of a failure of other defense mechanisms. If the increasing recognition of the existential differentiation of mother and infant or the integration of the accompanying emotional development fail, we later see, amongst other things, difficulties in localizing the self in one's own body, in personalization and in grasping reality.

directs it more inwardly, and permanently continues its attacks in its imagination. As a result, it persistently seeks a limit for its reactive rage in the outside world and remains caught in its fantasies of omnipotence and absolutes – "the world is all me" (Benjamin, 1988, p. 71). It is a fantasy that blocks further differentiation. According to Benjamin, the consequence of this failed destruction is splitting. Consequently, the key to resolving this split is the establishment of an external world which can be experienced and that recognizes reality. This can emerge through the self-activity and self-assertion of an attachment figure, who recognizes their subjectivity in the context of reciprocity.

"In successful destruction (when the other survives), the distinction between mental acts and what happens out there in 'reality' becomes more than a cognitive awareness; it becomes a felt experience. The distinction between may fantasy of you and you as a real person is the very essence of connection" (Benjamin, 1988, p. 71). For us as group analysts, the knowledge of our subjective limits, which are expressed amongst other things in a healthy and authentic "So far and no further!", is of central importance for the establishment of the outer world within the group and within the individual.

Two levels of mutuality distinguished by Winnicott are of diagnostic importance and relevant for treatment: the neurotic and the psychotic levels of functioning.

On a neurotic level, he expects that if the analyst shows ambivalence towards the child and a tension of love and hate, the child will respond in a conflictual way by splitting love and hate. However, this is short-circuited in the sense of a dichotomous thinking in which one can only be loved or only be hated. The tension necessary for the infant's development either dissolves or crumbles. Love and hate can be perceived but only separately from one another.

However, on the psychotic level the child enters a state in which love and hate coincide. In this case, the child may experience the analyst profoundly as someone who is only capable of one kind of relationship, namely a relationship of raw and dangerous simultaneous existence of love and hate. This means for the child that if the analyst shows love towards it, it is convinced that it will be destroyed in the same instance.

Based on clinical experience, we agree with both authors that the process of differentiation from existential separateness and dependency can only succeed in the tension of mutual recognition of the subjectivity of the other person. This mutual recognition paves the way for the development of signal anxiety and the integration of developing or existing hatred.

3 Enactment of hate and destruction

In the following case study, we describe scenes from the children's therapy group which meets regularly once a week, and from its accompanying parent therapy group that convenes every four weeks. In these scenes, existential experiences of dependency and separation are brought to life in the context of the stressful experiences the participants have in their relationships. The group of children and the group of parents struggle together with the group leader to transform and understand destructive processes.

3.1 Farewells and comfort stones

After a fairly constant set of participants in the children's therapy group over the previous few months, several farewells were now imminent. The children's responses to this varied. In one session they consoled themselves with a stone which, when pressed, could remove the pain caused by the separation but could also be used as a weapon against the person who had caused the pain. Up to this point it had been possible to integrate some things within the context of these recent experiences of separation and, according to the group leader's assessment, some things had to remain unintegrated. To ward off the inner pain but also to actively counteract the outside that was experienced as threatening, comforting things such as the stone, which the children named "comfort stone", provided a temporary, creative solution.

3.2 Separation and omnipotence

A boy who had been part of the group for a long time staged his farewell by lying down in a fetal position in the middle of the final circle that took place ten minutes before the end of every group session, jumping out again shortly afterwards, and saying that he had been dead and had resuscitated himself. He had had an especially difficult start in the children's therapy group because he experienced himself as a potential danger to others, namely as an earthquake destroying everything around him. Now, in order to detach himself from the group, he needed to feel omnipotence over life and death. Nonetheless, he could not prevent the group from actually experiencing his loss and that of another boy. Indeed, shortly after this group session another boy suddenly stopped coming to the group. He could no longer be taken there due to a car accident and then stayed away permanently without further explanation or accessibility to his parents. It was as if he and his family had disappeared from the face of the earth.

3.3 Snow White and the Seven Dwarves

After the summer holidays, a girl was admitted to a group that for a long time had only consisted of boys. After the initial round broke up, the boys wanted to build a house together. That seemed astonishing at first because previously they had tended to fight with each other. The girl had dressed up as a princess, and the scene made the group leader think of Snow White and the Seven Dwarves. As with the seven dwarves, arguments broke out among the boys over who had taken something from whom.

Presumably the children were initially frightened by the lack of integration of the past separations and the new situation. The boys sought mutual support in the group, but it was unclear who was allowed to take what place where. It all got too much for the youngest boy, who withdrew to the lower floor of a playhouse and wanted to be left in peace. The other boys responded to his desire for protection by barricading all the exits. Initially, it was still a game they all played in which the youngest boy always found a way out. Like the mouse in Tom and Jerry, he was always able to outsmart the others and make holes in their barricades. However, he soon found it too tiring, and in the end, he accepted his fate.

3.4 Cycle of omnipotence

Now the youngest boy stopped trying to counter the attacks of the others. As a result of his refusing to continue playing the cat-and-mouse game, the tension that had prevailed in the group thus far began to dissipate. The other children now really turned up the heat, and giving no thought to the boy's feelings, they completely barricaded him in. The cycle of omnipotence took its course. Now the group wanted to force the youngest boy to finally come out. The oldest boy then climbed onto the roof and jumped around energetically putting all his weight into it. The group leader began to wonder how much the group, each individual, and the playhouse could take and whether her intervention might be needed. She caught the oldest boy's attention and gave him a questioning look. However, he didn't seem to care that the beams were giving way or that the roof might not be able to take his weight any longer. He wanted to risk breaking through the roof, falling on the youngest boy, and injuring him. The initial game with borderline experiences had come to a head, all previous attempts to maintain a sufficient barricade in the game and as such boundaries, protection, and support were in danger of failing.

3.5 Invulnerability, submission, and protection

Now the youngest boy's best friend interrupted his involvement in the barricading and tore open the door to the playhouse. What made him do that, you might wonder? Did he want to free the youngest boy or give him the final death blow or coup de grace? The group leader sat behind him and both of them were able to look inside the playhouse. They could see that the youngest boy had created a basic shelter for himself and was hiding under foam blocks. The unbearable sense of helplessness and impotence filled the room. The group leader found it almost unbearable to see him looking so helpless. Was not his best friend now also rebelling against the unbearable situation? She got the impression that he wanted to attack his best friend despite or precisely because of his defenselessness and through this violation of boundaries to attempt to oust him and the related unbearable impotence out of the group. He rushed forward and given his weight and his rashness the group leader realized grave danger was imminent. Thank goodness the worsening of the traumatic events had not left her completely incapacitated, nor had the omnipotence manifested in the room enticed her into playing down her fear and not responding or responding too weakly. When the boy was about to kick his best friend, the group leader intervened by standing up and physically but also with a commanding voice preventing the attack. In the opening of the door of the protective space (playhouse) and the group leader's intervention and boundary-setting, the group had found the boundaries that are always sought in parallel to the orchestrating of omnipotence.

In order to put the group process to date to therapeutic use, we felt from our perspective that two things were necessary: on the one hand to allow the orchestration of the illusionary ideas of invulnerability and comprehensive notional protection of the group so that it could (perhaps for the first time) be experienced within the group, but on the other hand subsequently to disillusion these ideas and demands. We found out that through this interaction the children experienced existential separateness, the cycle of omnipotence that had arisen was interrupted, and the children recognized their dependence on one another. Only now could the traumatic anxiety be alleviated and signal anxiety become the basis for the ongoing group process. Now psychological elements gained in the process of retrospection could be used for new psychological growth. However, this would take up a lot of time and require many different sessions of working through the events. In the process, the group members struggled to establish a viable relationship with one another and repeatedly grappled with the question of whether it is possible to reach and experience objective hate.

In a joint discussion of the situation described, the oldest boy who had jumped onto the roof and the best friend of the youngest boy were evasive. Nor were they prepared to become involved in the tidying up afterwards. The girl was angry at the group leader for letting something like this happen. At the time it was not possible to understand the situation better.

3.6 Psychotic level

Initially, following this situation the group repeatedly operated on a psychotic level in which existential separateness did not seem possible, but rather love and hate, death and life became blurred. The next session was not attended by the youngest boy, who was ill. When he joined the group again, he first of all denied feeling angry with them and seemed oblivious and somehow remote. It was as if the other boys wanted to test how much the group, the group leader, and the space could stand. They waged mutiny against the group leader and kept out of her physical reach by huddling together on the upper level of the playhouse, as if in the crow's nest high up in the rigging of a sailing boat.

From there they shouted down and prevented any kind of regular session from taking place. The group leader was embarrassed that she had so little control over the group and that this was visible to everyone in the immediate vicinity and above all could be heard outside the group therapy room. At the next parent therapy group session, this was also the very thing for which she was criticized by the parents. Everyone seemed highly satisfied that when they had gone to collect their children and were waiting outside in the car park beneath the playroom window, they could hear that the group leader did not have the children under control despite what one might expect from a qualified person. This time it seemed clear to the parents that the group leader was not always up to her job. Despite her embarrassment over the situation, the group leader remained accessible and available to the parents and echoed their sentiments. Initially, the parents were relentless and avoided any discussion about their own inadequacies. It was only through the group leader's express appreciation for the parents that it proved possible to create a space for reflection on the parents' own need for boundaries, their own experience of boundary transgressions, but also the nascent recognition of their own transgressions.

In the children's group therapy sessions, the children continued to push the boundaries, and the group leader was tormented by self-doubt. In the intervision group, the group grappled to be allowed to develop an objective hatred towards the children. When is a boundary reached? What do we no longer tolerate as people? How much limitation should be imposed on the scope offered in order for the latter to be effective? We tried out power words that remained ineffective, but at some point, the group leader had truly had enough. When the children began to provoke one another, she yelled at them. Shocked by her verbal outburst, the children became very quiet and serious. They had not experienced anything like that before. One of them was so frightened he refused to join the final circle. The group leader was surprised by her own response, by the fact that despite having a cold she had been able to raise her voice, but also relieved she had been able to communicate to them that she had reached her own limit, albeit in an unstructured way. Was that not precisely the point? Something unconsciously known but unstructured, something unfixed seeks a structure and can, in the group process, be transformed into still unknown, but now structured, consistent space?

3.7 Personification of evil

In the sessions that followed, everything was calm to begin with. Some children withdrew into bunkers they had made themselves, which was just as difficult to bear as their previous provocations had been. The oldest boy told the group leader that he saw hell in her. For him, she now embodied the devil, who forced him to participate in this horrible group. He said he would like to squash her like an ant, but he couldn't do that because as soon as he destroyed her, he would be afflicted by a curse that would also destroy him, and after that he withdrew into his bunker.

We construed his bunker and that of the other children as reflecting the rudimentary human need for protection, which they had previously needed to fight for strenuously. In return, the group leader now willingly accepted the negative transference and lent herself as the representation of the evil object the group had previously been. This brought about a de-dramatization of the evil character in the group ego (on this, see also Quinodoz, 2002, p. 56 f.). Subsequently, the group's support-ego function could resonate more freely and develop more creative solutions. Afterwards a couple of boys really got wound up. This time, the oldest and the youngest had formed an alliance and together they took great sadistic pleasure in disrupting the peaceful play of the other children. Banging on pans, they produced a terrible noise which they themselves could only stand with tissues stuffed in their ears. Presumably this was their way of letting the group leader know that they themselves found their behavior unbearable. After a while, the group leader said she found the noise hellish and she could no longer stand it. First, she tried using words, and then she tried using physical contact with the noisy boys. Everyone wrestled over the pans, until finally it was possible for one of the two children to express the fact that what he was now doing to the others in the group was exactly what he had experienced on the part of his older brother. This time it was not necessary for the group leader to draw a strong boundary. She had been able to recognize that her subjective boundary had been reached. This allowed her to find her objective hatred and set the children an authentic boundary. She made her earache available to the children as a physical pain also expressed verbally, a pain which the children had themselves expressed non-verbally by stuffing tissues into their ears. This way, sharing space and time together became increasingly possible again.

3.8 Neurotic level

The next session started out with noise again, but this time the other children refused to put up with it. They no longer allowed their building blocks to be stolen, went on the counterattack, and defended themselves several times, stating that they had copied this from the group leader in the previous sessions. One of the noisy children found his own noise too much and ran over to the other camp. Another boy wandered away, seemingly pleased that he had finally achieved the desired and appropriate response to his behavior, one that was not exaggerated but preserved the boundaries.

In the next session, this boy then announced his final departure from the group. The group leader told him that she was reluctant to let him go as long as he felt she had put him in shackles. His initial response to this remark was an astonishingly calm one, and he withdrew into the playhouse. Finally, he hammered against all the boundaries of the playhouse and experienced that around him was not nothing but rather limitation. So as to make himself heard, he took the button-operated Indian war cry with him into the house. He confirmed the group leader's suspicion that he was a prisoner in his own prison. He said that despite his innocence he had been sentenced to life in prison. He didn't want to be freed, he felt good in his prison. Meanwhile the other children felt more confident and this time pitted themselves against him with relish. Again and again they dared to challenge him. They slammed the shutters of the playhouse to, and he promptly flung them open again. If someone had withdrawn their hand too slowly it would have been trapped, but now every player knew this, and also knew pain is painful and that you have to be prepared for people to respond to your attacks with protective and defense measures. Acknowledging vulnerability and separateness made the risk easier to assess for everyone and reduced the risk of real injuries.

3.9 Acceptance of reciprocity

In the last-but-one session before the upcoming farewell, the group members were able to appreciate each other better, and the noise level had become more bearable for everyone. The girl gave a ball to the boy who wanted to go, so that he was less lonely on his beanbag that seemed more like an island. The girl's spontaneous gesture in acknowledging the pain the boy felt about parting and her giving him a ball, perhaps as a good object, would probably not have been felt in the group in its dialectic of disintegration and new beginning, anger/sorrow, and hope without the preceding destructive actions and the jointly experienced social breakdowns. The destructive processes could now be reappraised in a way more conducive to development. Later, this ball hit the group leader so hard that it was painful. The girl who had thrown it apologized but also noted that the group leader should have taken better care of herself. In the boy's farewell session, the children used large foam elements to build a "millennium wall" occupied by Playmobil figures in different scenes that recalled many scenes from past sessions. A lot had happened before this understanding of oneself and the others in the group was possible, but also before common boundaries had been established enabling shared play. Responsibility for one's own invulnerability could now be returned to each individual. With this expansion of the scope of action, a separation from one another had become possible.

4   Discussion on framing and inner setting of the group

The paradoxical experience of first destroying something in order to rediscover it implies a constant incorporation of love and hate, of forming and destroying in relation to each other. Through this area of experience, it becomes possible to support the group in their journey towards greater differentiation, the recognition of reality, and their own individuation. In order to be able to utilize the psychological momentum that exists between tension and loss of tension, it is necessary amongst other things to consider the binary opposition of the elements of victim and perpetrator in the group as a social body. Or as children themselves sometimes put it: "If there's a God, there's a devil." And nobody wants to always have to embody just one aspect. What was significant for our work was that no one, neither we nor anyone else, is either God or the devil; rather, we are limited and limiting human beings. Just like the children and parents in our therapy groups, we grapple with painful feelings and in doing so contribute to a necessary de-idealization and de-dramatization in the therapy groups (Quinodoz, 2002). In this context, the willingness of the group leader to take on the negative transference and the momentary allowance of helplessness and potential traumatic shame also seems significant to us, as both are preconditions for psychological growth in the group (Weber, 2019). Working through these associated intense internal and external tensions in the group process requires continuous reflection on the projective identification in countertransference "because the effect hits us before we know the causes" (Eickhoff, 2007, p. 32). The psychological challenges involved go far beyond any permissive attitude. As we also saw in the descriptions, the group leader is much more strongly involved, above all emotionally, particularly in the moments when the group tries to push her out or negate her. If these emotional levels are not reflected on, if they remain excluded from a process whereby, they become conscious feelings, this can hinder the group leader herself and also the entire group in their collective analytical work and cause the therapeutic processes to lose any edge or come to a complete standstill. In order to alleviate the group's stress, delegations and fixations in perpetrator and victim roles or scapegoat attributions can be increasingly observed (Weber, 2019). The polar tension that a healthy psychological development requires collapses, and the cycle of omnipotence (Benjamin, 1988) is continued. This cycle is also kept in motion when the group, as a result of events within the group, can no longer experience its leader as vibrant in Winnicott's sense.

If rigidity and confusion persistently define the situation, then it becomes impossible to generate adequate resonant testimony given the pressure of projective identifications. The level of anxiety in the group increases. As the analytical function of everyone involved is weakened, it is important for the protection of everyone not only that violence in group events is flagged appropriately and in a timely manner but also that the reality of assaults in relationships is acknowledged and the group allows individuals to experience and express hate. This allows the group and each individual in it to acknowledge reality, to (re)discover the cognitive function, and to admit new creative solutions in the play and experiences of everyone. Just as feelings of love and hate are related to one another, in our therapeutic work we also experience the group and the individual in an existential field of tension with each other that is indissoluble at its core (Weimer, 2021). Identifying the associated ambivalent tensions in the group process and also in ourselves and recognizing their central significance for development enabled the children and parents from our therapy groups but also ourselves as their therapists to survive the attacks. From the perspective revealed here, we understand survival as one's own subjectivity discovered in intersubjective tension and maintained under pressure, which the group can experience as challenging and helpful and which allows all participants to feel alive.

> **At a glance**
> *Group analysis makes it possible* to manifest conflictual events that have been defended against through the manifold possibilities of transference within the group and to reappraise them over time. In this manner, aggressive impulses that were previously repulsed can be given manifest form again in the interaction and thus become available again in their potential for promoting development.
>
> By expanding the child therapy group setting to include an accompanying parent therapy group, *group analysis gains* a stabilizing effect and one that promotes development because the changes the children undergo tend to be more strongly supported by the parents.
>
> The methodological considerations described in this paper provide group analysts with a theoretical and clinical space for reflection on how to deal with potentially destructive impulses and the conditions of limitation beneficial to development.

Bibliography

Benjamin, J. (1988). *The Bonds of Love: Psychoanalysis, Feminism, and the Problem of Domination* (pp. 51–84). New York: Doubleday

Eickhoff, F.-W. (2007). Über den Prozess der Nachträglichkeit. *Europäische Psychoanalytische Föderation: Bulletin,* 61, 29–35.

Ferro, A. (2005). *Im analytischen Raum. Emotionen, Erzählungen, Transformationen.* Gießen: Psychosozial

Freud, S. (1915c/1946). *Instincts and their Vicissitudes.* In S. Freud, Standard Edition, vol. 14 (pp. 109–140). London: Imago

Klein, M. (1952/1999). Some Theoretical Conclusions regarding the Emotional Life of the Infant. In M. Klein, *The Writings of Melanie Klein,* vol. 3: *Envy and Gratitude and Other Works* (pp. 61–94). London: Hogarth Press

Quinodoz, D. (2002). *Worte, die berühren. Eine Psychoanalytikerin lernt sprechen.* Frankfurt/M.: Brandes & Apsel

Spielrein, S. (1912/1986). *Die Destruktion als Ursache des Werdens.* Tübingen: edition discord

Weber, C. (2019). "Übertragung und Gegenübertragung in der Kinderpsychotherapie," In S. Kudritzki, K. Salamander (Hrsg.), *Psychodynamische Behandlungstechnik bei Kindern und Jugendlichen* (S. 107–138). Frankfurt/M.: Brandes & Apsel

Weimer, M. (2021). Die talmudische Denkweise kann ja nicht plötzlich aus uns verschwunden sein. Todestrieb – eine Figuration dargestellt am Beispiel des Antisemitismus. *Gruppenpsychotherapie und Gruppendynamik,"* in: *– Zeitschrift für Theorie und Praxis der Gruppenanalyse,* 57, 2, 142–66

Winnicott, D. W. (1945). Primitive emotional development. *The International Journal of Psychoanalysis,* 26, 137–143

Winnicott, D. W. (1949). Hate in the counter-transference. *The International Journal of Psychoanalysis,* 30, 69–74

A Suicide Fantasy – Confusion, Speechlessness, and Projective Identification as Defenses of Tabooed Issues in Group-Analytical Psychotherapy with Late Adolescent Women Aged 18–21

Franziska Schöpfer

1 For dynamic administration

1.1 Setting

The analytical group with late adolescent women has been running consistently for several years and is semi-open. The group meets once a week for a hundred minutes in my practice.

1.2 Leadership in a pair

From the beginning, we – my colleague Christina Selle and I – have led the group together as a leader pair. I wanted to lead the group as a pair because of the special requirements of an adolescent group and the possible transference of parents, which can promote an intensified confrontation with idealized parental images and work on de-idealization. The age-related challenges of detachment from the family, the search for a partner, and the first autonomous steps into adult life can be tried out and worked through in this family-like setting.

In the current group, there were predominantly female group participants who lived without real parenthood or without family membership. Our setting was particularly helpful here for working through these life circumstances of childhood and adolescence with the experienced lack of response to developmental needs.

Since leadership in a pair carries the danger of a *"split transference"* (Behr and Hearst, 2009, p. 45), we take time after each group session for an extensive reflection in order to bring together and exchange different, split, or indeed congruent, matching transference phenomena again.

1.3 Girls' group

The decision for an all-girls' group creates the prerequisite to get into an intimate and familiar exchange with each other more quickly. In our experience, the challenge of a successful female identification and the psychological pitfalls of accepting a now sexually unambiguous body are often difficult for our female patients to master. The search for a positive female identification and the exchange about fears and conflicts that arise in the process – right through to the manifestation of pathological symptoms – takes up a lot of space in these girls' groups.

Irvin D. Yalom writes about this:

> "Members of homogeneous groups can talk to each other in a particularly authentic way because they all have certain experiences in common. This enables an authenticity in communication that therapists themselves are not always able to achieve" (Yalom, 1970/2007, p. 31).

With our decision for a homogeneous group of girls, we excluded a large field of exchange possibilities, opposite-gender reflections and resonances, as well as possible conflicts. But we expected this to alleviate the fears and resistances at the beginning of our group work (Behr and Hearst, 2009, p. 210).

Encouraged by our very good experiences, we have kept this setting up to now, although time and again the group itself fantasized about the participation of young men and questioned the chosen, homogeneous setting.

2 Thoughts on the age group of late adolescent female patients

Many late adolescent patients come to my practice with developmental inhibition that is also represented by the lack of satisfying social contacts or the lack of a well-functioning peer group. Either they are still too closely tied to the primary objects, so their own authentic autonomy development can only be mastered with massive feelings of guilt and fear of losing the object, or they lack a holding, a family bond, and have to go prematurely (pseudo-progressively) into an autonomy in which they cannot be sufficiently considered in their developmental needs. Often a neurotic compromise is then sought with the justification of social withdrawal and the devaluation of a peer group. Missing, disappointing, or even traumatically impacting peer group experiences usually bring feelings of failure. Not infrequently, this leads to a silent reproach with a mixture of feelings of (destructive) envy with revenge and resentment effects, which in turn creates dysfunctional relationship patterns. Either the pathological withdrawal organization is reinforced or on/off relationship patterns manifest, which each time lead to another experience of disappointment.

Holger Salge writes about the function of a peer group:

> "The peer group is the place that is physiologically sought out from puberty onwards in order to attempt a gradual detachment from the primary objects, to try out rivalry and competition, at the same time to stabilize identity, to create experimental spaces for the awakening drive world, to experience self-efficacy, to cope with feelings of shame, to endure the pain of separation. This list could be continued" (Salge, 2013 p. 123).

He goes on to state that:

> "Group psychotherapy can become the place where, secured by the setting and the framework, a catching-up peer group experience becomes possible for those patients for whom such an experience was not possible in the social field against the background of their personal psychological development. [...] In the course of treatment, group therapy can also become a place where, for the first time, with the help of identifying and observing the (developmental) difficulties of others, a genuine recognition of one's own life entanglements, fears of independence, and detachment difficulties becomes possible. [...] Only when it is possible for the young person to no longer deny and finally also mourn their own inner inhibitions in the use of the adolescent testing space can a reorientation succeed" (Salge, 2013, p. 125 ff.).

Our experiences with late adolescent group participants clearly confirm these statements by Holger Salge. I would like to add to these reflections by drawing attention to the aspect of the ambivalence often experienced violently in the process of detachment from the primary family. On the one hand, the young people already want to take steps that belong in an adult, responsible position. On the other, in the face of the inevitable crises that an adolescent detachment process brings with it, they are always existentially dependent on family support and belonging to a primary family that can give them protection and emotional security when it is needed. If this place of the primary family does not exist, family-like structures are needed for their progress in the development process, which replace the family in terms of support, protection, boundaries, and emotional security.

The analytical groups, which are often attended by our group participants for several years, perform a decisive transitional function for the success of a detachment process where integration into a supportive, reliable peer group has not yet been mastered. This is because in the group – as in individual therapy – strong parent-child transference is not necessarily driven. In the group, a variety of "sibling transferences" is stimulated and the orientation or identification takes place more in horizontal rather than vertical parent transference. This creates a much wider range of possible reflections and resonances, and the group members can have crucial experiences of efficient self-purposiveness, object use, self-object differentiation, etc. through their trial action in the group.

Following these considerations, I discern the great developmental possibilities that group-analytical psychotherapy offers, especially for the stage of late adolescence. In our groups, many participants were able to detach themselves from their family entanglements or to experience a family-like support within the group (as with siblings, group cohesion), often for several years, and to feel safe and a sense of belonging here. Many succeeded in developing an authentic autonomy up to adult positions of responsibility.

3   Current situation of the group

After two announced goodbyes and two spontaneous break-ups shortly afterwards, which were unsettling and difficult to bear (fragility of the group cohesion), the group was reduced to four participants. Now the four remaining group members were in a united mood: "The four of us really want to work here in the group, nobody should disturb us now". Since then, the framework was reliably adhered to, the participants related strongly to each other, and a good group cohesion developed again. Despite very different personalities, a mutual tolerance for conspicuousness, social difficulties, or inhibitions developed. Self-openings became increasingly possible, and reflections were experienced as less offensive and more benevolent. There were many different resonance phenomena, and humor was not neglected either. The *"free-flowing group discussion"* (Foulkes, 2017, p. 173), which, according to Foulkes, can open up *"access to unconscious processes"* in groups, found its time again and again in the group sessions.

4 The four participants

4.1 Imke

19 years old, had previously been in personal analytical therapy with me. At the beginning, she could hardly go to school, although she was in the middle of preparing for her high-school graduation exams. She had a pronounced but massively denied eating disorder (anorexia), which had already led to malnutrition with accompanying symptoms. Physically, she was so weak that she often could no longer cope with everyday school life and stayed at home (social withdrawal). She was extremely perfectionistic and had immensely high expectations of herself, so that she worked unreasonably hard to perform well in school and suffered from extreme fear of failure. She regularly had panic attacks when the pressure became too great. Imke's appearance and demeanor were almost the epitome of an anorexic: She was tall and very thin, almost androgynous, with a narrow, pale face and very light, straight hair. She was extremely friendly and approachable, seemingly always in a good mood, and well versed in language and intellect. Everywhere Imke went, she aroused sympathy.

Course of treatment so far: With the help of astronaut food, nutritional counselling, the personal analytical treatment, and her enormous ambition, she managed to pass her high-school exams – with excellent grades, of course. Imke had a younger sister (two years her junior) at home, for whom she felt very responsible, because her parents – since as far back as her childhood – had disappeared in their independence and were mostly absent. The two sisters were almost symbiotically connected. Imke also shouldered an inordinate amount of responsibility for her friends, an issue she successfully "conquered" during the analytical treatment, and showed herself to be a pronounced carer, with the difficulty of standing up for her own concerns or needs.

She usually took on this role in the group as well. With linguistically differentiated and psycho-dynamically relevant contributions with a structuring effect, she ensured a successful dialogue in the group. In order for her to be able to highlight her own needs and to take the space in the group for this, she usually still needed the support of the group leaders.

Imke was not present at the session in question because she had asked the group for permission to take her driving test that day. Since Imke had already reported various obstacles and great fears regarding the test, the group responded favorably to her request. For Imke's mastery of her unresolved basic conflict of "supply vs. self-sufficiency", this was a great step forward: She asked to be released from her responsibility towards the group in favor of her own concern.

4.2 Vanessa

20 years old, had been in personal analytical therapy for two and a half years before I could imagine taking her into the group. Vanessa herself had great concerns and fears about group therapy. She came at 16 years old and presented with borderline developmental disorder with manic-depressive episodes, marked attachment disorder, self-injurious behavior with dissociative states, and unclear sexual orientation. During individual treatment, she also took psychotropic drugs. Vanessa was the sixth of a total of seven children in a patchwork family. She had no contact with her biological father and had been sexually abused by her next older brother – together with a sister – when she was a child. Her mother was addicted to computers, alcohol, and drugs. In addition, there was a sister with cancer who received most of the attention in the family (hospital stays lasting years). The other children were neglected. Vanessa developed pseudo-progressively at an early age and had the gift of being "adopted" by her friends' families. With the help of her great adaptability, she spent time with them and learned a lot. In her youth, she joined a sports club and developed into a competitive athlete thanks to her ambition, her talent, and a dedicated coach. This helped enormously in regulating her ill-tempered affects. At the age of 16, she independently organized her move into assisted living through the youth welfare service. Shortly afterwards, she introduced herself to me. Vanessa's appearance was that of a competitive athlete: muscular, well-trained body, not very feminine appearance, short brown hair and glasses; everything about her seemed pragmatic. Her great insecurity or fear of closeness expressed itself in an extreme motor restlessness and a constant, inappropriate laugh, which she struggled to regulate.

Course of treatment so far: On the one hand, Vanessa immediately aroused my recognition and respect for what she had achieved and how she had endured her mental situation thus far. On the other hand, contact with her was initially very difficult or almost impossible due to her extreme motor restlessness and repeatedly agitated helpless or powerless feelings of countertransference. We were able to get through and endure several impulsive acts on her part to break off contact, so the quality of the bond between us now seemed reasonably stable. Vanessa graduated from high school during the personal analytical treatment (she was the only one in her family to do so). Afterwards she did a voluntary social year at a primary school, as it was her dream to become a primary school teacher. Vanessa was constantly involved in difficult, dependent relationship constellations. She started to study, but she overburdened herself with the standards she set herself. With advanced analytical treatment and crumbling defenses, she self-referred to a psychiatric clinic for children and adolescents. She could no longer tolerate or regulate her self-injurious behavior and suicidal fantasies. She stayed there for three months and learned about group therapy in a positive way.

Afterwards, she did an internship at the German school in Mexico City, and after six months – a foray into autonomy – she returned to personal analytical therapy, now with more courage and tolerance towards her dependency needs. She had great doubts about whether she could manage to study primary education but took it up again and did well after all. Through the positive experiences in the clinic with group psychotherapy, she now expressed the wish to continue with group psychotherapy with me as well.

In the group, Vanessa could only stand it if she moved her chair one meter outwards at a time and always in the same place, directly to my left – probably an indication of a dependent attachment pattern. There she had enough space for her motor restlessness or her fear of being taken over. The group tolerated this. Her contributions were often apt, somewhat pedagogically preachy, and not infrequently she acted as "co-therapist". I understood this role as masking: Vanessa showed herself adapted to her projected expectations and could not yet find an authentic self-opening (development of a "false self"). Just as Vanessa probably used to adapt to the family norms of her friends or the performance expectations of her coach in the sports club in order to experience belonging and recognition, she initially showed herself to be completely compliant with the group norms and with the group leadership. However, as she became more secure in the group, she then introduced more undifferentiated contributions with fecal language into the group. A few weeks before the session in question, she launched direct attacks against me: The group room was too messy, the chairs were lousy, I would only ever ask the other group participants, there was no room for her problems ...

In this context, Irvin D. Yalom quotes a text by Freud on the conflict: sibling rivalry vs. group cohesion:

> "Freud assumed that group cohesiveness stems, strangely enough, from the universal desire to be the favorite of the group leader. Consider the prototypical human group: the sibling group. It is dominated by strong feelings of rivalry: Each child wants to be the favorite and resents all rivals for their claims on the parents' love. The older child wants to take away privileges from the younger one or eliminate the child altogether. Yet every child realizes that rivals are equally loved by parents; therefore, one cannot destroy one's siblings without incurring the wrath of parents and thus destroying oneself" (Yalom, 1970/2007, p. 239).

Yalom himself writes further on this:

> [...] Oh, to be the favorite child of the parents, of the group leader! For many group members, this longing serves as an inner background against which

all other group events are silhouetted [...] – there is a background of envy, of disappointment at not basking alone in the glow of the group leader. [...] This desire to possess the leader alone, and the envy and greed that follow from it, are hard-wired into the substructure of every group" (Yalom, 1970/2007, p. 241).

Vanessa was contradictory and destructive in her communication and bonding skills. On the one hand, she wanted more attention from me as group leader or from the group and rivalled with the other group members for my favor. At the same time, she attacked me and showed the defense mechanism of splitting (good/bad mother or group) or split in her transference between us group leaders: "I can't do anything with Ms. Selle, she is not interested in me either!" For Vanessa, it was about the experience of the attacked object (mother/group) surviving these destructive attacks and not taking revenge on her, but rather remaining in a relationship with her (see Winnicott). In individual treatment it would probably not have been possible for Vanessa to attack me so directly or to show her split object representations so clearly. The group cohesion that had grown in the meantime gave her the necessary support for her actions. It is possible that Vanessa acted as the mouthpiece of the group and formulated aggressive impulses against the group leaders. This behavior calmed down in the weeks before the session in question, and Vanessa increasingly reported more freely about herself, e. g., about the shame in her cross-border, chaotic relationship entanglements. The group reacted spontaneously with emotional reflections that brought Vanessa's defended emotions into the open and perceptible and raised the question of setting boundaries or crossing boundaries in the group.

It bears noting that Behr and Hearst write about borderline patients in groups as follows:

> "Through denial, projective identification, and splitting, the underlying defense mechanisms are revealed, challenging the whole group to simultaneously support and confront the patient in caring efforts ... The group setting creates ... a constant and reliable framework which, over time, enables the patient to experience the other group members as strong enough to endure his projection-induced persecutory fantasies ... interventions must be distanced enough to allow the patient to withdraw from time to time so that he does not feel overwhelmed or overwhelming, for this would lead to psychological problems" (Behr and Hearst, 2019, p. 86).

Vanessa was able to feel included, important, wanted, and accepted in the last sessions.

4.3 Amelia

19 years old, who had been in the group for a long time with a six-month break, came to me for personal analytical treatment when she was 15. At that time, she was clearly depressed, had hardly any social contacts (social withdrawal), did not talk to her parents, and felt little wanted or seen. She had kept herself in her creative world, drawing extensively and writing her own songs, for which she accompanied herself on the piano or with music programs on the PC. But she was unhappy. In addition, she became entangled in endless power struggles with her father, who, in his neglect and his attitude of denial, was an unbearable imposition for the entire family.

When Amelia was about five years old, her father suffered a severe burnout with suicidal tendencies. Before that, he had earned a lot of money with his computer company. This was followed by several months in hospital and the bankruptcy of the company. The mother had to step in financially with her parents and supported the family with her work. Soon after the start of the personal analytical treatment, the mother separated from the father and moved into her own flat with Amelia. The younger brother (two years her junior) stayed with the father. Amelia described her bond with her brother as superficial and not very emotional. Amelia's appearance at that time corresponded perfectly to the term "grey mouse": She was small and petite, her curly brown hair tied up in a poorly groomed state, her face pale and not very expressive. The language was quiet, but differentiated and clever in thought. By now she was much more visible, thanks to an all-white outfit, right down to the short-cropped hair dyed white. She immediately stood out and spread a "special aura" around her. She even changed her call name to "Snow" in a foreign language. She was communicative, usually happily masked, and made smart comments.

Course of treatment so far: Amelia was the youngest when she joined the group at that time. For a long time, she was subordinate in the hierarchy of the group members and was rather quiet. Only by chance did the group learn about her creative projects at that time, which had meanwhile developed into real work projects. Increasingly, she thawed out in the group, showing humor and understanding for the others. She easily did very well in her high-school exams, worked on her song project (completed 14 songs and posted them on Instagram), and her manga project, and dreamed of Italy. Then Amelia left the group unexpectedly and without a personal goodbye to go to Milan as an au-pair. After six months, she contacted me again and asked to talk to me, saying she was not well. She had quickly found her stay in Milan to be a failure and had had difficult months with severe self-doubt. We agreed that she would join the group again.

By now, Amelia had become a vehement advocate of group therapy and claimed "elder status" within the group. It was usually Amelia who started the group, finding it hard to endure the initial silence. She was characterized by stable emotional defenses and defense against self-reflection, at least in the group sessions. Apparently, however, she was able to use the resonances and reflections of the group for herself in the "quiet chamber" and thus always find her way back to her needs and emotions and progress in her development. In the meantime, she had taken up a design degree and went about her tasks with great diligence. In doing so, she showed a compulsive tendency to overwork – just like her father – and reported exhaustion and loss of appetite. She lived a strictly timed, ascetically structured daily schedule so that she could succeed with her workload. She avoided downtime, and her social contacts were exclusively related to work projects. When faced with unforeseen demands or social events without a work structure, such as a party, she repeatedly experienced panic-like anxiety. The group repeatedly brought in feedback that Amelia was placing too great a burden on herself or had too high expectations of herself, did not engage enough in the teamwork desired by the university and thus did all the project work alone or did not include other fellow students with their competences. Amelia mostly reacted rationally and defensively in the group but was able to act on the admonitions from the group to some extent.

4.4 Hannah

19 years old, came to the practice with pronounced social anxiety and depressive phases. On bad days, she could not leave the apartment and could not attend school. On good days, she was able to make contact with her familiar friends and take part in everyday school life, but with considerable concentration problems and inhibitions about expressing herself in class. She had massive problems falling asleep and often looked for "controlling objects" (friends or her boyfriend) with whom she could sleep better. Until then, she had had a very close dependent-symbiotic relationship with her mother, to the extent that she appeared retarded in her ego functions. Her drive was clearly reduced, she appeared childlike, helpless, and naïve. Violent mood swings produced an unpredictable self-experience in her, her self-esteem regulation was dysfunctional, and not infrequently she attempted regulation via oral incorporation of a good object with regular binge eating. The mother constantly derided the value of Hannah's father, the parents lived separated, and Hannah struggled to establish an independent relationship with him.

Hannah's outer appearance was dominated by her excess weight, dark complexion, and very black hair. At first, although a tall woman in real terms, she came dressed like a little girl, with a short skirt and monkey-swing braids in her hair. She put on a cheerful demeanor. When I asked how she was, she was always fine! She told funny stories and consistently concealed conflict or difficulty. At the same time, her voice was soft and her language undifferentiated, which, however, was not due to a lack of cognitive abilities, but rather to an inexperience in linguistic exchange. At home, people hardly spoke to each other, let alone reflected. Family communication was characterized by denial, undoing, or avoidance. Hannah only learned to verbalize conflicts or difficult emotions now in therapy.

Course of treatment so far: In the personal therapy sessions, I first activated the (German) father, who, with his overstructured attitude, formed the antithesis to her absolutely chaotic mother. Hannah said she was afraid of him and avoided contact. She had no inner permission to emotionally distance herself from her mother or to use the father as an alternative, triangulating, developmental object. During her high-school graduation exams, however, the father (with my support) showed himself to be helpful and was able to assist Hannah in her exam preparations. With further help from therapeutic drugs, she managed to pass the exams, which was "no mean feat" and contrary to her and our expectations. Afterwards, Hannah felt liberated on the one hand, but meanwhile she had no plan for herself at all. She felt under pressure to do something meaningful. She started working but couldn't master the necessary drive and self-regulation to stick it out. She decided to study languages at short notice and started with enthusiasm, but the huge university campus scared her. Nevertheless, she managed to get a foothold in her courses.

In the middle of the semester, her mother demanded that Hannah accompany her on a trip to her country of origin for three weeks and visit the part of the family there. Hannah did not want to go, but also did not know how she could resist her mother and so went with her. This conflict only became clear afterwards. When Hannah returned from the trip, she fell into a new and severe depressive phase. She could no longer keep up with her studies, lapsed into listlessness and meaninglessness, and had violent suicidal impulses.

In the group, Hannah has so far been fairly silent; she was still very embarrassed to talk about herself and to claim the time and attention of the group for herself. She often responded to the other group participants with naive amazement, as if a whole new world would open up for her through the contributions of the others. In the personal therapy sessions, she had already shed her cheerful, childlike masquerade, but in the group she only managed this hesitantly. However, in the last group sessions especially, she voiced her fears, and the group reacted sympathetically and helpfully, although Hannah was not yet able to report on the deeper emotions such as senselessness and depressive emptiness with suicidal thoughts.

Hannah could spontaneously respond very emotionally to the contributions of others and was often surprisingly quick-witted and humorous. The group showed sympathy for her sense of personal failure and of failing in society, and in this way she brought something warm and human to the atmosphere.

5 Case vignette from the 180th group session (matrix)

This is the 23rd group meeting for this group composition.

At the beginning of the meeting, only the group leaders and Hannah are present. Imke is absent today because of her driving test. Amelia had texted to say that she would be a few minutes late. Vanessa is absent without excuse; she arrives seven minutes late.

This is an atypical situation for this group; so far, the framework has been reliably adhered to by all. Silently, I wonder about this.

At the beginning of this three-way constellation, Hannah tells us that she has now increased the dose of her medication (in consultation with the child and adolescent psychiatrist), that she has managed to talk to her father about the planned stay in hospital, and that he has reacted with understanding, contrary to her expectations. Her depressive mood is slowly stabilizing. Vanessa then joins about seven minutes late, and she takes her seat noisily without explanation. Hannah soon falls silent. A little later Amelia arrives and takes a seat. She asks Hannah again about the conversation with her father, because she had only half heard it. Hannah answers briefly.

Amelia starts immediately and tells the group about her work project in her studies. She is working on it non-stop, even on weekends, to get it done. She is actually doing it with two other students in the team, but they don't want to work as much as she does, which disappoints and annoys her. Otherwise she would have nothing to report.

Vanessa says, after a short pause, that she doesn't want to say anything today.

A silence develops that lasts longer. A subcutaneously irritated-aggressive mood becomes perceptible. Surprised by this resistant silence, I feel irritation and anger rising inside me and spontaneously think: "Then we can all go home!" I am surprised at my violent reaction, I have never experienced such an angry feeling before in the group sessions, and certainly not during longer pauses of silence.

Finally, Amelia begins to speak, as she has often done before in such pauses of silence; the others do not participate either linguistically or emotionally.

She now reports in more detail about her drawing for the interactive drawing-animation video game on the topic of bullying that is to be developed, an assignment from her university for her team. She drew a scene for the beginning of the game where the protagonist – the victim of bullying – hangs himself. This is the consequence in this game if one does not help the victim of bullying, as needs to be made clear at the beginning of the game as a warning or threat.

Amelia reports emotionlessly about how she had to draw every minimal change in facial expression until finally the rope came down from above. That was quite exhausting. There are also studies that show that the draughtsman adopts exactly the same facial expression as the drawn face.

The group has now awakened from its stupor of silence and asks:
- Why would this scene be at the beginning of the game?
- Why did she have to draw it alone? What were the other two students contributing to the project?

While Amelia is answering the questions from the others, images involuntarily arise in me of what it must be like to draw someone, line by line, who is about to hang himself. I am seized by an inner flood of terror, horror, and fear effects. It seems absolutely terrible to me to have to cope with such a drawing task. At the same time, I perceive Amelia blithely and seemingly unscathed in her feelings about her drawing. The affects raging inside me seem inaccessible to Amelia and the rest of the group. My gaze wanders to Christina (co-leader) to see if she has similar emotions to mine. But I find no resonance with Christina either. I am violently irritated.

Cautiously, I now dare to ask Amelia how she had perceived her facial expressions when drawing, whether she had also experienced such an "imitator effect". But already another, louder question comes from another side, so that mine is "buried" and with it my attempt to gain access to the averted affects. Once again, I try to create an inroad for the group and Amelia into the unbearable affects that have not been felt so far and that have obviously been deposited with me alone. I make my fantasies about drawing this scene and the possible accompanying affects available in language:

"If I imagine having to draw a scene like that, it would probably overwhelm me and flood me with difficult feelings, with fears, with horrors …"

Amelia denies this input from me, she has not had such feelings. Vanessa and Hannah now offer lively participation in the verbal resistance and say that this is quite normal. In such video games one would constantly be exposed to such destructive scenes and would not have any feelings of horror (*"symbiotic cuddling tendency"*, Lehle, 2018, p. 129).

Meanwhile, an association comes to me – a sudden spark – which links the present scene with Amelia's biography: Amelia's father was violently suicidal during the time of his burnout. Did he want to hang himself? Does Amelia know about her father's condition at that time? She was five years old. I suspect she doesn't know consciously.

Amelia then goes on to report, unimpressed and with little emotion, that they were also preparing a scene where you would only hear a car running over a pedestrian, also intended as a "future vision" of the video game if you were a player without empathy. There they planned a "black-screen". So you would see nothing, only hear.

Now, spontaneously, I finally find words for the overflowing emotions and say that this is even more terrible than the sequence described before. One's own imagination would provide plenty of images for such an acoustic scene. And such fearful fantasies would not let you go!

The other participants come back into the conversation and discuss what is more terrible: a visual game or an acoustic one with a "black screen". Now everyone participates. The *"free-flowing group discussion"* (according to Foulkes) is restored; the language inhibition is lifted. Once again it becomes clear to us group leaders what kind of quality of images can be seen in the usual video games nowadays, and we express it. Scary!

A spontaneous question from Amelia to Vanessa about her relationship entanglements shifts the focus away from Amelia to Vanessa. Vanessa can and will now talk in detail about how much she has become entangled in a destructive oedipal triangular relationship, how much she suffers, and how impossible it is for her to find a way out of these dependencies. At the end of her report, she describes a whole bouquet of psychosomatic complaints that have been plaguing her in the last few days: heart palpitations, shortness of breath, dizziness, and nausea, and this was also noticeable here in the group session. Vanessa opens up and shares herself very authentically for the first time in the group.

Now the group can sympathize; there are audible groans, shaking of heads, and emotional comments like the one from Hannah: "I would have left long ago", or from Amelia: "nobody keeps any boundaries". Hannah takes an emotional interest in Vanessa's report. But Hannah has reported very little about herself today, although she is the most unstable of all at the moment.

After the group session Christina (joint leader) and I tried to reflect together. Very quickly it became clear that we were in very different emotional states: Christina was seemingly light-hearted, felt rather emotionally distant, was rationally creeped out by the idea of the video games and the images delivered there, but otherwise she was fine.

My state was completely different: I felt emotionally confused, completely exhausted, had a huge appetite (for the "good object"?), and at the same time there was an undigested "ball" in my stomach, and I had to moan a lot. The fantasies and imaginings of Amelia's described scenes occupied me with an emotional weight of lead; I couldn't get rid of them at all. I was shaken and felt helpless.

The first thing we could observe was that a regressive pull with a massive splitting process had obviously manifested itself in the group session and was now showing itself in the very different emotional perceptions and states of the group leaders.

What had happened?

6 Discussion on the group process

6.1 Regression and the basic assumption of dependence

I understand the difficult beginning of the group as a scenic expression of the quickly manifesting resistance to the unconscious group theme. Two participants arrive late; the group remains in silent resistance. A rejection reaction arises in me, which I do not express. Already here I lacked the therapeutic distance, the words, and the free-floating space of thought. Otherwise, I could have formulated a helping intervention, such as: "How difficult it is for us today to talk to each other, to say something about ourselves! And perhaps that is our group topic today, because it seems to be the same for all group members." Christina remains stuck in the emotional group defense; she is identified with the "silent mother" and is thus in the defense mechanism of undoing or denial. We all seem to be immediately caught speechless in diffuse fears, the whole group descends into a regressive state and thus into a non-verbal "projection level" (five levels of group communication, according to Foulkes, 2017, p. 33). On this "projection level", the group members experience *"one's own repulsed desires and drives in others, parts of oneself that are still too unbearable to admit to oneself at first"* (Foulkes, 2017, p. 106).

Mirroring processes can intermediate and allow us to perceive this initially unbearable parts of ourselves in other group members *"in order then slowly to be able to integrate it in oneself"* (Foulkes, 2017, p. 106 ff.). Nebbiosi reflected on Foulkes' idea of a group matrix and the organizing patterns of a group as follows:

> "In general, a group with good cohesion can regulate the affective level of its interactions. If one or more group members brings a particularly intense affective state (e.g., depression, agitation), it can be shared by the group and then scaled back to a tolerable level" (Nebbiosi, 2003, p. 766 f.).

If the group is unable to do this because the traumatic emotional background is too strong, what then sets in is what Nebbiosi calls *"emotional conformism"*:

> "Expressions are now only expressible in a conformist mood that avoids affect and to which the group has unconsciously agreed, so that change no longer takes place" (Nebbiosi, 2003, p. 766 f.).

Bion's theory of *"basic assumptions"* (Bion, 1971, p. 107ff) as basic, unconscious organizational patterns in groups used to ward off archaic fears, along with the

resulting blocking of the members' ability to work as a group, can also help us understanding the processes here. According to Bion, one basic assumption of the three he identifies tends to determine the group mind-set, while the other two fade into the background. These three basic assumptions are:
1. the basic assumption of dependency,
2. the basic assumption of fight and flight,
3. the basic assumption of pair formation.

What is perhaps characteristic of the group situation described above is the *"basic assumption of dependency"*. Sandner writes in this regard that:

> "In the basic assumption of dependency, the whole group behaves like an immature, helpless child who is totally dependent on the care of an adult. The group leader is seen as all-powerful, as someone who will solve everything in the best possible way. Own activity is neither necessary nor promising, nor is communication among the group members. The group leader knows what is good for everyone and will get everyone what they need" (Sandner, 2013, p. 80 f.).

The peculiarity of the participants' interactions is as follows:

> "The group is hardly able to use verbal communication, language as a means of trial action and reality testing. Rather, language is used concretely as a means of unconscious action in the service of basic assumption." ... Summarizing, we can say: In the basic assumption group, all processes take place largely along the unconscious primary-process fantasies of early childhood. There is no reality check in the group; rather, all the desires of the group participants gather – figuratively speaking – in a kind of group ego (group mentality) that would prefer to do nothing at all, have everything, and not be frightened in any way by the superego" (Sandner, 2013, p. 81 f.).

For his part, Lehle elaborates on this:

> "A magical expectation prevails that feelings of insecurity or threat in the individual can be eliminated. There is a symbiotic 'cuddling tendency' in which any unpleasantness is excluded. There is also a pronounced tendency to 'work alone' with the group leader. ... The prevailing group mood is lethargy, depressiveness, and lack of clarity. There is a high level of anxiety, latent readiness to flee, and an inability to solve problems – this is delegated to the group leader" (Lehle, 2018, p. 129).

In other words, within a very few minutes, the group had unconsciously entered a regressive-resistant state in which *"emotional conformism"* and the *"basic assumption of dependency"* predominated. The ability to work (according to Bion, 1969: *"working group"*) was no longer given.

6.2   Splitting processes and the suppressed group theme coming into play

The game designed by Amelia works with sadistic feelings of guilt on the part of the player if he or she does not behave or play in a morally or politically correct way. In the true sense of the word, it is no longer a game, since a "real game" is characterized by an open outcome, whereby the player's action would not lead to a sadistic punishment or moral condemnation at the end but would keep various options open. Amelia's game, however, works with clear divisions into "good or evil", and there is only one morally "right" game solution to succeed.

The unconscious group theme, which is obviously associated emotionally with massive resistance and archaic fears and therefore cannot be negotiated directly, has risen to the surface in indirect form with the help of Amelia's emotionally distanced report about her drawing (sublimated expression of the unconscious group theme): *"A suicide fantasy, which appears as the only way out at the end of destructive relationship experiences"*.

In this emotionally distanced form, the other group members can participate once more and show lively interest, the group can find its way out of its speechlessness. It seems as if the "tabooed topic" gets placed out in the open. Amelia acts here – as so often in earlier sessions – as a mouthpiece for the group.

In relation to Amelia, I understand this meticulous description of a suicide as an attempt to reconstruct her traumatically experienced emotions in a sublimated manner (they were not sufficiently well contained at the time) and gain access to the emotions she had split off, such as her structure-threatening fears of losing objects. The feelings that were flooding in at that time (according to Bion, split-off *"beta elements"*, see *"container-contained model"*) now flow into the group (see Mario Erdmann's concept of anachronicity in adolescence). Here in the group (as in the family back then) there likewise initially seems to be no successful resonance for this among the other group members, and the experience of dysfunctional communication (*"emotional conformism"*) is repeated. It is a re-enactment in the group. Only with me (as the responsible therapist) have the split-off or rejected *"beta elements"* landed and been deposited as if in a *"container"*. Presumably there are not only Amelia's aversions, but also those of the other two group members, who are themselves dealing with suicidal impulses. The group leaders may also be dealing with their own rejected self-parts. All these undigested *"beta elements"* are floating around in the group.

6.3 Projective identification, the phenomenon of resonance, and the function of containment in the group process

At this point in the group process I am confused, speechless, emotionally shaken, and do not know how to deal with it, how to bring these hard-to-bear affects (*"beta elements"*) that have landed with me back into the group in a pre-digested, metabolized form, (*"alpha function"*, according to Bion). I am currently (like all the other group members) on a regressive, speechless communication level (*"projection level"*). I can find no access to an emotional therapeutic distance that could enable me to have a free flow of thoughts again. I experience myself as absorbed by the group regression and preoccupied with incompetent, powerless, and helpless feelings of countertransference.

The whole group is weighed down by the theme of destructive relationships or the insufficiently good *"containment"* of unbearable affects from the pre-linguistic early childhood period.

The *"phenomenon of resonance"* (Foulkes) and the concept of *"projective identification"*, according to Melanie Klein or in the extension by Bion and later especially by Fonagy (Fonagy, Gergely, Jurist, and Target, 2004), can help us to understand what was happening in the group and with me as one of the two group leaders:

> "'Projective identification' is the name Melanie Klein gives to a defense mechanism of the paranoid-schizoid position that is closely related to the concept of 'splitting' and involves the tendency of the early childhood ego to protect itself from unpleasant feelings and fears by splitting off unwanted, threatening, or destructive elements and projecting them into the maternal object. According to Lazar, projective identification serves not only to 'promote disturbing things out of oneself' but also to protect good and valuable parts of the self from 'inner damage or even destruction' (Lazar, 2004, p. 42)" (Lehle, 2018, p. 101).

Mathias Hirsch writes on the *"resonance phenomenon as a container function"*:

> "The members of the group will be able to produce adequate expressions of affect much more directly than an individual therapist, when the patient in question has by no means yet had access to his or her split-off affects. This

is where the long-known resonance phenomenon in the group can be classified. Often, terrible traumatic experiences are reported, but without any affective agitation. Then a first step in the integration of the traumatic affects will be their experience by another group member who experiences the horror, the anger, and also the shame and the pain instead of the reporting patient and expresses them affectively. ... If violent affects caused by projective identification occur in a group member, they can often be attributed to the 'transmitter' much more convincingly than in individual therapy. The resonance phenomenon can be explained by projective-identification induction" (Hirsch, 2008, p. 74 ff.).

Lazar emphasizes the importance of both components of this psychological defense mechanism:

"There is the projective and the identificatory part. The latter 'sends' signals, as it were, via the various sensory channels ..., which are 'received' and processed by the psychic apparatus of another person. The prerequisite for this is the willingness and ability of the 'receiver' to receive these signals: 'Only when he identifies with the projected content does the desired effect occur in the object.'" This is what constitutes "successful" projective identification according to Lazar (Lazar, 2004, p. 43).

Behr and Hearst write about this:

"One function of the leader at this stage and more or less throughout the existence of the group is to accept the projections and projective identifications and keep them to himself in order to give them back to the group in a modified form at the right time. This refers to group projections as well as individual ones. The return of these projections is then used to expand and deepen the transpersonal and interpersonal communications within the group ..." (Behr and Hearst, 2009, p. 116).

At this point, it was not yet possible for me to verbalize or metabolize the split-off affects and return them to the group. The projective identification had fully occupied me.

6.4 Return to the working group

It was only through my spontaneous, emotionally vehement statements on the idea of a "black screen" and acoustically learning of self-destructivity that language connected with the associated affects came back into the group. The *"free-flowing group discussion"* that then began enabled a return to the group's ability to work. Vanessa's situation was narrated, illuminated, commented on, and discussed empathically. The painful realities of a love triangle and the shame of failure could be named, and the other two group members could take their individual position on it. For Vanessa, these were valuable reflections. Then the group could say goodbye in a balanced mood and with a functioning reality check.

Sandner writes on the working group:

> "Bion understands a 'working group' to be a differentiated group in which attempts are made to achieve the group goal set in each case through continuous clarification of reality within and outside the group. ... In order to progress from the initially spontaneously forming basic assumption group to a differentiated group, it is necessary that the members of the group become active and enter into a mutual clarification process. ... What Bion calls a basic assumption group or working group is of course never present in pure form. There are always mixtures of both – ideally simplified – group forms. Nevertheless, there is a constant struggle within the group to remain in an infantile (regressive) stage on the one hand, and to develop a differentiated structure on the other; that means to examine what is really going on in the group" (Sandner, 2013, p. 81 ff.).

7 Final consideration

I chose this group session as an example because it gave me food for thought for a long time. My entanglements in transference and projective identification and in the negative pull of regression were more immediate and violent than I had ever experienced before as a group leader. The way out of these entanglements was to express my unfiltered emotions of fear and terror, something that opened the door for the patients to also find their way out of their defensiveness. In the following group sessions, I was able to gradually return the defended affects to the group in a metabolized form, where they could then also be taken up and worked through. This experience made it clear to me once again how much we as group leaders are part of the group dynamics.

At a glance:

1. The methodological considerations described in this article, which relate to the context of group-analytical psychotherapy with adolescents/late adolescents, lead to the idea of a consciously chosen "pair leadership": The possible projective transfer of parents to the two group leaders strengthens the patients' inner-psychological confrontation with the idealized parent image and their de-idealization. In this family-like setting, age-appropriate challenges of detachment from the primary family and thus the first autonomous steps into adult life can be tried out and worked through.

2. Group-analytical therapy groups with a focus on female adolescents create the prerequisites for participants to enter into an intimate and familiar exchange with each other more quickly. The challenges of a successful female identification and the mental cliffs in the task of accepting the now sexually unambiguous body are often difficult to master. The search for a positive female role model brings with it fears and conflicts. In the girls' groups, reports of neurotic symptom formation and compromises take up a lot of space. This can create a climate of connection, relief, and protected space within the group, in which shame-ridden topics can also be tackled. Participants are thus encouraged to authentically open up.

3. Group analysis in this context facilitates an experience of catching up with a reliable peer group for the patients who have not been able to make this important identification with peers sufficiently well in their biography so far. Within the peer group, a gradual detachment from the primary objects can be attempted with simultaneous stabilization of the identity and the experience of self-efficacy among peers (group cohesion, sibling transmissions). Group analysis enables a bridging function for the success of the detachment process.

Bibliography

Behr, H., Hearst, L. (2009). *Gruppenanalytische Psychotherapie. Menschen begegnen sich.* Frankfurt/M.: Klotz

Bion, W. R. (1969). *Experiences in Groups and Other Papers.* London: Routledge

Fonagy, P., Gergely, G., Jurist, E. L., Target, M. (2004). *Affektregulierung, Mentalisierung und die Entwicklung des Selbst.* Stuttgart: Klett-Cotta

Foulkes, S. H. (1964). *Group Analytic Psychotherapy: Method and Principles.* London: Routledge

Foulkes, S. H. (2017). *Praxis der gruppenanalytischen Psychotherapie.* Hohenwarsleben: Westarp Verlagsservicegesellschaft mbH

Hirsch, M. (Hrsg.) (2008). *Die Gruppe als Container. Mentalisierung und Symbolisierung in der analytischen Gruppenpsychotherapie*. Göttingen: Vandenhoeck & Ruprecht

Lazar, R. A. (2004). Psychoanalyse, "Group-Relations" und Organisation. Konfliktberatung nach dem Tavistock-Arbeitskonferenz-Modell. In M. Lohmer (Hrsg.), *Psychodynamische Organisationsberatung. Konflikte und Potentiale in Veränderungsprozessen* (2., verb. und um ein Nachw. erw. Aufl.; S. 40–78). Stuttgart: Klett-Cotta

Lehle, H. G. (2018). *Freiräume des Spiels. Psychoanalytische Gruppentherapie mit Kindern und Jugendlichen*. Frankfurt/M.: Brandes & Apsel

Nebbiosi, G. (2003). Organizing patterns in a dyad and in a group. Theoretical and clinical implications. *Psychoanalytic Inquiry*, 23: 750–770

Salge, H. (2013). *Analytische Psychotherapie zwischen 18 und 25. Besonderheiten in der Behandlung von Spätadoleszenten*. Berlin and Heidelberg: Springer Medizin

Sandner, D. (2013). *Die Gruppe und das Unbewusste*. Berlin and Heidelberg: Springer VS

Winnicott, D. W. (1984). *The Maturational Processes and the Facilitating Environment*. London: Routledge

Winnicott, D. W. (1989). *Playing and Reality*. London: Routledge

Yalom, D. J. (1970/2007). *Theorie und Praxis der Gruppenpsychotherapie*. Stuttgart: Klett-Cotta

The Dynamic Links between Groups of Children and those of Primary Carers

Drudgery and Duty or Findings and Freedom?! Reflections and Experiences from a Parents' Group Accompanying Analytical Children's Group Therapy[1]

Matthias Wenck

I felt disappointed, sad, and dejected, with undertones of annoyance and anger. Lea's mother had just made it clear once again in the parents' group that her daughter would be leaving the children's group at the beginning of the Easter vacation. My colleague and I, who run the children's and parents' groups together, had been aware for some time of how difficult it was for Lea's mother in particular to get involved in the group activities. Yet we had just regained some confidence. In one of the previous sessions, Lea's mother had been given a lot of sympathy and understanding by the other members of the parents' group. The fears, anxieties, and intense struggles of a mother with a "damaged" child had become palpable and evident. Lea's mother had told us about her journey so far as parent to a daughter born with a cleft lip and palate, also known as cheilognathouranoschisis. About the shock following the birth, the difficulties feeding the baby, about the hopes before the surgical interventions and the disappointments that followed them. The last operation in particular was supposed to produce a result that would make Lea look like an undamaged child, but it was not successful. From our point of view, Lea had settled in well in the children's group. She had given up the habit, for example, of hiding her mouth behind her right hand. And now she was to be removed from the group and, as we saw it, terminate her therapy! What did this all mean? We'll get to this later.

First, I would like to quote from the "Kommentar Psychotherapie-Richtlinien", the commentary to the German Psychotherapy Guidelines: "[T]he involvement of the attachment figures who have a certain influence on the child's neurotic disorder is an indispensable component of [...] child psychotherapy," "[...] the objective [...] is not, for example, the independent [...] psychotherapy of a parent, or couples' or family therapy, but intensive support from the attachment figures [...]," and "the aim should be to change the intrafamilial constellations in the family of the treated child, [...] furthermore, to raise awareness of role assignments and the repetition of one's own disturbed

---

1 This article is based on a presentation at the symposium of the Munich Association of Psychoanalysis (*Münchner Arbeitsgemeinschaft für Psychoanalyse e. V.*) on February 23, 2019.

behavior patterns that have their origin in one's own family" (Dieckmann, Dahm, and Neher, 2018, p. 72).

The task of therapy is "the clarification of typical coalitions of family members among and against each other which determine the intrafamily dynamics as well as the elaboration of less stressful patterns of upbringing through understanding and insight." And a final objective is: "In critical threshold situations, mobilizing one's own childhood memories as well as one's own successful and failed attempts at resolution is just as much a part of elucidating behavioral patterns of an intrafamilial nature that have thus far remained unclear as is the revival of the confrontation with parental imaginings" (Dieckmann, Dahm, and Neher, 2018, p. 72).

If, as claimed by S. H. Foulkes (1978), the founder of group analysis, the human being is born from the very beginning into a network of communication processes that inevitably and profoundly influences them, then the above-quoted remarks from the commentary read like a plea for parent or caregiver groups. What I personally always find inspiring about groups, especially children's groups, is that I can feel the liberation and developmental support provided by a space with a clear framework, in which everyone can be the way they are right now, the way they feel right now, and which creates the possibility of showing this, of communicating it, and thus also sharing it. This is very reminiscent of the peer groups that are so important for children and young people in their development.

In a therapy group, the central element (the medium that makes knowledge and change possible) is the group, not the counterpart, who is the group leader or the therapist, as in individual therapy. In the latter, in my view, there is always a much more pronounced hierarchy: here the "ignorant" sick person and there the "knowing", healthy therapist. In the group, at least according to Foulkes' concept, the therapist or leader recedes much more into the background. The interaction and communication between the participants acting as group members "on an even footing" is the impetus for insight and change.

The group should provide the protected space in which parents can talk about themselves and their difficulties and about what is going on for them on the inside. Facilitating and securing this space is the task of the group leader. In addition to establishing the time and place and ensuring there is enough seating, the leader must ensure above all that time is kept to. They make sure that if communication stalls, "the train starts rolling again". This is a reminder that Foulkes talks not about a group leader, but rather a conductor, i.e., a guide, a supervisor on a train, or even the servant of the group (Foulkes, 1978). The attention of this conductor is also directed at whether there are any tendencies towards exclusion in the group, and they try to make these known and thus changeable through appropriate interventions. The parents have the possibility, or at least an option, to exchange their experiences in a group of people with children who are also special, who are difficult or worrying, and to see that there are people who are in a similar situation. They can discover that they are not so exceptional and that their situation is not quite as particular as they perhaps always thought so far.

The effect created by the group is known as universality. The particular consternation and suffering of a situation, which until now has always been regarded as serious and perhaps also irresolvable, is not so special after all. However, this experience can also be very disturbing. So disturbing and so destructive of one's own self-image that, as in the case of Lea's mother, for example, the therapy is terminated. My colleague and I suspected that Lea's mother found the experience of acceptance and compassion for the difficulties involved in having to change her own self-image as so distressing that she had to end the process. On the other hand, in Lea's case, over the last few weeks of her belonging to the group we had clearly perceived that her self-esteem had improved tremendously. She also seemed to be kinder and more caring towards herself. On previous occasions in the parents' group, her mother had complained that Lea was almost always in a bad mood, that she often crossed the street carelessly and thus put herself in danger. In this parents' group session, both parents had been able to pick up on the group leader's thoughts that a person who does not like themselves could be careless with their own self and in doing so could even put their own life at risk. In this parents' group it had become clear that the most important overriding goal of Lea's therapy was to overcome her latent suicidal tendencies. As far as we group leaders were able to perceive, this seemed to have succeeded. Could it be that no longer having to worry in such a way about her daughter had caused difficulties for the mother herself, in the sense of a crisis of meaning or even identity? And if so, how could we have countered this in order to avert the premature termination of the therapy? We had to "content ourselves" with the "progress" in Lea's development, which was indeed not insignificant. We hold onto the not unjustified hope that this experience will be an impetus for Lea to handle herself and her life differently in the future.

Despite this experience and the fact that we perhaps were not able to "hold" Lea's parents adequately, we have found and continue to find that in the overwhelming majority of cases the experience of universality brings relief and prompts change. Analytical group therapy is, or so studies to date show, the psychotherapy method with the greatest effectiveness (according to a PowerPoint slide, compiled by Ulrich Schultz-Venrath for a seminar at GRAS e.V. on

September 29, 2007). The positive experience of universality is bolstered by the experience of cohesion in the group. Yet it is questionable how a feeling of cohesion can develop in a group that takes place every four weeks and whose composition continues to change. I would like to counter this by saying that I myself am always amazed at how I have developed and felt an intense sense of cohesion for and within the group in two large groups that each take place only once a year at a workshop for children's group analysis. While it is true that I am in a different position as a participant in these groups than are the parents, it makes it clear to me that it's not just the rhythm of time and repetition that is key to developing a sense of cohesion. And my experiences in the parents' group reveal this as well. Here is one small example:

In a group session, my colleague noticed a beaming smile on a mother's face and addressed her, asking if the smile was a reaction to what she, the group leader, had just said. "No," the mother replied, "I wasn't listening to you at all, I was just enjoying watching my husband so much." The couple had lost sight of each other in their concern for their baby girl, who was born with a heart defect, and with the help of their daughter's experience in the children's group and their own in the parents' group, they were able to let go of the worry and reconnect with each other.

I wrote about my feeling of cohesion in the workshop group and about the fact that there can be doubts about whether such a feeling can develop in the parent/caregiver group. I believe the potential difficulties need special scrutiny from the group leader. It is one of their tasks to pay attention to whether a sense of protected space and a feeling of group cohesion can develop in the group, and to ensure that it does. They can do this, for example, by repeatedly pointing out the special nature of the structure of this group. In this way, the difficulties in dealing with the group and its special rhythm get their appropriate and allowed place in the experience of the group members and do not have to be denied and repressed. And with the end of denial and repression, there is space for other experiences.

For the experience of universality and its effect on the inner image of each individual group member, of course, it is imperative that the group leaders also pay attention. Yet the effect cannot be accurately estimated and predicted in advance. It can be a great relief to realize: I am not alone; I am average, like others. Yet if my self-image is fed exclusively by the uniqueness of my suffering or my "badness and imperfection", then the experience of the universality of my thoughts, feelings, and the conclusions that arise from them is a severe, sometimes unbearable rupture in my self-image which then leads to therapy being discontinued (as with Lea's mother). The difficulty of changing a firmly established self-image, even only in small parts, is of course also something known from individual therapies. In the group, I always find it to be more painful, because it is not just me who is affected but a group of people.

What does the "Commentary on the German Psychotherapy Guidelines" have to say? "The goal should be to change the intrafamily constellation in the family of the treated child," (Dieckmann, Dahm, and Neher, 2018, p. 72). It fits with this that a group can be experienced like a model of family. Within the group, behavior, communication, and interaction with other people becomes directly visible and tangible. This is different from the individual therapy situation, where the experience is limited to two people. It is therefore necessary that in the therapist themselves, an inner space of experience and fantasy opens up that allows imaginations of intrafamily interaction in the most diverse ways. These can then flow back into the process between therapist and patient, where they can be made useful for change. Because this process takes place in the therapist, it is, in my view, much easier to imagine oneself having understood something – or, more clearly, having something in hand, being able to control something. From my point of view, this is a temptation that always comes quickly and is worthy of attention. In the group, in the interactions and in the communication of the group members, the other things also going on in life happen in a directly visible and tangible way. The group is therefore much closer to everyday life and makes it clearly visible. Since, however, the group with its members also offers a wide variety of transference possibilities, there is much more at work in the background and in the unconscious, which can probably only ever be grasped and understood in small parts, and never in its entirety. The group leader is thus called upon or even compelled to rely much more on the group, on what happens in it – or in other words, they have much less in hand and are much less of a central figure. They are mainly observing, occasionally giving comments or interpretations, or putting into words what they perceive. The change in therapy happens through the interaction and communication of the group participants. There is the couple, for example, who used to come to the group together. The mother always expressed suffering in what she said and was, one might say, depressive in her mood. The father, meanwhile, was calm and friendly, preferring to hide behind questions, but also depressed. The distance between the two became palpable, the tortured communication maintained only with difficulty. And then they appeared together only rarely, and after several months the man in the group was able to talk about the fact that they had separated. He continued to be a calm, friendly, and more questioning presence in the group, but seemed more relaxed and reported on his own dealings with their four daughters. The other parents reacted neither with pity nor critically to his revelation of the separation, but let it stand as an occurrence that can happen and is also part of everyday life. The condemnation that was possibly feared and was perhaps behind the long delay in communicating the serious change in the family's circumstances was nowhere to be seen. Even if all this was not explicitly expressed, it can be assumed that it had an effect.

Or the mother who always comes alone, because her husband is a busy manager who travels a lot and probably doesn't want to face the process in the group or rejects the necessary therapy for her son as a flaw. Her intense striving to be a good mother to her two sons, always trying to be available and make life beautiful for the children, becomes palpable. And it also becomes clear that this intense striving has to do with the fact that she requires a screen behind which to hide her suffering in her relationship with her difficult, sometimes very categorical and ego-centered husband. On the other hand, the status secured by her husband with his successful career is something that pleases her, and sometimes she seems a bit conceited. This is probably the origin of a sometimes somewhat tortured facial expression when there is input from the mother of a boy in the children's group whose circumstances are simple and poorer both educationally and economically. Yet recently, this facial expression has changed. Sometimes there is even evident recognition. This success is the outcome of the group work, which makes the perception of other people's otherness both necessary and possible. The experience of this otherness stimulates questioning one's own often firmly established ideas of what is right and to come to different and new conclusions. So the group is very similar to a family. There too, it is necessary to put up with people who have different ideas about life and how to deal with it. The only thing is that we as parents can very easily cling to the conviction that we know what's right and that we have to pass this conviction on to our children. Yet if we are to believe the words of the Persian poet Rumi, who lived from 1207 to 1273: "Out beyond ideas of wrongdoing and rightdoing, there is a field. I'll meet you there," then perhaps dealing with children is more about providing them with a clearly defined space within which they can move freely and gain their experiences and discoveries about how life works.

This brings us back to the space that the group offers and constitutes. If the aim of participants in a parenting group is discovering role attributions and repetitions of their own disturbed behavior patterns, the cause of which lies in their own parental families, then it is necessary for the group to provide space for thoughts, feelings, and memories, as well as the expression of such, and thus their communication in a way that is as uncensored as possible. This is a tall order and requires time for the experience from which trust can develop. After all, when new parents join the group, fear is the predominant feeling. The fear of being judged – above all devalued – and condemned for mistakes made in dealing with their own children, which have now led to the children being psychologically disturbed and in need of treatment. We find parents in the group to be very reserved at first, anxiously orienting themselves and recounting the efforts that have already been made. In their experience of the others, who open up about shameful things and things that were previously considered ineffable, the messages then begin to change. Of course, this developing openness requires the support of the group leader. Their interventions and comments are sensibly directed to the fact that it is okay if showing oneself is difficult and that time is needed to overcome it. And it is certainly helpful if the hidden or reciprocal themes and feelings are also addressed again and again. For example, that the flip side of love is hate and that this flip side needs its place to be communicated in a socially acceptable way. This was the case with Lasse's mother, who kept constricting her son with great concern for his progress in school. In one session, she began to complain at length and vehemently about her unsatisfactory relationship with her husband. She talked about her thoughts of separation, about her anger and resentment, about how little she felt supported and thus then rejected. She spoke of how similar she found the father and son to be and how abandoned she felt. The group listened sympathetically and gave space to the complaints, neither passing judgment nor evaluating.

It was like a dam bursting, but it did not lead to her feeling like she had to contain herself. Ultimately, the mother herself was able to see how much she had attributed to the father and son by way of fixed role conceptions. She could see how her own wishes and ideas had influenced and distorted her view of her partner and son, and she was thus able to discover the other side of both of them, what was good about them, and let Lasse go his way and become successful.

Foulkes writes: "The deepest reason why [...] patients [...] can reinforce each other's normal reactions and wear down and correct each other's neurotic reactions is that collectively they constitute the very norm from which, individually, they deviate. [...] Each individual is to a large extent a part of the group to which he belongs," (Foulkes, 1978, p. 29). If everyone is part of the norm, then any departure from this pre-given norm is an impetus to change the norm, to create a new norm. Every member of a group is, in their way of being, in their differentness, an enrichment to otherness despite or indeed because they are a threat, an impetus for change. This otherness harbors the discovery that a different way of dealing with life, with its demands, does not naturally lead into the abyss, but represents a possibility. A possibility that has consequences, but what possibility does not have consequences? And if the otherness can be seen as a possibility, then there are already two possibilities, a more, a gain. Sure, this comes with the freedom to be able to – or indeed have to – decide. That means, of course, that I can also find such freedom to be tortuous. But the group opens a space for model learning, for practicing self-efficacy. Participants can use the other group members to try out new things. There is feedback on expressed thoughts and reflections. Of course, even here in the less frequent parents' groups, there is a need for the group leaders to constantly encourage and open up the space. However, since attitudes and previously experienced spaces are also reflected in the unconscious, in the matrix of the group, and thus have an effect, with long-lasting groups this support work will no longer have to be as intensive as it was in the beginning.

Another example: Daniel's mother, a tall pretty woman, often seemed very tense and recounted almost without exception in the parents' group her worries about the academic progress of her son, who was 13 years old when he joined the group. She herself had graduated from high school and had a good job. Daniel is the product of a relationship with a Polish farm worker who, after the couple's separation, works on a farm near where Daniel and his mother live.

Daniel was a tall boy who seemed rather quiet, calm; one could also say sometimes sluggish in the group. He did not defend himself much against attacks, trying instead to evade or appease when there were quarrels. He liked spending time with his father. Fascinated by the large farm machinery, he had discovered his passion for the youth wing of the Federal Agency for Technical Relief and spent a lot of time there. He had already failed to reach the class target at secondary school once, and now in his repeat year it was close again. His mother tried repeatedly to push him and encourage him and was constantly worrying about him. In the group she found a lot of understanding for her concern and for the effort involved in enduring the anxiety caused by the path her child had chosen. However, the parents also talked about how the situation at home had eased once they had begun to stop controlling their children, to give them responsibility for their progress in school. This process of the mother complaining and the others sharing their experiences took a long while. At times, it seemed to have little effect on her, and at others she seemed moved by it. Daniel achieved the class target. However, he continued on what his mother saw as a difficult path at school. Yet in the second year of therapy, she also talked about her son's commitment and reliability in taking care of the technical equipment for the choir in which she sings. And in the last parents' group when Daniel's therapy ended, she reported that she was able to let him go, she could trust him to follow his own path. She could see his reliable and committed side and allow him to shape his own life.

I have tried to show you the impacting factors and how they take effect, their reality in a group. These are cohesion, universality, protected space, expression of thoughts and feelings, image of family, feedback, social learning, model learning, self-efficacy, and autonomy. However, the group is not just a place for the impacting factors to take effect, and it is more than the sum of its participants. A group, and not only a therapeutic group, is a living organism that is constantly changing. You can feel that. Many of you will be familiar with it, a spontaneous feeling of either being secure or also being questioned in a group, and how these feelings are always changing.

Exposing oneself to a therapeutic process (individually as well as in a group) always means having or developing the willingness to question oneself. Every person has communication, problem-solving, and relationship patterns within themselves that have evolved over the years. Changing something about this is, in a certain sense, also a "process of destruction". In other words it is something that is misaligned, that must be destroyed, but destroyed in a positive sense! This process becomes a constructive one when it is possible to let the group – here the parents' group – become a place where life-limiting self-judgments can change. Parents with the firm and agonizing notion of having failed in their task of bringing up a child and who therefore feel shame (and you know that many parents feel this way!) can feel safe in a group where there is space to form a "working group" with people in a similar life situation, with similar difficulties, in order to discover and develop new ways out of the dilemma.

The task of the group leader, who knows about the potency of the group, is to let this "potency" become effective, to let confidence arise from despair and self-accusation. If this succeeds – and in my experience it succeeds more often than it fails – it is a sometimes exhausting but also gratifying process for all involved. With this in mind, I ought to change the title of my article so that it is not "either or", but rather "both and": both drudgery and duty, but also findings and freedom.

> **At a glance:**
> The parents' group allows parents:
> - to discover role attributions and the repetition of one's own dysfunctional behavior patterns, the causes of which lie in one's own parental families.
> - to take the otherness of the other group members as a prompt to question one's own firmly established ideas.
> - a space for thoughts, feelings, and memories and their expression in a way that is as uncensored as possible.
> - a space for model-learning, a practice of self-efficacy. Participants can use the other group members to try out new things.

- realization and the positive experience of universality. One's own suffering and personal challenges are put into perspective and classified.
- cohesion.
- to change their perspective and experiences with their own children.

Bibliography

Dieckmann, M., Dahm, A., Neher, M. (2018). *Kommentar Psychotherapie-Richtlinien* (11th, updated and supplemented ed). München: Elsevier

Foulkes, S. H. (1978). *Praxis der gruppenanalytischen Psychotherapie.* München/Basel: Ernst Reinhardt

Children's Group for Primary School Children – Group Analysis in a Family and Educational Counseling Center under the Aegis of Diakonisches Werk

Horst Wenzel

The group work presented here is as a service embedded in an institutional context under public law that states: "Every young person has the right to support for their own development and to an education that helps them to become an independent and socially responsible person" (Arbeitsgemeinschaft für Jugendhilfe, 2014, p. 17). This legal right to support lays the foundations on which parents and their children can resort to group therapy as a form of institutional educational and family counselling free of charge and without filing an application. In the educational and family counselling arm of Diakonisches Werk, I have for the last seven years also provided a mixed therapy play group for primary school children on this basis.

The counseling center is located in a listed building that was completely destroyed during World War II and then rebuilt initially with three floors. The fourth floor was added 30 years later by expanding the attic to create space for the educational counselling unit.

My announcement of the children's groupoffering is sent specifically to schools and is also distributed in the social network of the counseling center. In this announcement, I explain that this group is for children whose parents are looking for support for their children in addition to school and daycare centers. The group takes place once a week for 90 minutes. It is free of charge and is meant to roll over, whereby before every summer vacation period a concluding celebration is held together with the parents and other family members. No cost for parents. Participation requires that I get to know the family before the first group encounter and that the parents are willing to take part in the parent group, which meets once a month.

In a letter addressed to colleagues, I also explain: When putting the group together, I consciously forgo providing psychosocial diagnostics because the concept of the group is based on the idea that the children's difficulties are an expression of relationship experiences. As the group progresses, these difficulties are worked on indirectly in the activity that the children themselves decide to pursue. Of special significance here is the resulting and gradually unfolding group dynamic, playfully enacted as a group fantasy and based on the ideas the children have. On the basis of how the group stages games, the children's internalized relationship experiences that they have brought with them are then expressed. This group approach is based on a mixed concept, which consists of elements of the group work undertaken in Haus Schwalbach and on group analysis according to Foulkes and Bion. Since elementary-school children need sometimes to be able to rely on swift intervention by the group leader, the Haus Schwalbach group concept can be an important addition to Foulkes and Bion. The group leader is thus able to develop an approach that is appropriate to the children. The leader's thoughts and emotions move within Foulkes' matrix, anticipate particular scenes in which the children deal with intense feelings of fear by viewing these as attempts at defense and self-regulation and sets boundaries in an appreciative way as a means of helping the children to help themselves.

Understanding of the group concept can be fostered in the parents' group meetings. This way, the parents are more easily able to ensure the children's ongoing participation. If a child is missing in the group, this is regarded as unconsciously staged by the family and as a trigger of transference in the children's group. When a child is absent, this can imply to the other children that there is no supportive framework in the group, which the group needs for the process to be beneficial. In other words, the group leader's activity focuses on both the children and the parents. These linkages are according to Foulkes, aspects of the dynamic group matrix (meaning aspects of the unconscious network of communications and relationships in the group) will be described in greater detail below using case examples and commentaries. The scenes I describe are shortened and do not reflect the entire course of a group session. I mention only those children and parents and such aspects that are necessary for understanding the sense of an unconsciously staged scene.

First, I will describe aspects which are helpful for creating the secure framework for the group. It is self-evident, the aids that I describe in the following (namely the "talking stick" and the "island") do not in themselves suffice, because it is also crucial that the group leader is alert in any session to monitor any transferences with reference to whether s/he should go into action in order to ensure the children feel safe.

1 The importance of the "islands" and the "talking stick" for the group and for the group leader

Each of the children's group meetings begins and ends in a circle, where all the members of the group, including the group leader, sit on green pillows which we call "islands". This allows everyone – including the group leader – to arrive emotionally in the group, to perceive each other, and to be perceived. A talking stick, which stems from a ritual among Sioux lies in the middle. Anyone who wants to say something with the group can pick up the talking stick.

The stick is intended to help the children find words to communicate, and it helps them to train their ability to step out of the group's emotional center and develop their own ability to mentalize (Rahm, 2004, p. 75). It also prevents all the group's energy, including that of the group leader, being used up too early (cf. Lutz, 1976). The regular use of the islands and the talking stick at the beginning and end of a meeting thus serves specifically to create a secure framework for the group. This framework makes it possible at the end of a session for the children and the group leader to reflect and mentalize what happened during it, jointly to seek words that help the children to convey their own thoughts and feelings to one another. From my point of view, there can be no underestimating the importance of this reflective circle because for the children it resembles a mirror that enders fears more visible and tangible as they come into contact with their internalized conflicts. The group becomes active thanks to the mild traumatization provoked by the minor initial structuring of the group by the leader (cf. Haar and Wenzel, 2019). The minor structuring by the leader causes the group to react with polarization cf. (Foulkes, 1974, p. 31), which in turn advances the group.

The children's group fantasies that gradually evolve can be seen as trials in presenting inner conflicts and creatively transforming them into a new, joint scene. Important here is that group leader waits and leaves the children the time for their own steps in personal development. This stance on the part of the leader can be challenging for him, as the children tend to touch the leader's unresolved blind spots that the leader should have already mentalized. Recurrent group scenes can be stem from the fact that the leader has not yet thus mentalized. It was Heidegger who described this aspect with his distinction between care "that steps in" and care that "strides ahead" (Rogers & Schmid, 1991, p. 51). The therapist is ideally someone who has strode is a step ahead, i.e., can stride ahead of the group. I shall give an example below of a group interaction where the leader steps in instead of being ahead.

Sometimes it is necessary during the sessions for the group to convene on the islands, for example when there has been a dangerous situation during a game that can only be reflected on together in a calm setting. This fosters the development of the inner space which the children need in order to tackle their own aggressivity. At the end of the group session, the children are sometimes very creative in using the islands: They stack them to high towers, take it in turns sitting on the top, ask for the talking stick, and describe their experience of the session that has just taken place. Looking down from above can help the children to gain more emotional distance from the stressful group process and then go home more relaxed. The talking stick, too, is sometimes used in a creative way: At times, children use it to emphasize their need to be treated with respect. Two examples illustrate this.

After a boy experienced the use of the talking stick in the group several times, he found a small wooden stick in a box and asked me: "What is this?" I told him it was a talking stick and he thereupon asked if he could take it home. Because of what I have heard in the parents' group, it was clear what his reasoning was: At home, in his family, there was confusion over the roles. The boy's sister had assumed responsibility for raising him by frequently putting him down with insults whenever he tried to say something. Here, in the group, the boy witnessed how the use of the talking stick could playfully causes the children to listen to each other and learn to thus treat each other respectfully.

With regard to the talking stick, in terms of instinctual drives it can be viewed as a phallic symbol. Sometimes the children use it that way, for example when a child wants to prevent the others from talking. The leader construed this scene as the child's unconscious staging of the wish to demonstrate power. This example scene is discussed below as a part of an unconscious group fantasy. Another group scene also suggests at first glance that a demonstration of power is involved. On closer inspection in light of the social life of the children at school, however, a different picture emerges.

Three boys in one of the groups have great difficulty in school in resolving social conflicts with other pupils on their own. At the time, when they talk about these conflicts in the group, many primary schools in the district are having problems with violence among the children. The boys also recount that they repeatedly seek support from their teachers, but instead are left alone with the problem. In class they have already become the scapegoats needed to take the burden off the difficult group dynamics. They are now actually afraid of going to school. Without the leader taking action in the group there is the risk of the boys getting all worked up in the issue. He therefore prompts the children to use their creativity and to continue searching for adults at school whom they can trust. The group leader also talks in the parent group about their children's situation at school and notices that the children's despair resembles that of their parents, since there seems to be no way out for either. By this point, the boys have passed by taking their places on the islands by way of the mutual welcome at the beginning of the group and instead, one of them grabs the talking stick and they take turns running in a circle over the islands. In the transference they are indicating to the leader: Running around with the talking stick is important, has the effect of mirroring the situation at school and helps them symbolically respond to the lack of respectful treatment there. Now, seated in the group, they narrate in greater detail the individual quarrels with other children and listen to one another attentively. This sequence is repeated several times over a few weeks. Finally, the boys say there is no longer any such violence at school or at least not such that they feel exposed to it, they seem more satisfied and open to school lessons. In the parents' group, the parents offer feedback, saying that their children are now more able to talk about their problems a little more swiftly and to ask for help.

From the perspective of the group leader, the above sheds a particular light on the archetypical meaning of the talking stick in the group. Foulkes describes four levels of communication in the group, and the archetypical level is the primordial level (Sandner, 2013, p. 39). All processes of transference and countertransference meet at the archetypical level. And the talking stick symbolizes this context in a special way, because it represents both respect for everybody and the big picture. The use of the talking stick is known, for example, to be used in Cherokee culture, the roots of which go back 8,000 years. All matters serving the welfare of the Cherokee can require the use of a talking stick, for example when far-reaching political issues have to be discussed, but also when imparting traditions to children. Anyone who holds the talking stick and who is talking to the others is, according to the ideas of the Cherokee, expected to talk about matters that come from their heart, truthfully. The wood of each person's own talking stick is meant to symbolize a quality that person feels best defines their character and how they see themself in the eyes of the Creator. Such qualities of character are, for example, a love of truth, a wish for peace, strength, wisdom, harmony, good relationships with others, great healing powers, caring for others, being a provider for others, a strong will, the ability to unite opposites, the sense for spiritual truths, and a sense of the Great Mother (cf. Over-Hill Indian Nations, no date).

2   Case example with group fantasies that build on one another

The islands and the talking stick help the group to deal with the minimal structuring of the sessions by the group leader, so initial fears of each beginning do not become too great: Everybody finds their place on an island and can see for themselves that it is possible at the beginning of the group to communicate if they so want.

Two girls and three boys aged eight to nine years, who come from divorced or separated families, meet for the first time in the group after an introductory meeting, each held respectively with the particular family. The group leader greets each child at the entrance to the group room. As he does so, he realizes that Julia (name changed) ignores the hand he proffers and avoids looking at him. Her facial expressions communicate to him the idea that he has no say, and that he is blocked by her. This moment is actually the beginning of the group fantasy (cf. Meyer, 2005). The countertransference of having nothing to say is something the group leader will relate to later scenes in the group.

All the group members, including the group leader, then sit on the comfortable islands he placed in a circle before the arrival of the children. These islands give them sufficient space. A talking stick lies on a big cloth in the middle of the group. The group leader is the first one to take the stick, and he greets the group. Julia takes it right after him and talks seemingly endlessly about herself, then about her path to the group, and in the end, she tries to define what kind of game the group should play first. No one takes up her suggestion. Somebody says, "I'm not saying anything here!" Another one talks with regret about his football game, that he had to interrupt to come to the group. Finally, Julia takes the talking stick again and tells the group once more about her school. The group leader has the impression that Julia is talking without emotional relation to either the school or the group. She again proposes what games could be played, but none of the children adopt her suggestions. After this welcoming round, the boys play at sword fighting with growing enthusiasm and without taking any notice of the Julia, having discovered a box of swords at the back of the group-room. The two girls sit on the floor to one side, looking bored. This sequence of scenes is repated several times at the subsequent group meetings. When Julia again tries to define what the group should play, the boys threaten her with exclusion. The group leader feels the group is stuck and unable to move forward by itself. However, he initially has no idea how the group can progress. He feels powerless and decides to use his experience of the group and what he knows about the families. He has the impression that within each family there is a dynamic of power and powerlessness, respectively in the behavior of each parent toward the other. This had come to light in the initial meetings with the families. He also discerns power and powerlessness within the group, in the behavior of the boys towards the girls and of one girl towards the others. The boys play without the girls and even go so far as to try and exclude Julia. There still are no words, the group leader thinks, that come to the children's minds and could help the group as a whole progress. He therefore says to the group, "Julia determines today, and the group surely has an idea about how to handle that." The scenes with the group being stuck at the beginning, and the feelings of powerlessness that apparently concern the group as a whole, are repeated in the next group sessions. Eventually one of the boys says to Julia, at a moment when she is once again trying to determine what the group should play without asking the others, "You always decide. Today I want to decide!"

The reason why, in the beginning, the children initially could find no words and could only exclude Julia, the determiner, is that every child is affected here by their own conflictual experiences. These evidently need to be parried as a whole by the group unconsciously using a psychosocial compromise: (cf. Heigl-Evers & Ott, 1995). Julia, who always tries to determine things and who brakes the process of the group, needs to be excluded. Not one of the other children is therefore to realize for themselves that similar exclusions happen often in their own family. This probably would have been too painful for them in this situation. The group leader has developed a picture of this on the basis of the discussions in the parent group. Using the figure-ground concept (cf. Haar & Wenzel, 2019, p. 83) he intervenes and relates the group's behavior to Julia's. The boy, who now finds words when Julia again tries to determine things and becomes active without trying to exclude her, is no longer stuck in his fixed role. And in the same way, the group as a whole is no longer blocked. At that moment when the boy's never-ending swordfights start to really bore the girls, Lara (name changed) asks to talk to the group leader. In this one-on-one, she talks about her fears which prevent her from addressing the boys directly. The group leader understands Lara's feedback from the context of the reason given for her joining the group, when he met her and her family for the first time in the introductory meeting. During it, Lara's mother had worried that her daughter would in future not be able to assert herself. She had also talked about similar difficulties during the parents' group meetings. It therefore seems to make sense to the group leader that Lara asked him for the one-on-one. Possibly when she had called on the group to develop ideas it also prompted her to go into action herself. He encourages Lara to express her criticism in the next group session and assures her that he will protect her if the boys offend her.

The boys once again fight with their swords. Lara says loudly, so that everyone can hear her, "I want to build a hospital and I need you, Mr. Wenzel, to carry the wounded fighters away from the battlefield!" Her idea was to install the hospital in the corner of the room, where we previously had a secure spot with pillows and blankets. The two girls arrange the latter so that it now forms a separate area. Then they take bandages, plasters, and a stethoscope from the first aid kit. When a fighter goes down, Lara, the self-proclaimed doctor, asks the group leader to help her carry the fighter to the hospital. One of the boys, who is still 'unhurt', now attacks the hospital and tries to destroy it. Quickly the group leader shouts out, "Stop, the Geneva Convention applies here! The hospital cannot be destroyed!" The boy who attacked the hospital and the other fighters accept the intuitive super-ego response of the group leader and now want to receive medical treatment, just like the first fighter who went down.

The group leader notices there is closer contact between Julia and Christian (name changed), one of the fighters, who is now wounded. Christian seems to like Julia using the stethoscope to hear his beating heart, and how she tells him everything is "okay" and provides him with an arm bandage. The two other boys also accept bandages and in the process look happy. Finally the girls ask the boys for medical treatment and a bandage, which they provide with obvious joy. In the reflecting circle at the end of this group session, Julia asks whether she can take a bandage home with her. The healing power of the group is perceptible the leader thinks. After that, the children complete with their bandages meet their parents, who are waiting for them at the entrance. They greet their children with amazement. Looking back, the group leader is not surprised by the fact that, from then on, none of the children misses a further group session, even though this was previously not unusual. In the following session, the group leader announces that the group has to give up the room where they have been meeting because it does not meet current safety standards. This decision is surprising for all the children and for the group leader too. It makes them sad because they are losing their safe place and they want to know why. The group leader explains that there is no escape route in the event of fire – for example, the semicircular windows on one side of the room are too small to get through. Conversion work is not possible because it's a listed building. The group leader also mentions that he will try to find a new room and that the children can decide what they want to take with them to the new room.

The group leader himself is very involved and emotionally touched by the loss of this room, which is furnished for children. It is separated by two big columns, has sloping walls on both sides, and offers lots of space for the group's toys to be stored without the children– all this makes him pensive and sad. He is not able to communicate this to the children.

In this session, the children build two castles opposite each other. On each castle they put a cannon and shoot until there is nothing left of either castle's structure, and the center of the room is completely covered with small fragments of the castles. In the end, Julia says to the group leader, "Mr. Wenzel, you clean up!" Given his own feelings of dismay, the group leader does not grasp the group's symbolization until the supervision session covering the group session: The children created one castle to represent the group and the other to represent the institution. The total destruction of both castles until there is nothing left and the request for the group leader to clean up most probably go together in the children's perceptions. The group leader, as the representative of the institution, is responsible for their now being deprived of a place to which they can retreat where they can together feel safe and protected. The institution, which previously symbolized the protective, safe arms of the mother in the positive sense both for the group and the leader, takes this away. The sadness about it has not yet been granted a space. But the anger has emerged, as symbolized by the children in their destruction of both castles.

It turns out that the group can move to a room in the same building, and this happens shortly after this session. It is possible to use a room in the basement, which is a bit smaller and brighter. The children tell the group leader that they would like to take the columns that divide up the old room with them, because they can put their legs in the air and rest them on the columns. In this way, the children are able to turn the adult world upside down. They had done this several times at the end of the group sessions, breaking out into joyful laughter as they did so. Pondering this, the group leader considers the importance of fun and joy when the children take part in the group. Fun and joy help the children open up in the group. The experience of fun and joy in the group also prevents the children from unnecessarily reinforcing the indexical roles assigned them in their family systems. Will the new room convey a feeling of safety, and will it again be a holding environment that fosters fun and joy? In other words: Will the children be able to link the inner developmental steps they have made in the previous room with those that lie before them?

In the next group session, the children build a dormitory in the new room, put themselves in beds, which they have made out of blankets and pillows, and demand of the group leader, "Mr. Wenzel, turn off the lights!" Once again, the leader is unable to speak. He could have answered, "Can somebody please take the role of a ward nurse? Time for everyone to calm down" (Haar & Wenzel, 2019, p. 121). This idea only occurs to him later when reflecting on the situation he analyzes his own dismay. The problem, therefore, is that not just to what extent the children have lost an inner space of maternal qualities, but also whether this applies to the group leader. His prior naive trust in God is shattered. By constructing the dormitory, the children have staged the limitations of the group leader, who, when the children were busy destroying the castles and building the dormitory, was not able to mirror the mental context.

In the three following group sessions, the children symbolize the room as a dormitory. Then they symbolize a family, where Julia takes the role of a mother and Christian the role of a child who eats – on behalf of the whole group. With squeaking noises, he imitates a whining child that cannot get enough and insults his mother. These insults are repeated in the following session by a prince talking to his queen. "Stupid queen-mother," the prince insults the queen. Apparently, the children are now playing a royal court. Their development has made a leap in terms of individuation. The group takes another step, too. As the queen of the court, Julia is initially able to lord over the princes and the princesses. In a fierce dispute with his queen-mother, the prince accuses her of giving him too little attention. After this, the queen seeks to retire to her chambers, the prince follows her and at one go tears down the walls of pillows behind which the queen is trying to hide herself. The queen, recognizing her "son's" intention, calls for the group leader, "Mr. Wenzel, you have to help me!" But the group leader comes too late. The prince has already torn down the walls, which supposedly serve the queen as protection against danger. In this way, not only is the queen's protective space torn down, but so are the autistic walls put up by Julia, who came to the group with these walls around her. In the final group session, Julia and Christian tell the group about fierce quarrels: Julia with her younger sister, Christian with his slightly older brother. The other group members take part, too, talk about their families, and listen attentively to one another.

What becomes clear here is that they relate far more strongly to one another than in the scenes of power and powerlessness at the beginning of the group process. The group holds a celebration to celebrate the successful group process and talk about the holidays, during which there will be no sessions. All family members are invited. At the beginning of the celebrations, the group leader asks the children what they will do on the free Thursdays when they would otherwise be attending the group. In this way, he helps the children bridge the time till the next group session after the holidays.

3 Mental representations: The group fantasies staged by the children and the leader's entanglement in the children's games

Due to the leader's minimal structuring of the group, a regression is triggered that prompts the children to bring their internalized relationship conflicts to bear in the group and enact them. The group tries initially to stead itself by finding a scapegoat. With the intervention of the group leader, it proves possible to hand the role of the powerful decider over to another child such that the group's initial attempt to solve things by excluding one of them was not realized. In the meantime, the group is able to endure the initially almost intolerable group tension.

In the knights' battle, the boys are struggling for domination with the sword as their penis symbol. The knight represents the desire or the thirst for adventure, as well as immature masculinity and struggle. The knights are from a psychological perspective clad in armor: They withdraw emotionally from the outside world and make themselves unreachable. It's very likely that in this fantasy the children are repeating their experiences of power and powerlessness within the family. At the beginning of the session, the girls are ignored by the boys in the same way as their mothers at home are excluded by the fathers from decision-making. The hospital, an idea one of the girls had, is a symbol of the mother and a place where you are cared for and looked after, and thus helps the group move one step forward. The group moves from a regressive phase onto a progressive phase. The children's wounds from home can be treated here. With the battle between the two castles, the group makes another attempt to move. The castles initially arise as symbols of power and isolation, with protecting, sheltering, and holding qualities, and the children's destruction of them symbolizes how they experience their situation in the here-and-now: The loss of the first room threatens the group as a whole, hence the group attacks the Diakonisches Werk as an institution and destroys it.

The instruction "Mr. Wenzel, you clean-up!", underlines the children's experience. The acting-out by the group leader in this situation initially prevents the group from working on the children's and the leader's anger and sadness. With the fantasy of the dormitory, the group once more goes into regression, but draws strength from this and makes another step forward by inventing the court: Enchanted mental dignity and new mental independence and expressiveness appear, for example, when the group works on oedipal subjects: a prince blames the queen, who withdraws because of her emotional isolation and her missing connectedness to herself. Since the children are beginning to trust one another, the prince can tear down the walls of the autistic queen without damaging her. In the end, in the reflecting circle the children are thus able to talk about their family backgrounds, consisting at the moment of sibling rivalry.

At the leaving celebration, the children invent a circus as the final group fantasy: Emotions, drives, and the body can be shown and expressed differently than in everyday life, but in a controlled manner. In this way, the children create an inner space as a contrasting foil to everyday life and to normalcy. Feedback the children give one another in the last reflecting circle before the holidays takes the form of mentalization. For example, one child says to another: "You can play well, even if you are sometimes not in a good mood." This can be read to mean: Just because this child is in a bad mood, a game does not stop. It also means the children are now able to distinguish between their own feelings and the feelings of another. The children's fantasies that move the process forward (the hospital, the two castles, the circus) show that the children can constructively contribute. Partly with the support of the group leader but mostly by virtue of their own creativity, the children have been able to make recapitulating new experiences.

In the following, I describe how a group of boys gets out of stressful situations, initially with the support of the group leader and later of their own volition, by inventing rules themselves. The boys' group emerged after the two girls bid farewell to the group.

At the start of a meeting, four boys decide to have a pillow fight in the dark. After a short time, it becomes clear: The group can only partially comply with rules that are intended to limit potential overstepping. Suddenly one of the boys asks the group leader to take part in a game as a lava monster. In this group, the leader consciously assumes this role for a short time. He is declared a lava monster which then has to stand in the middle of the room. The children set no other rules. The boy who had asked the leader to play the lava monster now takes hold of the lava monster's hands, looks at him carefully, as if to see in his eyes whether he is well disposed, smiles briefly, and finally does a somersault; he then stands up in front of the lava monster, looks into his eyes again, smiles once more, and the lava monster smiles back.

In the parent group, the group leader was told beforehand by the mother of this boy about the father's aggressive attacks on the son. This knowledge helps the leader to understand the boy's transference on him and thus the meaning of this role assignment. Since groups tend to use individual members to brood on a group issue that concerns everyone until it matures, this boy has a special function in that group: At a time when the group as a whole is ready to so do, he is the first to be brave enough to make physical contact with an adult male role model in such a way that this contact does not derail. The leader knows from the parent group that all the boys have at some point had the experience of lapses on the part of their fathers, some verbal, others physical. In other words, this is an issue for all the boys.

The group leader is therefore not surprised when all the other boys also want to do this somersault with him. In this way, the leader assumes a position that enables not only this boy but the others, too, to experience a new relationship. In a next step, the children inform the leader that he is no longer a child and thus release him from this role. The group then experiences another step in its members' development, since the boys now invent rules that are intended to contribute to the game being structured in a way that serves to promote a gain in pleasure. The reflective rounds in the circle at the end of each session prompted the insight, as the boys were able to think more carefully about what they considered to foster boredom. For example, they now determine how long the boy who is the new lava monster has to hold another boy captive on the ground before the captive boy also becomes a lava monster. There is no need to describe the symbolic meaning of the lava monster in more detail, since the evolutionary step taken by the group as a whole, with the introduction of rules to which everyone feels bound, becomes clear in the course of the coming sessions, and everyone respects these rules. The children can now each perform their own positively connoted super-ego acts on the basis of their own particular experiences.

Now I will describe how this group of boys responds to a frightening situation by forming pairs.

After a round of greetings, the boys cannot agree on what to play. Instead, one of the boys gets up from his island and declares: "Pillow fight!" A wild melee quickly ensues. The boys run after each other and throw little pillows. Eventually they form a heap and test how much pressure the boy lying on the bottom can withstand. When one of the boys refuses to lie at the bottom of the pile, the game stops. Now the other boys try to convince him that it's fun and that he should join in, but they are unable to motivate him to continue playing the game.

The boy fetches drawing materials, sits on the edge of the group room, and starts drawing. Another boy lies down next to him and also starts drawing. They talk and look at each other's drawings with interest. From time to time, they also look over to the other boys, who are continuing their game and fighting with each other. After a short time, only two boys continue fighting. The third sits on the ground near the group leader and shows him Playmobil figures. The two boys who are drawing maintain the connection with the other boys by turning around every now and then and following the action of the other boys attentively. At the end of the group meeting, both present their pictures in a circle so that everyone can see them. The picture by the boy who was the first to stop playing action games and started drawing shows a picture of fighting red and black stick figures. In the other boy's drawing, there is a seaworthy ship that has several decks. There is a smoking chimney on the roof. On the upper deck are individual figures, not directly in contact with one another. Three couples appear on the lower deck, spatially separated from each other by a wall. One of these stick figures is shown with heavier strokes. In this way, all group members, including the group leader, are captured in the picture.

The first boy to drop out of the game had stick figures fighting each other in his picture. For the group leader, who knows the boy's family and school background, this acts as a representation of his own state of mind and also as a mirror of the group's status: The boy experiences destructive situations everywhere. The picture by the second boy lying down next to him can be understood as a continuation of this representation: The drawings look like questions and answers. Fear and ultimately destructive relationships in the one image are answered with the possibility of entering into constructive relationships. Three couples sit in the ship and promptly show themselves in the group itself. Fear made the boys drop out of the game and form pairs. Since the couple can basically be seen as the nucleus for the formation of relationships, the two boys show the other boys how the group process can proceed. In this respect, the idea that arises from the action game, namely to create a unifying ship in which everyone has their place, serves to promote relationships and to develop the coherence of the group. The group leader is seen as a person of special responsibility due to the stronger accentuation of the drawing. Presumably, the children noticed the concern of the group leader, who was thinking about how this game stimulates sexual fantasies, adding something uncontrollable to the group process, and so they began another form of expression: drawing pictures, albeit one that likewise took the group process one step further.

The following case example shows how a single action by a child at the end of a group session can be understood as a creative contribution that moves the group forward. As already described in other examples, it also makes it clear how the group broods on something, as it were, until this is expressed in the seemingly sudden interaction of a child:

At the beginning of a session, four children in a mixed group who are already familiar with one another select Playmobil toys with which the boys will build a town and the girls will build a nearby farm. They pay close attention to the development of the buildings, occasionally watching one another attentively. One of the boys prepares for a trip on a horse, bids farewell to his playmate, places a fire-breathing dragon in front of the town, rides past the farm, chats with a farmer at the fence, and then continues on his trip. At that moment, the other boy grabs the fire-breathing dragon and throws it across the room, breaking off its head. Asked about the significance of the dragon in front of the town, the boy replies with a reproachful undertone: that indicated to the group leader that he should really know, "Honor, of course!"

The archetypal meaning of the fire-breathing dragon, which comes to the group leader's mind as the evil mother, in the meantime creates a tension that explains the actions of the boy who threw the dragon: He, having got to know his playmate's sometimes moody and patronizing mother in the drop-off and pick-up situations and also through the stories in the children's group, apparently assigns the dragon a similar meaning as does the group leader. By killing the dragon-mother, the boy has an enabling effect on his playmate, who was previously so concerned with identifying with personal aspects of his mother that she inhibited his development. The boy had not been able to see through this until then, because he believed he could see honorable aspects in the dragon. In other words, the dragon-thrower encouraged his playmate to develop more personal autonomy. It can be assumed that the other children, who experienced and observed this scene, also grasped the symbolism of the destroyed dragon and were therefore also able to find encouragement in the act.

> **At a glance**
> *Group analysis enables* a growth process in institutional educational and family counseling for the children and the parents, the group leaders, and the institution, if all those involved are seen as part of the group matrix.
> *Group analysis becomes more important* in the framework of an educational and family counseling center if it elevates archetypal forms of expression relating to the group matrix to a first-order form of communication (Foulkes, 1974). Since the group process constantly requires the group leader's willingness to get emotionally involved in the group process, reflection time is necessary for the preparation and follow-up of the sessions. In this way, the work can be placed on a secure basis.

Bibliography

Arbeitskreis zur Förderung der Kinder- und Jugendlichengruppenanalyse (2014). *Curriculum für Kinder- und Jugendlichengruppenanalyse*. Darmstadt: Rehani Druck & Verlag

Foulkes, S. H. (1974). *Gruppenanalytische Psychotherapie*. München: Kindler

Haar, R., Wenzel, H. (2019). *Psychodynamische Gruppentherapie mit Kindern*. Stuttgart: Kohlhammer

Lutz, C. (1976). *Praxis der Gruppentherapie mit Kindern*. Stuttgart: Bonz

Meyer, W. (2005). Überlegungen zur Zusammenstellung der analytischen Gruppe. Analytische Psychologie. *Zeitschrift für Psychotherapie und Psychoanalyse*, 3, 249–162

Over-Hill Indian Nation (no date). The talking stick. https://overhillcherokee.com/talking.htm (last accessed March 29, 2022)

Rahm, D. (2004). *Integrative Gruppentherapie mit Kindern*. Göttingen: Vandenhoeck & Ruprecht

Rogers, C. R., Schmid, P. F. (1991). *Person-zentriert. Grundlagen von Therapie und Praxis*. Mainz: Matthias Grünewald

Sandner, D. (2022). *Society and the Unconscious*. Berlin & Heidelberg: Springer

The Rhythmic-Triadic Setting in Group Analysis

Katrin Stumptner

1 Prologue

For many years I have been working as a group analyst with adolescents and their caregivers in what I call the rhythmized-triadic setting (Stumptner, 2019). It was during a trip in 2010 that access to the complexity of this setting opened up for me as an active factor in group analysis in the process of detachment between generations.

The rhythmic-triadic setting is characterized by the fact that, in parallel to the weekly group sessions with the young people, I meet their caregivers every six weeks. The background to this model is based on the notion that only where there is attachment can there then be detachment. Before I delve deeper into the examination of this complex group-analytic work, however, I would like to begin by describing something that happened on the aforementioned trip. This experience led me to a broader understanding of the inner, intersubjective intertwining of parallel group processes, which I, as a representative of the groups in my leadership role, experience reflexively.

To set the scene: It was a balmy summer evening in a small Basque town. It was at that time, a time of "in between", when the brightness of the day increasingly gives way to the dark hours of the night, that I was enjoying my aperitif, free of all obligations and in a glorious state of reverie. I was sitting on a little wall at the edge of the marketplace and felt free. Still quiet, the entire large square lay before me. Time seemed to stand still. Yet as the evening progressed, the square developed more and more into a stage, and I became a fascinated observer, allowing myself to be drawn into the unfolding scenic play.

Groups of old people gathered scattered chairs, sat down together, and waved for an aperitif. Groups of couples, women, and men assembled, standing here and there together, laughing, chatting, and also enjoying the end of a long workday over an aperitif in a visibly relaxed atmosphere. Teenagers and young adults emerged, sometimes from one side of the square, sometimes from another. They greeted each other, shouting loudly, posing cheerfully in front of one another, and joining sometimes this, sometimes that peer group.

In between all these lively goings-on, children whizzed around: small and bigger kids, running, jumping, on scooters and blades. They used the standing and sitting adults to structure their play space and enriched this place with their exuberance, their joy in playing, and with their enthusiasm to let their joyful voices resound over the square and to hear them in turn. Within this convivial gathering, the different generations seemed to be connected with one another, and yet each group also stuck together. On closer inspection, it was the exchange of gestures, a look back and forth, a nod, a little smile, that signaled a bond across the boundaries of this sticking-together. I felt like I was in an atmospheric concert, a spectacle of generations, pulsating with vitality, with moments of tension, and yet well-tempered. The separation between the generations shaped itself before me in a fascinating choreography with a multitude of protagonists, which at the same time pointed along almost invisible threads to a sense of inter-generative belonging. Threads that show themselves most clearly in the active games played by the children, who visibly enjoyed these gatherings in the marketplace. They moved freely between the groups, unobserved yet seen, and protected at the same time. The children got into surprisingly few arguments, and despite the high speed of the game, they seemed to be magically protected from disruptive accidents.

My silent participation in this complex scene triggered a lot of resonance within me. The playful dynamics between closeness and distance, the obvious separation between generations in a simultaneous, atmospheric connectedness enlivened me. Scenes from the groups in the rhythmic-triadic setting at my practice came to mind and intertwined with one another. The image of the marketplace as an *intersubjective gathering place* for the generations created an inner meeting space in me as the leader of both groups. In the marketplace of this small town, a three-generation structure (von Friesen and Wilke, 2016) is staged as a dynamic, large group event without any recognizable large group leadership.

The marketplace formed the shared stage. This event was reflected in me like a symbol of the imaginary space between the generations: each separated from the others and yet connected. Separated in their different perspectives, and connected in the respect shown for the boundaries of age. Only the children move between all these levels. It is they who still shape the link between the generations as a matter of course. They have formative scope in which they depend on the open and benevolent support of adults.

2   The setting

The opening of imaginary spaces in the sense of an *inner marketplace* between the generations is significant in this work. Through the interweaving of the intersubjective experience of the parallel group processes in the group leadership, greater scope of access opens up within the participants of the groups on the sensory-symbolic level in a clear demarcation between the generations.

Intergenerational belonging, connected by invisible threads, is what Foulkes calls a "network of interrelations" (Foulkes, 1992, p. 19). "This network of interconnected transpersonal processes is the actual frame of reference or unit to be observed." The matrix, in the diction of Foulkes: "is the hypothetical fabric of communication and connection in a given group. It is the basis that ultimately determines the meaning and significance of all events and upon which all communications, verbal and nonverbal, are based" (Foulkes, 1992, p. 33).

The protagonists are, as mentioned at the beginning:
- a group of young people (in a circle of chairs) who meet once a week for a two-hour session. Where it seems appropriate, creative media (e. g., writing, painting, design, music) are incorporated.
- a caregiver group (in a circle of chairs), which gathers for a two-hour session every six weeks.

The dynamic process of the adolescent group is at the center of the psychodynamic work, with the dynamic process of the caregiver group supplementary to this. The parental generation opens the view into the family matrices of a three-generation structure (von Friesen and Wilke, 2016, p. 46). In the leadership of both groups, this requires the recognition of the generations in their cultural-social diversity of narratives, stories, needs, challenges, and tasks.

It is the simultaneity of the rhythmic group processes that opens imaginary spaces, in the sense of the inner marketplace between the generations, in the leadership. With the knowledge of all protagonists about the parallel group processes, from their respective perspectives the participants of both groups begin to turn to the projectively conflictual, dynamic processes of the family matrices on the peer level[1]. In the course of group processes, rapprochement and confrontation at the peer level both lead to a mitigation of projections between the generations and to an intersubjective experience of belonging to the respective peer group. With growing group cohesion in both groups and the more stable experience of bonding at the respective peer level, the tense conflictual issues in the transmission diversity of the groups become more concentrated.

---

1   The "peer group" (see "peer group" on Wikipedia, no date) is described by Salge (2013, p. 123) as follows: "The peer group is the place that is physiologically sought out from puberty onward so that, within its protection, the person can attempt a gradual detachment from the primary objects, try out rivalry and competition, simultaneously stabilize identity, create experimental spaces for the awakening of drives, experience self-efficacy, cope with feelings of shame, and endure the pain of separation. This list could go on."

In the course of the parallel processes, this leads to detachment between the generations and opens up interstices in the sense of imagination and thinking spaces within the individual participants. These autonomy processes are gradually transferred onto the real family and social contexts. Both the caregivers and the adolescents alike succeed more and more often in leaving each other alone, in better bearing their feelings of frustration and disappointment, and in negotiating these inner tensions in the respective groups and finding words for what is bothering them. Perceptions of each other crystallize more clearly as they begin to enact themselves projectively in the context of the respective groups. In the dynamic matrix of the respective group, these can now be negotiated, better understood, sorted, and classified together against the background of the family matrices (Stumptner, 2018). The boundaries between generations are formed, repeatedly marked, and increasingly understood and recognized in this repetitive marking. The quality of family communication and of cultured argument improves in the course of these rhythmized processes of argument.

3 A brief look at the theoretical background

In the interactional events of the family matrix, the caregivers' notions of themselves as parents and of their child have a modulating effect on the development of the child's sense of self as part of a community (Stumptner and Thomsen, 2005). According to their age, the required developmental steps and needs, and the constitutional competencies, the child explores the ego in the "we" in further phases of detachment. The family constellations are repeatedly challenged in these developmental phases, and the steadfastness and continuity of relationships are put to the test. In the relationships, the child seeks recognition in their independent, psychosexual being and wanting.

According to M. Buchholz, these developmental steps are "'self-assertion' in the literal sense" (Buchholz, 1990, p. 121). In these phases, the caregivers are inevitably confronted with the transgenerational-family relationship constellations they have personally experienced, which, in the three-generation structure (von Friesen and Wilke, 2016, p. 2, p. 46), can lead to thoroughly necessary, but also lastingly confusing, role diffusions between the parental positions and the child's needs and perspectives (Stumptner, 2015).

If the caregivers "in their parenthood" (Misselwitz, 2009, p. 42) are themselves confronted with unresolved and "stressful separation and abandonment experiences" (Misselwitz, 2009, p. 42) from their own history during these detachment crises with their adolescents, the family situation comes to a head.

Pressure to act as well as voicelessness increasingly take hold. In shared helplessness and despair, feelings of love and hate can often no longer be adequately differentiated and lead to misunderstood interpretations. A vicious circle begins to perpetuate itself, in which young people and caregivers reinforce each other in their tense interactions. Mistrust between the generations grows and isolates.

In a lecture to the British Psychoanalytical Society in 1946, S. H. Foulkes put it this way: The concept of the group is "perhaps the first useful instrument for getting an adequate view of the main problem of our time: the tense relationship of the individual to the community" (cited in Kreeger, 1977, p. 27). In the dynamic matrices of the parallel groups in the triadic setting, the entire "microcosmic" (Foulkes, 1948, cited in Hearst, 1998, p. 35) world of each group participant is mirrored and reflected in all participants, including the group leader, who acts as a witness. Both groups weave the "communication web" (Foulkes, 1978, p. 105) of the three-generation fabric. Processes of remembering and telling in resonance with likewise affected persons of the same generation (peer level) are shared. Within the triadic setting, the group leader moves in a continuous change of perspective of this large-group process, as in the inner marketplace, as a participating link in the field of tension.

Between a rock and a hard place, the group leadership repeatedly moves in the conflict zones of the generations. Participants of both groups try to elicit secrets of the other from the group leadership. The radical recognition of confidentiality in the sense of abstinence, communicated in both groups, opens up independent communication spaces in the peer group processes. The goal is a dynamic movement "from the symptom to the underlying conflict" (Foulkes, 1978, p. 34). The fostering of a willingness to engage in conflict, which is supported by an increasing concession and expression of diverse perspectives, helps with the recognition of and more conscious respect for generational boundaries and, as a result, with more honest confrontation of personal as well as family crises.

Possible intergenerational lines of conflict often occur at the beginning of a group or in transitional phases at the group boundaries, such as when old group members say goodbye or new ones start. Parents arrive too late or cancel the caregiver group session. Adolescents are unexpectedly excused by their parents, who then do not show up for the group. The adolescents simply don't turn up, arrive late, or leave early. In the transference, the group leader as guardian at and on the group boundaries is repeatedly entrapped and challenged. Translating these enactments as traded messages by understanding their "unconscious nature [...] and the meaningfulness of symbolic expression" (Foulkes, 1978, p. 104) as messages in the complex dynamic large-group process of the two parallel groups repeatedly marks the boundary between the groups. In this transference-countertransference process, the psychodynamic tension of pleasure-displeasure experiences is mapped in traded provocations and voicelessness to ward off feelings of shame, sensations such as overwhelm and physical tension, and feelings such as mistrust, anger, fear, and grief. In the sense of Bion's containment model, according to which the ability to think what is already there – "to think the already existing thought" (Bion, 1962, p. 83) – is developed by a counterpart who ensures what Bion calls the "alpha-function", the projectively induced "beta-elements" become progressive processes in the group if the group leader holds, reflects, and translates them into the respective group in a meaningful way and according to the psychodynamic process at a fitting time. Here, beta-elements mean unprocessed, "undigested" material, impressions, and events that cannot be mentally processed. The alpha-function "digests" beta-elements and thus makes them mentally tangible ("thus made available for thought"; Bion, 1962, p. 7). These mentalizing transformation processes of previously unconsciously-projectively impacting topics in the dynamic matrix of the respective group enable an expansion of communication and open up *inner scope* for the participants, in which bodily sensations and feelings are more clearly perceived and communicated in mutual mirroring and resonance phenomena. In a developing space of imagination and symbols – according to Dietlind Köhncke, the *imaginary in-between space* (Köhncke, 1997, p. 121) – the group participants discover, as if on an expedition into the *realm of the family,* extended spaces of imagination and thinking within themselves and towards others. According to Bion (1962, p. 7): "Alpha-function transforms sense impressions into alpha-elements which resemble, and may in fact be identical with, the visual images with which we are familiar in dreams." Independent communication cultures develop in both groups, and confrontational processes of "self-assertion" are tested in both groups. "We" representations in the ego and notions of the ego in the "we" begin to interact in a more pleasurable and mutually challenging way. This expanded self-awareness is increasingly transferred outside the groups, into the families of origin and expanded social spaces. Caregivers begin to move more confidently in the role of their parental authority and increasingly endure the adolescents' projective affective and tension states in identity and autonomy crises, without turning them into their own affective states. They thus more consciously assume the alpha-function according to Bion's containment model. This acceptance of the generational boundary enables the adolescents, who are likewise becoming more self-confident, to assume more self-responsibility on the peer level in the continuing process of self-discovery, in accordance with the necessary crisis of detachment.

The experience of frustration transforms more and more into a lustful urge to discover. This does not make the challenges between the generations any easier, but the perpetuation of painfully inhibiting, transgenerational issues recedes into the background and the generations begin not to lose sight of each other, according to the imagined image of the marketplace, with simultaneous respect and recognition of the diversity of perspectives.

To summarize: In the triadic setting, a field opens up between the two poles created by the two parallel, rhythmically working groups with the same group leadership in the search for the ego in the "we". In the course of this, the connection between the generations is re-established in the intersubjective field of the groups. At the beginning of the group processes, the diversity of perspectives in the groups working independently of each other becomes apparent in the confrontational process of the respective dynamic matrices. "This succeeds through the radical acknowledgement of not-knowing, of strangeness and a common search for orientation" (S. Alder, oral communication, December 27, 2021). In the process of simultaneity of a connection in the peer groups and a separation of the generations into two groups, current dissonances between the generations become accessible in the respective peer group's dynamic process of more differentiated reflection. In the searching, finding, and narrating of the images, symbols, and words shared with each other in the story, in the recognition of the diversity of narratives in the peer groups, an imaginary in-between space (Köhncke, 1997, p. 121) opens up in the group leadership and in all participants of both groups, in which the struggle for the ego in the "we" experiences a meaning and can be recognized. Phantasms in the generational structure sort themselves out and find their place in the time and space of the systems; they are mourned and discarded.

4   Example

In a group of four transgender adolescents aged about 16, I, as the leader, experienced a disconcerting, disembodied feeling of "we" in the first sessions. The shrouding of the adolescents' bodies expressed their trepidation about not feeling located in relation to others, and the search for a transgender sense of self in the "wrong body" (according to one participant) brought the participants in this group together. The four young people moved communicatively on a level of mutual self-affirmation of an assumed identity that can be located neither externally nor internally in the historical context and in the here-and-now. Everything seemed insecurely constructed, both on the peer level, the horizontal level, and on the vertical level of parental transmission to me. Their self-chosen names were still fresh; they told me that their parents often got confused or avoided calling them by name and used "the wrong female pronoun". Within the countertransference, I sensed a deep, physical confusion and a need for orientation. They seemed to have fallen out of context, like young birds who got lost while learning to fly and can't find their way home. When they talked about their school context, their positioning seemed more secure. Being a student is an identity, and many teachers in Berlin schools are already familiar with transgender transformation in the institution of the school. They make it relatively easy for young people to come out and move as a trans person within the institutional framework. Yet there was no sense of belonging on the peer level, either in the masculine or the feminine world of senses and sexual awakening of physical signals. They were currently in between, in transit space, neither fish nor fowl. In the group, they began to talk with one another like actors, as if they were trying to physically-habitually fit into the male role. They hailed one participant's account of having been addressed as a boy at the kebab stand like a stage victory in an arduous mountain climb. At the same time, he talked about sending his female friends at the kebab stand ahead to order for him so as not to be betrayed by his feminine-sounding voice. They seemed creative and at the same time tense and controlled in everything they showed of themselves. The original first name was presented as a "dead name" and was not allowed to be heard in the group room. In the first group phase, everything revolved around reassuring oneself in the gaze of the others, as if in a mirror of the transgender self. The search for a psychosexual identity was expressed between the participants in the group in fictional ideas of another body and a deeper voice. For the time being, the connection to the past acted as a taboo. They communicated in the here and now in a technical language "whose meaning seems emptied by designer meanings" (Wilke, 2015, p. 276) and signaled to me that I did not belong. Within countertransference, I endured the madness in the current identity conflict. In the parental transference, I experienced the necessary exclusion and simultaneous witnessing of four adolescents' struggle to shed their skin in the sense of self-assertion. In the early group phase, the transgender language seemed insubstantial, the new words searching for a sensory-bodily filling of shared relational experiences. I found this palpably desperate search for the ego in the gaze of others touching, and it made me sense the need for connection in the self and for belonging in the "we". Their courage to carefully discover themselves in the protected space of the group, the deep desire to be recognized and acknowledged and to finally feel physically identical with what they have long felt within their own bodies, stood side by side in the center of our group sessions.

The parallel caregiver group opened up the view into the family stories and into the painful world of the adolescents' warded-off feelings of fear, anger, grief, and isolation. The parents of the transgender adolescents began to connect through the search for the children they had lost. They formulated feelings of helplessness, sadness, and a painful sense of separation from a previously physical-spiritual shared familiarity and intimacy, from ideas shared with and by each other. Questions about transsexuality, about historical, social, and cultural references were asked and led the caregivers to their own history and to their stories with their children. They talked about the birth and naming of their children, the name that was then no longer to be spoken in the presence of their children. Childhood scenes were exchanged as if at a funeral service, and at the same time current scenes of voicelessness and, in turn, painfully uncertain arguments between the generations; the shyness in the encounter with their unfamiliar children, with whom they no longer blithely share the habitually well-trodden common ground (Alder and Alder, 2021, p. 396), but seek to revive the previous naturalness of connection and intimacy in a changed tonality. Everyone worked towards recreating access to the previously familiar in the process of transformation. The caregivers found themselves to be a peer group and wove a tapestry with body and soul, through which the inner marketplace in the triadic setting between the generations began to revive.

An increased number of enquiries about transgender youth in my practice prompted me to ask myself what I could offer them. Me, as an adult therapist incarnate, with no experience of a bodily transit space. The narrative of Foulkes' beginning as a group analyst in his practice[2] encouraged me to bring trans youth together in a group setting. At the same time, this meant I also had to bring the caregivers together in a parallel group. As a group analyst, I leaned into this experience, and my attitude – not knowing and not having to understand – helped me here: "I also don't think we should try to understand everything. That would confine things: approving, forgiving, sanctioning; it would set them in stone. Following Bertold Brecht's doctrine of the meaning of alienation, we can say that not understanding something can mean just the opposite: freedom of choice, the possibility to change and act differently [...]. Being able to bear this is equally important for the experienced therapist" (Foulkes, 1992, p. 28). All impressions, communications, social currents, mutual mes-

---

2   Foulkes observed that his patients struck up lively discussions in the waiting room of his practice and began to share their personal concerns with each other. This prompted him to establish an outpatient group with these patients. In addition, such an intervention allowed him to treat multiple patients in the same time period.

sages, transgenerational information, and events in the variety of transference in group processes "involve the network of interrelations" (Foulkes, 1992, p. 29).

This parallel process of the adolescent and caregiver groups, via the imagined interstice within the therapist, opens up access to the inner marketplace of the encounter between the generations, in whose field of tension a language can be found, both simultaneously and yet separately, for what was previously experienced in voicelessness with each other. Parents, like their children, go through a process of tremendous transformation.

Fear of strangers is no longer at the center. In both groups, the oedipal, age-appropriate processes of detachment have come to the fore. Caregivers have begun to be more compassionate and confident in their parenting responsibilities and to respond appreciatively to the shared hardships and fears in this challenging process of transformation with their children. The young people appear more open and more differentiated from one another in their ambivalence. The initial, necessary lockstep of the transgender adolescents seems to have loosened up. Pleasurable, age-appropriate topics such as music, school, and parties, but also fear-inducing future topics emerge more strongly in their experienced simultaneity. The topic of sexual identity is negotiated shyly, but it is the determining keynote of the discussions in the dynamic matrices. As one adolescent participant aptly puts it, "I avoid looking at myself naked in the mirror." The current, outer female body image does not correspond to the inner sense of I-am-a-boy that has long been felt, and the goal is the fit between inside and outside. The issue takes the generations to mutually shattering limits of autonomy and responsibility, with hormone treatment and further operations on the horizon. A possible decision provokes wanting and inhibition, fears of the effect of the desired consequences, and the need for finite implementation. In the dynamic matrices of both groups, the possible, real physical interventions from very different perspectives and backgrounds lead to painful confrontations in these complete processes of detachment. As a group leader, I find myself in the in-between space of the diversity of perspectives of the current, dynamic confrontation of social transformation processes and discover again and again my trust in the group processes and the necessity of the attitude as quoted in the Foulkesian sense, of freedom through non-understanding (Foulkes, 1992, p. 28).

In the protected setting of the group, the young people begin to formulate their needs and to find images, words, and metaphors for their emotional worlds. The young trans people's search for meaning, for a body-coherent positioning and a coherent body-self experience in connection with their origin in the social here and now, is condensed in the setting of the parallel groups. In the intersubjective experience of the therapist, in extension as an imagined marketplace of the generations, a triangulating, transgenerational search and demarcation process opens up for the caregivers as well as for the adolescents in the transgender process of transformation. In both groups, the encounter with like-minded people contributes to a supporting and sustaining cohesion on the peer level. As a group leader of both groups, I move as a witness and translator in the inner marketplace as well as in the transit space between the genders and the generations searching for reassurance in letting go.

> **At a glance:**
> *Group analysis in a rhythmic-triadic setting:*
> - involves caregivers in a group process that runs parallel to the child/adolescent group (two peer groups working in parallel).
> - opens the view into the field of tension and the complexity of the diversity of perspectives in the generation structure.
> - brings to light unresolved, projective-transgenerational roles – entanglements "stage" themselves in the dynamic matrices of the respective peer group.
> - expands the ability to mentalize; each generation finds access to "their language" in the further process of reflection in the relevant peer group.
> - opens up the "imaginary in-between spaces" in the parallel group processes, where the generations begin to differentiate and recognize each other.
> - fosters an increase in the sense of connectedness and belonging in the intersubjective experience of the respective group, thereby triggering the detachment processes of the ego-in-the-we experience between the generations.
>
> *Methodical extension of the group analysis*
> - involves the conscious inclusion of the caregiver group in the group-analytical process in the work with child/adolescent groups.
> - due to the complex, dynamic processes involved in the management of this setting, calls for a solid group-analytical approach.
> - integrates the parallel group work with children/adolescents and caregivers into group-analytical further training.

Bibliography

Alder, M.-L., Alder, S. (2021). Analytische Perspektiven auf Großgruppenprozesse während der psychohistorischen Trialog-Konferenzen 2015 und 2017. *Zeitschrift für Gruppenpsychotherapie und Gruppendynamik,* 57 (4): 387–408

Bion, W. R. (1962). *Learning from experience.* London: William Heinemann

Buchholz, M. B. (1990). Die Rotation der Triade. *Forum der Psychoanalyse,* 6 (2): 116–134

Foulkes, S. H. (1978). *Praxis der gruppenanalytischen Psychotherapie*. München: Ernst Reinhardt

Foulkes, S. H. (1992). Gruppenanalytische Psychotherapie – Mit einem Nachwort von Georg R. Gfäller. München: Pfeiffer

Friesen, A. von, Wilke, G. (2016). *Generationenwechsel: Normalität, Chance oder Konflikt? Für Familien, Therapeuten, Manager und Politiker*. Berlin: LIT

Hearst, L. (1998). Der Wandel unseres historischen und kulturellen Erbes in der Gruppenanalyse. *Luzifer-Amor*, 11 (21), 30–47

Köhncke, D. (1997). Die Gruppe als Möglichkeitsraum. Gedanken zur Kreativität des therapeutischen Prozesses. Gruppenanalyse – *Zeitschrift für gruppenanalytische Psychotherapie, Beratung und Supervision*, 7 (2): 103–127

Kreeger, L. (Hrsg.) (1977). *Die Großgruppe*. Stuttgart: Klett

Misselwitz, I. (2009). Krippenerziehung in der DDR – Kindheitserfahrung und eigene Elternschaft. *Psychosozial*, 115 (1): 31–48

Salge, H. (2013). *Analytische Psychotherapie zwischen 18 und 25. Besonderheiten in der Behandlung von Spätadoleszenten*. Berlin/Heidelberg: Springer Medizin

Stumptner, K. (2015). Wir tragen unsere Wurzeln in uns. Ambulante Gruppenarbeit mit Jugendlichen und Eltern. *Gruppenanalyse – Zeitschrift für gruppenanalytische Psychotherapie, Beratung und Supervision*, 25 (2): 149–169

Stumptner, K. (2018). Immer wenn ich getötet werde. In S. Reck, C. Reck (Hrsg.), *Worte und Bilder*: 135–41. Heidelberg: Universitätsverlag Winter

Stumptner, K. (2019). Ohne Verbindung keine Entwicklung: Gruppenanalyse mit Kindern, Jugendlichen und Bezugspersonen – Ein institutsübergreifender und transgenerationaler Entwicklungsprozess. In C. Seidler, K. Albert, K. Husemann, and K. Stumptner (Hrsg.), *Berliner Gruppenanalyse. Geschichte – Theorie – Praxis* (S. 231–246). Gießen: Psychosozial

Stumptner, K., and Thomsen, C. (2005). MusikSpielTherapie® (MST). Eine Eltern-Kind-Psychotherapie für Kinder im Alter bis zu vier Jahren. *Praxis der Kinderpsychologie und Kinderpsychiatrie*, 54 (8): 684–99

Wikipedia (n.d.). Peer group. https://de.wikipedia.org/wiki/Peergroup (last accessed April 5, 2022)

Wilke, G. (2015). Konflikt und Potenz innerhalb und zwischen Gruppen. *Gruppenpsychotherapie und Gruppendynamik – Zeitschrift für Theorie und Praxis der Gruppenanalyse*, 51 (4): 270–287

The Dynamic Network Provided by the Institutional Context of Schools, Youth Welfare Agencies and Hospitals

The Meaning of Shame in the Context of School Groups

Ursula Proebsting

Shame is a universal affect. Every human being experiences it, and it exists in all cultures, even though shame triggers may well vary culturally (Hilgers, 1996, p. 26). Shame is part of being human (Marks, 2007, p. 11). In the school context, we encounter shame in both overt and covert forms on a daily basis. Because it can camouflage itself so well, we rarely notice it. The desire to hide is an essential component of shame (Wurmser, 1990, p. 42). If we as teachers look at school situations from the perspective of shame, we can learn a lot about people's motivation, understand situations better and, in the best case, become more capable of acting. Shame can hinder development and lead to false self-assumptions, withdrawal, and breaking off contact. However, it can also be developmental to a moderate extent. Shame can cause us to adapt our behavior to the community and confirm membership.

1   Forms of shame

The triggers of shame are very diverse, as are the forms of shame. The social scientist Stephan Marks lists six forms (Marks, 2007, p. 13 f.):

1. *Conformity shame* occurs when one does not conform to the generally prevailing expectations and norms.
2. *Group shame refers* to the shame of belonging to a group, e.g., a nationality or a political grouping.
3. *Emphatic shame* empathizes with the shaming of others. For example, children defend their classmates while the teacher scolds them in front of the group.
4. *Intimacy shame* has a protective function. It prevents us from exposing ourselves to others; it protects our privacy.
5. *Traumatic shame* arises from massive injury to the person, from psychological or physical experiences of violence. Thus, the feeling of being unlovable and thus existentially threatened can arise through permanent rejection and humiliation. Hilgers calls this form of shame "existential shame" (Hilgers, 1996, p. 26). It is the feeling that arises when one is not perceived, as if one does not exist (Hilgers, 1996, p. 26). Existential, pathological shame conveys the lasting feeling of being fundamentally wrong (Schnee, 2013, p. 4).

6. Finally, Marks mentions *shame of conscience,* which is triggered by wrong or criminal actions. Shame, here, is not to be confused with guilt: Shame is a feeling, while guilt is more of a fact. The feeling of guilt as a result of shame means the ability to take responsibility for the misdeed.

2   Effects of shame

Shame is an extremely unpleasant affect that is experienced in an intense physical way. This affect is accompanied by blushing and emotional numbness and triggers the desire to curl up and die. The gaze is averted, one literally freezes. Flight or fight impulses are triggered. According to Wurmser, a central component of the shame effect is fear, which can range "from quiet suspicion to overwhelming panic" (Wurmser, 1990, p. 78).

Shame interrupts contact with other people. In the state of shame, one can no longer put oneself in the other person's place (Schnee, 2013, p. 5). The shame effect is warded off by projection, aggression against other people, arrogance, or contempt for others (Marks, 2007, p. 71 ff.). If children frequently attract attention at school through aggressive or disruptive behavior, this may therefore be a defense against shame. Aggression and provocation distract from the fear of failing, from the feeling of not being able to keep up and then ultimately no longer being part of the community.

3   Shame at school

People, both the students and the parents and teachers, bring their unconscious shame stories to school (Marks, 2007, p. 182). The traumatic shame is continued in the school and acted out defensively there. Behind cool, emphatically bored, or provocative behavior "hides a traumatized young person who is psychologically fighting for survival" (Marks, 2007, p. 183). To break this vicious circle, teachers need professional distance in order to be able to recognize the person behind the mask of shame defense. However, if the teacher also brings an existential shame experience with her to school, then she may lose touch with the students in shame-inducing situations.

Often a whole group or even a whole school class adopts the disruptive, shaming behavior pattern. The entire class boycotts the lesson, and the teacher feels humiliated, paraded, and shamed. Such a dysfunctional group is driven by conformity and group shame. Those who do not participate are excluded

(Marks, 2007, p. 183). This dynamic can quickly take on a life of its own and cannot be controlled by mere sanctions, as these perpetuate the humiliation and shame and tend to make the situation worse. Bonding, community-building measures that give children a sense of achievement can better mitigate these dynamics because they strengthen the self-esteem of individuals. Shame occurs when there is a threat to belonging to a group or community. If pupils feel that they are lagging behind others in their learning progress, they fear that in the worst case they will have to leave the class, e. g., to repeat it. A teacher who has to hide her weaknesses from her colleagues may fear that otherwise she will no longer be a full member of the staff if they become visible.

4   Positive aspects of shame and its opportunities

Shame can also be used and overcome. After all, it is also a natural affect that accompanies development. "Shame is a sting that calls for coping with reality as long as the person concerned sees sufficient possibilities for coping and acquiring new competences" (Hilgers, 1996, p. 309). Hilgers illustrates this with an example: When learning to ride a bicycle, falls and mishaps inevitably happen. These are painful experiences, but they spur on new efforts. At the moment of the fall, the mental pain is equal to the physical pain. It is the humiliation of being seen to fail, of having been interrupted in the development of autonomy. In an atmosphere of pampering, which is tantamount to neglect, these mishaps are avoided and false fantasies of grandeur are encouraged, for example: "Riding a bike is boring anyway, I'm about to get my driving license!" (Hilgers, 1996, p. 309). In a stable pupil-teacher relationship, however, failure is not a misfortune; it can also activate the motivational systems. Under the encouraging, benevolent gaze of the teacher, one can start countless new attempts until one has reached the next competence.

Successful learning processes require successful relationships that are fed by recognition. If there is no prospect of recognition, the motivational systems shut down. (Marks, 2007, p. 189)

5   Case study 1: Baran in a vicious circle of shame defense

Baran (name changed) is a boy aged 10. His parents are of Russian origin. He attends the fourth year of school. He immediately stood out in the first year of school because of his behavior. He constantly shouted in the classroom, annoyed his classmates, hid under the table, refused to cooperate, and topped it all off with a mask-like grin. He could never make eye contact with the teacher. He regularly drove his teachers up the wall. He also quickly found imitators in his class, with the result that lessons sometimes became impossible.

Baran's brother had also attended our school and had shown similar conspicuous behavior. His mother always felt overwhelmed and was often desperate. The father had been in Jordan for long periods of time as a soldier and expected his sons to function when he went home – this only increased the pressure. Most of the time, the parents then passed on the pressure and the feeling of failure to the school. The parent meetings with them were always very aggressive, and it was difficult to keep to the framework and make agreements. The mother tried to compensate for the problems with Baran by engaging in parent work, to become a part of the school community. She succeeded well; here she could belong on a different level and establish good contact with other parents and the teachers.

In the first years of school, Baran had a sensitive, patient teacher, Ms. Weber (name changed), who took him as he was. If he could only work for ten minutes a day, she was happy about it, praised him, and otherwise did not push him. Eventually, there were also longer phases in which he could concentrate, so on some days Baran even worked quite well the whole morning.

Ms. Weber seemed to realize that behind the defensive behavior was a very nice boy, for Baran probably brought a deep, existential shame with him to school already, which caused him to behave in such a conspicuous manner. With Ms. Weber, however, he apparently felt like a full part of the class community. But then Ms. Weber went on parental leave, he got a new teacher, and on top of all that, the school was closed due to the pandemic.

Baran's new teacher, Ms. Schulz (name changed), was seconded to our school and came from another type of school, specifically a junior high school. She was not very familiar with elementary school education and fended off her insecurity and foreignness in the new system by emphasizing casualness and apparent self-confidence.

In her year-group team, she kept herself rather isolated from her colleagues in her work. She closed herself off to their tips and help and developed her own concept, which soon overtaxed the children in her class. Tasks she thought were easy were still too difficult according to the standards of the elementary school. She usually fended off advice from colleagues and the school administration with the unspoken message: "Don't worry, I'll manage. But just leave me alone!". The shame of not belonging and the struggle to survive in the new school also shaped her relationship with Baran.

Baran quickly seemed to sense that Ms. Schulz was very insecure towards him. In the early days, he again provoked during the lessons in his usual way. For him, the strenuous work of relationship-building also had to begin again from scratch. Ms. Schulz seemed hardly able to cope with Baran's attacks, yet she tried with all means and tricks to build up trust with Baran. But the successes lasted only for a short time, because Ms. Schulz was afraid that Baran might win in the end. And then Baran's mother intervened, criticizing Ms. Schulz for every little thing. She kept writing very aggressive, insulting emails. Regardless of whether Ms. Schulz made demands or went easy on Baran, everything was wrong from the mother's point of view. Ms. Schulz got into a cycle of justification, fear, and shame. To me as the head teacher, she often presented things she had done well, as if I should be constantly convincing myself that she was a good teacher. It seemed as if she wanted to hide her difficulties behind this.

The issue continued during the time the school was closed. Baran, like other children, now had lessons at home. He spent all his days with his mother, who soon felt overwhelmed with the learning situation. Baran probably developed the behavioral problems there as well, just like at school. Ms. Schulz put together a comprehensive learning plan for the children for four weeks. Since she wanted to do justice to all the children, she prepared differentiated plans. This brought her criticism from Baran's mother, who found the tasks too difficult, too much, and too demanding – because Baran also refused to do them at home. Moreover, Baran's mother found other parents whom she dragged into her discontent.

Ms. Schulz fell seriously ill during the time of the school closure and could not be reached personally for weeks – certainly a consequence of inner overload in addition to a physical disposition.

During this time, I once had a telephone conversation with Baran's mother. She called me as the head teacher because the teacher could not be reached due to illness. She had Baran diagnosed. He was diagnosed with dyslexia. To me, this diagnosis seemed like a way out of the dilemma of failing again and again. The mother wanted Baran to change classes for this reason, she would have preferred to have him repeat the class. She hoped that I would agree with her. But I refused: A partial performance deficiency is no reason to change classes, and I also thought: Escape is no way out.

One thing the mother said during this phone call stayed in my mind: "Baran feels totally lost". This statement summed up how it must feel for all involved: Both the mother, Ms. Schulz, and Baran felt "lost" in a seemingly hopeless cycle of shame defense. The mother accused the teacher of failure, while the teacher was afraid of failing and projected this back to Baran and his mother. The mother was afraid of failure towards her husband and saved herself through the diagnosis. Thus, the diagnosis of "dyslexia" could be the cause of the failure and not herself as the mother.

In order to help Baran, Ms. Schulz needed the opportunity to create distance from the situation. Only through self-reflection could she get out of the cycle of "reproach-shame-blame-justification" and meet Baran and his mother differently.

How do we move forward? My attitude as a group-analytical school head teacher is: In order to develop further, you have to stay in the existing group and endure the conflicts. Ms. Schulz, Baran, and his mother are part of our school system, and maybe the school as a large group can help them to endure the shame and to develop further.

I observed Baran during our "Respect Days". This is a project week that aims to strengthen the school community with a variety of activities. There, Baran had something to say! He was helpful and was also a leader of his small group, which had to complete a task together. He brought other children along and kept an eye on everything. He was completely accepted. And his teacher Ms. Schulz recently told me that she had finally managed to distance herself from Baran's mother by saying a clear "no". The latter wanted her to keep a daily notebook on Baran. Ms. Schulz justified her firm "no" by saying that she wanted to take Baran out of the "firing line". The relationship work with him should not be destroyed again and again by daily reporting and fear of punishment at home. Apparently, Ms. Schulz has already succeeded in getting some distance from the situation.

6 Case study 2: An example of overcome and integrated shame: Prince[1]

An elementary school colleague from another city told me about a case from her class that is a good example of how to deal constructively with feelings of shame for personal development.

The pupil Prince, also 10 years old, was in his third year of school. He came from the Congo and lived with his mother in a shelter for immigrants and refugees. Due to his skin color and immigrant history, he certainly already brought the issues of belonging, identity, and group shame to school. He had come to my colleague's class as a difficult pupil from the parallel class and was to be given a new chance here. He once introduced himself to his new teacher with the name "Deutsch". He wanted to belong! Later he insisted on the German spelling of his name, "Prinz". The teacher always accepted his name changes with interest and goodwill.

---

1 This name could not be changed because it fits the person and the case study without any alternative in terms of content.

His teacher had taken him to her heart from the very beginning. He was cheerful, friendly, and physically very strong. His laugh was striking, especially because of his widely spaced teeth. The children in the class quickly accepted him into their community. But Prince was still impulsive, so he was always getting into fights with other children.

Once a week, the class council took place in the class. The children wrote down incidents and complaints during the week and put them in the class mailbox. In the class council, the notes were then read out, discussed, and solutions to problems were sought.

At a class council meeting, Prince showed his exasperation at always being the subject of complaints. Shaking his head, he sat in his seat and spoke to himself: "Always Prince, Prince, Prince! I can't hear it anymore! It's best if I don't come at all!"

The children gave Prince honest feedback in the following conversation: "You just have to pull yourself together more! Then it will work out." Prince was able to accept this. However, when one child suggested writing down every time Prince had behaved well as reinforcement, he protested indignantly. He didn't want anything given to him! His positive behavior should be just as normal as that of the other children.

The most important point as to why Prince was able to overcome his shame is that he was basically given the feeling of belonging. This is shown in an exemplary way by the teacher and is transferred to the class atmosphere and the children's behavior towards Prince. In this way, the feeling of being fundamentally wrong does not get a chance. In class, it is possible to openly address mistakes and name disruptive behavior. As with riding a bicycle, each child gets many chances to try again and again – but limits are also set. The children are also allowed to say when they have had enough. Prince doesn't have to feel existentially ashamed, because the teacher and the children convey to him: "You don't have to become a different person, you will always remain part of our community, but you just have to try to behave differently."

If we look at the forms of shame that appear here, then in this case the focus is primarily on conformist shame and conscience shame. Apparently, Prince does not bring an existential shame issue with him to school. But Prince feels that he does not conform to the norms of the group with his behavior and he suffers from it. This shame is used in a way that promotes development, in that it is first endured by the class and the teacher and not immediately warded off. Prince expresses his desire to withdraw, to hide from the world. But the group helps him by showing him ways out. Thus, at this moment, the children largely feel emphatic shame with Prince and can empathize with him instead of additionally shaming him even more through reproaches. Existential shame can lead to a vicious circle of mutual humiliation and shaming. The way out can be for a person involved to break the circle for themselves. Self-reflection clears the way for getting back in touch with the others. This includes the painful process of realizing one's own part in the situation. If this does not succeed, all participants remain in projections. Shame can only be overcome if one remains in contact.

7 Group-analytical aspects and practical considerations

Group analysis enables those working in schools to gain confidence in the power of the group and to use it in a way that promotes development. Fundamental to the perspective of group analysis is the social nature of the human being: The individual is seen as the result of community development (Foulkes, 1992, p. 164). Consequently, individuals can also change in school groups if the conditions for this are created. This leads to the following thoughts on practical implementation for work in schools.

A group-analytical stance on the part of the head teacher can shape school events and set good group processes in motion. It can create space for teachers to self-reflect. The head teacher must provide the resources and time frame for this and also be available as a competent person. By creating a safe framework for teachers, the head teacher can in turn provide a framework for students to endure their shame effects and work through them in their class groups.

Other ways to pause and reflect on and understand critical shame situations with others are through supervision or peer counselling. However, in such professional settings, shame in front of colleagues can also be an obstacle to self-reflection. In this case, it is more advisable to use non-school settings.

In the classroom, a teacher can help the children to bear feelings of shame and to develop further through a participatory culture of discussion and a fundamentally accepting attitude. Cooperative forms of work are suitable for enabling children to experience that everyone can take over an important function for the others. They can build self-esteem (N. Green and K. Green, 2005, p. 64).

Parental work also plays a major role in overcoming shame. Basically, school management and teachers should convey to parents that they are part of the school community and make an important contribution to the children's learning success. The school must not compete with the parents as if the school were the better parental home. Then there is a danger that parents will project their shame onto the school in a scathing and accusatory way. However, if parents are given the feeling that they are important experts for their children, then there is also a chance to establish good contact in the children's interest. Parents also benefit from the feeling of self-efficacy. Thus, they can work together productively in school and festival committees and contribute to the framework within which school life takes place.

> **At a glance:**
> *In the school environment, group analysis enables* conflictual processes to be endured and observed and thus to be understood. It represents a fundamental attitude of the leaders in the system that makes them capable of acting. Group analysis creates trust in the group, which is itself the effective factor for change (H. Behr and L. Hearst, 2009, p. 112).
>
> *Group analysis gains* confirmation of its effectiveness in *the field of work in schools*. Basic concepts of group analysis can readily be applied to school situations. For example, the administrative framework is an important effective factor for the productive work of groups (H. Behr and L. Hearst, 2009, p. 52). This includes the spatial and temporal structure that the school management has to create for the class groups. Within this, the transformative group processes can take place: socialization, exchange and resonance, support and containment, and communication and mirror phenomena (U. Finger-Trescher 1991, p. 133).
>
> *The following methodological considerations are suitable for the school setting:*
> Conflict situations are in most cases not immediately solved by quick action. However, they can be better understood through a group-analytical approach. Before action comes waiting, endurance, and understanding. Often this already brings about a change before pedagogical or educational interventions take place. This does not mean that action becomes superfluous. As in the therapeutic context, the role of leadership in school is crucial to guide the class towards a productive resolution of its conflicts so that they do not end in destructiveness. It is necessary to find good middle ground between letting the group process run its course and the necessary intervention by the class teacher (H. Behr and L. Hearst, 2009, p. 115).

Bibliography

Behr, H., Hearst, L. (2009). *Gruppenanalytische Psychotherapie – Menschen begegnen sich*. (1st edition, 2009). Eschborn. Dietmar Klotz GmbH
Finger-Trescher, U. (1991). *Wirkfaktoren der Einzel- und Gruppenanalyse*. Stuttgart-Bad Cannstadt: frommann-holzboog
Foulkes, S. H. (1992). *Gruppenanalytische Psychotherapie*. München: Pfeiffer.

Green, N., Green, K. (2005). *Kooperatives Lernen im Klassenraum und im Kollegium.* (3rd edition, 2007). Seelze-Velber: Erhard Friedrich Verlag GmbH

Hilgers, M. (1996). *Scham – Gesichter eines Affekts.* (4th edition, 2013). Göttingen: Vandenhoeck & Ruprecht

Marks, S. (2007). *Scham – die tabuisierte Emotion.* (8th edition, 2019). Düsseldorf: Patmos

Schnee, M. (2013). Scham und Beschämung in der Schule. *Gestalttherapie – Forum für Gestaltperspektiven,* 1: 58–80. http://psychologische-beratung-koblenz.de/wp-content/uploads/2017/07/Scham-und-Beschämung-in-der-Schule-.pdf (last accessed January 22, 2020).

Wurmser, L. (1990). *Die Maske der Scham* (3rd edition, 1998). Heidelberg: Springer

Group-analytical Approach in Inpatient Educational Support

Tilman Sprondel

What is the use of group analysis in inpatient educational support? This question is addressed to two target groups at the same time: to social education workers, especially those who work in the field of residential youth care, and to group analysts working with young people. However, the question arises in different ways.

For social education workers: Is this an attempt to launch another (possibly ephemeral) methodological approach?

1 The view of the group

First of all, it is about something very elementary: We social education professionals should become aware of the form of living the young people are placed into in the youth care facility, i.e., the residential group. We have learned to understand each young person as part of the system of his or her family of origin, to look for individually "suitable" solutions, and to handle each case according to criteria of efficiency and transparency. We have tried – not least for reasons of justification to state authorities (payers) – to do justice to all this, and have unfortunately often forgotten in the process the organized form in which we work with the young people, namely the group. Not in a psychotherapeutic group that meets for 90 minutes at weekly intervals, but in a residential group that lives under one roof for a very large part of the day and all night. So we are talking about a *way of life,* which, for each individual member, is something qualitatively quite different from a form of *therapy.* Why has this circumstance been so much out of sight? (It was not always so.)

Some assumptions: Social pedagogy follows the pressure of social isolation. If difficulties in life and suffering are not experienced as individual failures, then the social system runs into problems of legitimacy. This also affects the youth welfare clientele and their relatives. Subjectively, on the side of the professionals there is the terror of the group, the fear of the "puer robustus sed malitiosus". Do we not see how powerfully destructive those from the margins of society can be when they band together – burning asylum seeker housing, storming the Capitol, carrying out nationwide pogroms 80 years ago, etc.?

Time and again, right-wing populists succeed in mobilizing groups of socially marginalized people against their own interests and spreading fear and terror in the majority society – and that is why such groups are scary to us, and we prefer to think of these people only as individual cases.

On the other hand, we cannot do without the group. Residential care (with a few exceptions) cannot be implemented in a meaningful way in an individual setting. This is not only because of the costs, but also for two other important reasons: First, because in the individual setting a high level of resistance can be felt that torpedoes an educational alliance. Ernst Federn describes the problem from the therapist's point of view: "When you treat an adolescent, you have to know one thing: Either they have an appointment, in which case they won't come, or if they do come, they won't talk. Or third, they want something. If you are willing to get involved in the latter, you can treat adolescents" (quoted from Becker, 1995, p. 15). And second, because already here, in the question of the setting, the power and appeal of the group unfolds: The initial agreement of the clientele is often only attainable through the prospect of living with a group of fated comrades. I have repeatedly experienced young people who came to the presentation only under noticeable pressure from the social worker, but then became so curious and "hooked" by their perception of the real existing group that they were able to engage in this step. Whenever possible, we[1] have had the initial tour of the house conducted by, or at least with, one of the residents during introductions for people who have been recommended for admission.

2   The appeal of the adolescent group

What are the causes of this attraction? One assumption is obvious: It is about the "universality of suffering", as Yalom calls it, i.e., the experience that one is not alone in the world with one's misery, but that there are fellow sufferers. This factor, which Yalom describes as particularly potent at the beginning of the group process (Yalom, 1970/1996, p. 25 f), becomes effective for young people in youth care not only when they are admitted to the facility, but as soon as they are introduced to it – thus the group process begins as early as this point. The attraction of the group is charged by another moment: Until the presentation in the youth care facility, the adolescent not only saw himself/herself as alone and quasi-unique in his/her misery (or grandiosity), but also, so to speak,

---

1   This refers to the team of the small facility for residential youth care that I managed and supported (1998–2015) (author).

fallen out of the world. The childhood world, however positively or negatively its psychological connotations, is lost, while the adult world is experienced as at least alien, if not hostile. This, of course, also includes communications with the state authority, namely the youth welfare office, which have taken place up to that point. This is an authority exercised by the adult world that these young people find themselves at the mercy of, because of their own plight, and feel increases their plight. Very few young people feel themselves to be legally entitled or negotiating partners with their own ideas and rights. In the eyes of most young people who are inexperienced in this respect, a youth care institution is not a tangible living space, but rather the content of a social threat (conveyed by parents, teachers, media, acquaintances): If you don't behave well, you'll go to an institution! For this reason, too, it is very important on the part of the facility to insist that an admission decision is not made in the interview, but only afterwards (in agreement with the young person, if necessary following longer communication).

The existence of not only an actual house with all the necessary facilities, but also of young people who already live there, often represents a turning point in the lives of young people and, above all, in their experience. One is no longer alone. This experience alone usually creates enough attraction to persuade the young people to agree to be admitted. Of course, this can also be used destructively, in the sense of "we're all no good". One young person who had already been living in the house for several months said in a group meeting, with the corners of her mouth pulled down in contempt, "We're all just talking garbage here!" More often, however, one witnesses an interested, curious, i. e., constructive processing of the experience that is the community of fate. More than once, I have experienced alliances between young people from completely different backgrounds, who would probably never have met without the common experience in the residential group. Yet they supported each other in exploring new areas of life or in coping with their respective developmental tasks, notably – and this is important – within an alliance that was not hostile to the adults but clearly excluded them, emphasizing its peer character.

At this point, it might be useful to take a look at the life-historical meaning of adolescence. "To be and to remain adolescent," according to Erdheim, "means to pass from the order of the family to the order of culture." Therefore, the "social place where adolescence" takes place is "important for coping with the problems that arise" (Erdheim, quoted in Rudnitzki, 1996, p. 363). This, mind you, applies to all adolescents. The serious background for the described attractiveness of the residential group lies precisely in the precarious life situation of the young people concerned here: They have not been kept in their respective families of origin, for whatever reason, and are therefore dependent on the residential group. Ilse Seglow said about her therapeutic work: "My main talent is to see a patient's potential, their ability to develop into a different person from the way they are. In order to do that, they have to be re-born. I always experience a re-birth with patients and find I become an alternative mother. That's my strength. My success as an analyst is that I can give patients a second chance at birth" (Seglow, cited in Rohr and Cogoy, 2020, p. 169). Even without the somewhat pathetic tone ("rebirth"), this description applies to the path of the residential group residents. The difference, however, is that they must be able to count on the support not only of one person, but of the peer group in which they live, in order to cope with their upcoming developmental tasks. This step is also obvious to them because they do not have to switch in their affection from the real to the "alternative" mother and thus commit a perceived betrayal, which would naturally be highly shameful, but have an alternative available that is neutral in this respect and combines with the charm of setting out into a new stage of development. "One withdraws love energy from parents and shifts it to the peer group" (Schröder, 2000, p. 163). This step, characteristic of adolescence, becomes imperative for the residents of the youth residential group.

Adrian[2], 15 years old, came from a distant big city on the instigation of his psychotherapist – who, I learned only years later, was also a group analyst. He arrived for the initial contact together with his mother (his father had died), and his whole posture, facial expression, and speech made it clear that he felt extremely uncomfortable and would prefer to leave immediately. At home, he used to spend his day in front of the PC; school was "dead" for him, and he left the house only to walk the dog. With some effort, I managed to persuade him to spend the night with his mother in a nearby guesthouse. Upon his return, his mother resignedly told me that he definitely did not want to come. In a process that lasted about three months, the mother and I, by means of old-fashioned letters, succeeded in persuading him to come after all. I grabbed him by his pride and his abilities and "incidentally" told him something about the group. Everything together – curiosity about the group, the realization of his own lack of prospects, the support of his mother and, last but not least, a deeply hidden love of life – finally brought about his consent. Contrary to my fears, "arriving" at school proved to be almost trouble-free. He quickly found a friend who was just as enthusiastic about computers, and as a result "LAN parties" took place in various houses, including ours (this was at the end of the 1990s). On Friday afternoons, various family station wagons drove up, a young guy and PC equipment got out of each of them, and they gathered in Adrian's

---

2   All names changed.

room (which was quite large) with up to five participants. They then spent the weekend playing PC games. The PCs heated up the room, which soon stank of sweat; food was eaten rather incidentally, and that remained so until Sunday afternoon, when all the highly satisfied participants ended the event the same way it had begun. Things went quite well at school, but the situation at home was a cause for concern. Adrian's older brother had taken up residence there in the meantime after completing his training and discontinuing his studies, and he was living similarly to the way Adrian had previously. Cooperation with parents had to be sought here. In sometimes pretty frequent telephone calls (up to three times a week), it was possible within more than a year to convince the mother that she would have to turf out this big brother if Adrian was to become something. Finally, after she had visited several times for a few days and we had been able to talk to her in person, she managed after a good year to organize a somewhat smaller apartment for herself, in which there was now "unfortunately" no more room for the big brother. This did Adrian a lot of good, and his uncertainty about whether the exclusively regressive path in life might be better disappeared. He graduated from high school, narrowly missed winning a school award, tried in vain to get into a post-secondary school, finally completed an apprenticeship successfully, and also met his future partner at our institution. Eventually, he moved into his own apartment, later with his partner, and after some time his mother followed him, moving into the neighborhood. The path "from the order of the family to the order of culture" was successfully followed, as far as possible within the framework of the residential group. Three factors were decisive: 1. the experience of the residential group, i.e., of peers with similar life difficulties and struggles; 2. the "two-track" work with the adolescent and at the same time with the mother; 3. a youth welfare office that trusted our work and let us do it, even in the case of temporary "failure" – the process lasted about four and a half years!

3   Changing perspectives among the young people

The described attractiveness of this step to switch to the residential form of the peer group goes hand in hand with the possibility that this group is regarded by its members as a rewarding place to live and no longer (only) as a forced community. The latter view seems obvious at first: The young people usually did not come to the group of their own accord, but were brought by the youth welfare office; they ultimately have no influence on the composition of the group or on the staffing; and the social attribution, in which labels such as "difficult to raise" and "depraved" still play a role, is a factor. Even more fatal is the more or less subtle pressure on professionals to stigmatize young people in development reports and in discussions about support plans, because only in this way is there a prospect of (further) assistance (= funding) being granted. However, the prerequisite for a facility to change from a place of stagnation to a place of living and development for its residents is the emergence of new ties of a professional, temporary nature (i.e., not quasi "new mother against old mother"), and this is only possible if, at the same time, there is a change of perspective among the young people themselves, a shift in self-definition from the object of the measure to the living and developing subject. In social pedagogy, the professional discussion on this point ran along the lines of shifting the focus towards everyday life as well as the living environment orientation. "The question for social education work geared towards everyday life can therefore only be whether it succeeds in using institutional and professional resources to help addressees to lead successful everyday lives and in doing so avoids the risks classically associated with modern social work, which repeatedly disavow such a goal" (Thiersch, 1986, p. 42). "Lifeworld orientation" refers, among other things, to the fact that the educators have to tie in with the subjective lifeworld of the clients in order to be able to reach them and to offer the necessary ties (i.e., not to hold them in their often-precarious living conditions). This lifeworld is already found in the residential group by every newcomer: It is, in a constructivist way, the result of construction and negotiation processes in the group as "work in progress" – or, in group-analytical terms, a component of the group matrix. This is precisely the strength of the residential group.

Katja, 15 years old, came to us in a very untypical way: The request did not come from the youth welfare office, but from the drug counseling center. The drug counseling center had been informed by the owners of a nearby trendy music bar that Katja had fled there and was living without the knowledge of her parents and the youth welfare office. The initial interview thus took place under quasi-clandestine conditions in the rooms of the drug counseling center, without parents or the youth welfare office. This staging in itself expressed Katja's enormous urge for independence and autonomy. She had escaped from the highly pathogenic milieu of her parents' home into the drug scene under dramatic circumstances and had then been placed by the youth welfare office in a special drug facility far away from her home. There, she had been persuaded by fellow residents to commit burglary and, frightened by this development, had escaped to the aforementioned bar. Subsequently, it was possible to bring together Katja, her parents, and the youth welfare office and to take in Katja, who immediately felt keen. The expectation of the youth welfare office had a highly stressful effect, with the decision taken that since Katja was so independent, a five-month stay would be sufficient. This unrealistic idea was naturally applauded by the independence fighter Katja, and we did not yet have her trust to the extent that we could have argued against it. We had to earn her trust, and the opportunity presented itself immediately. She was still of school age, but under no circumstances was she willing to attend. We went along with it, got her one practical training course after another, and gradually and subtly steered her toward an apprenticeship that matched her strong manual-creative skills. We succeeded. During the conversation at the company at the end of the second practical training session, the boss said she would offer Katja an apprenticeship, "but only if you stay at Juvita for another year." Katja immediately jumped up and left the room crying and slamming the door – the injury initially masked the affiliation. She actually stayed another three years or so, successfully completed this demanding – and rare! – apprenticeship, became entangled in relationship dramas again and again, and finally travelled the world with her journeyman's certificate. Her unwillingness to compromise and her struggle for recognition and independence left their mark on the whole group and had a particularly favorable effect on girls, who were more inclined to define themselves by their feminine "market value".

For the educators working in the institution, it is crucially important to recognize and promote this value of the group. This presupposes some professional qualities, which unfortunately threaten to fall into the background in the course of the neoliberal empowerment of social pedagogy and therefore merit some presentation space at this point. The recognition of the importance of the clients' lifeworld is compatible neither with a one-sided orientation towards the secondary virtues significant for proving oneself in the world of work nor with a dominant orientation towards the strongly individualizing "house numbers" of, for example, the ICD-10. Social pedagogues will have to insist on this in order to maintain their own professional perspective and to avoid slipping into an (even worse paid) quasi-medical auxiliary activity. We cannot succeed by *treating* clients; we can only *work with them,* which does not involve acting out, but often negotiating. This, however, gives rise to another professional requirement for social pedagogues – namely partiality on behalf of clients. Beyond the "fringe group strategies" fashionable in the 1970s (which in essence represented an abuse of the clients), partiality is a necessary quality of social pedagogy, including and especially in work with young people, and without it the necessary professional bond does not come about, since most young people have a very keen sense of it due to their vulnerability. The currently dominant orientation toward slogans such as "demand and promote" completely misses the clients' lifeworld and creates counterproductive stigmatization pressure. It is therefore very welcome, for example, that the International Society for Educational Assistance (*Internationale Gesellschaft für Erziehungshilfe,* IGfH) recently devoted an entire issue of its monthly magazine to the topic of partiality (IGfH, 2020). In conclusion, for the reasons mentioned above, the group-analytical view of educational assistance is not a possible fad, but first and foremost a return to the core of social pedagogical professionalism.

4   Group management as a team

For group analysts: In the practical, everyday implementation of socio-pedagogical and group-analytical professionalism in the youth residential group, we encounter a specific feature of this field of work, which clearly differentiates it from psychotherapeutic work. A pair or co-leadership as a standard in group work with adolescents – as recommended, for example, by the "Guidelines" of the Working Group for Group Analysis with Children and Adolescents (*Arbeitsgemeinschaft Gruppenanalyse mit Kindern und Jugendlichen* 2021, p. 52 ff.) – presents itself quite differently here. Due to the task and the resulting time structure (seven days of approx. 18 hours per week), we are not dealing with a pair of leaders here, but with an entire additional group, namely that of the educators. Each residential group needs at least four full-time staff (i.e., likely five or six people), and they are rarely on duty at the same time (and if so, then only in pairs). For the pedagogical potency and effectiveness of a (facility with a) youth residential group, the basic attitude and communication style of this group, including participants themselves, are of crucial importance. Not for nothing does Makarenko, for example, emphasize the importance of the tone of interaction and the community and quality of the educators[3]. If even just a pair of leaders in the psychotherapeutic group offers a rich field for the development of conscious and unconscious fantasies among the group (such as parents, boss and secretary, husband and mistress, etc.) (cf. Neumann and Zimmermann, 2010, p. 199), then this applies all the more with such an extensive staff. At the same time, the members of the staff group also provide a model and identification for the young people, as does the whole group, especially in its style of interaction, for the interactions of the residents. It is therefore a matter of *two intertwined groups,* between which there is a gap in maturity, age, training, and responsibility.

---

3   For example, Makarenko reports that he was offered 40 positions for educators to run his institution, each earning 15 rubles; however, he insisted on working with only 15 educators, who would each earn 80 rubles.

This has considerable consequences for the composition of the group of educators. If similar conditions apply as in co-therapy, i. e., "basic sympathy, no anticipated rejection, no doubts about the abilities of the other person" (Neumann and Zimmermann, 2010, p. 197), the gender ratio (and if possible, also the age difference) should also be roughly balanced in the team of educators in a co-educational facility. In the case of social education workers, regardless of their previous training, special care must be taken to ensure that the basic prerequisites of partiality (see above) and the associated professional curiosity are met. A fearful and rigid attitude, a (hidden) stigmatizing attitude, or a overly strong reliance on methodology (frequent forms of defensiveness) are not only counterproductive for the work of the person concerned, but can also paralyze the entire team. In pedagogical work, these are significant, demanding, and surprising topics for newcomers. Hardly any social pedagogue has any therapeutic or group-dynamic self-experience or corresponding basic knowledge. As a rule, everyone is alone as they are confronted with young people whose basic personal makeup includes a high degree of sensitivity to the weaknesses of others, basic mistrust, and manipulativeness due to previous experience that has hardly been beneficial to them. This quickly triggers fear, even in stable personalities, and inevitably leads to mistakes in the work.

5   Interlacing groups

The crucial question then becomes how this is dealt with in the team. If latent aggressions, such as competitive tendencies, are dominant, this leads to disturbed communication, which has a direct impact on the work with the young people and can quickly become dangerous. Instead of becoming a model for the young people for constructive and solidary handling of life's difficulties, the pedagogues, caught in the traps of their own defenses, then actually get caught in the maelstrom of destructive impulses brought in by the young people and act in the sense of the social unconscious, without noticing that they have become victims of a manipulative mechanism. The centrifugal forces that unfold in the process usually end up causing someone to have to leave the house, be it a resident or a staff member. Since this does not solve the problem but, speaking in terms of group analysis, merely removes one node from the network (and symbolically exposes it to extermination), the destruction can continue to work. Bion's basic assumptions ("dependence, fight-flight, pairing," quoted from Finger-Trescher, 1991, p. 109) continue to have an effect, and often they then claim yet another victim, who succumbs to the pressure, "remains on the rampage", or, as a common "skeleton in the closet", lastingly burdens the group with feelings of shame and guilt as well as hidden aggression. Due to the heavy biographical "burdens of the past" among the young members of the group, as well as the frequent lack of self-awareness and the limited psychological training among the social educationalists, such developments are not uncommon in youth welfare residential groups, with the familiar "facilities careers" a sad result of this. Therefore, one of the most important tasks of management is to create and use an atmosphere in the team meetings that is conducive to real collegial exchange (with as little competition as possible).

For in the real-life situation at the place of work, each pedagogue is usually alone. She or he encounters the young people as a *person,* not as a *professional,* which makes it necessary to build up a (temporary) bond. However, this results in a characteristic that is frightening for many pedagogues, namely the unplannable nature of the work in the sense of an input-output mechanism. Rather, "one should acquire a technique of identifying opportunities that arise or do not arise and then exploit these opportunities" (N. Luhmann, quoted in Feuling, 2017, p. 53). Otherwise, young people can be expected to feel "managed" and respond accordingly. This can take different forms, from obstruction, hostility, open disinterest, etc., to an exploitative demanding attitude: "What you do for me here is a matter of course – that's what you're paid for. If you really care about me, then be there for me in your free time, too," said one young person. Being thrown upon oneself in this way is hard to bear, especially for young, idealistic, and insecure educators. They are psychologically unprepared for it and as a result tend towards either self-exploitative behavior, sometimes to the point of burnout, or bluntness and indifference towards their clientele. Bettelheim says that "although all staff members agree on the views underlying our treatment efforts, these very views make it necessary for each individual staff member to put them into practice entirely according to his or her own personality" (Bettelheim, 1971, p. 32), and further: "They [the staff members, T.S.] must also learn to become part of a single-minded unit and, moreover, what may seem even more difficult, at the same time to preserve their own personal character. In short, they must learn to become *more* themselves, not less" (Bettelheim, 1971, p. 32; emphasis in original). Making this demanding path possible is the task of the pedagogical team and its management.

For me, an important indication that we as a team were on the right track, and therefore effective for the young people, lay in the extent of our ability to also talk about our counter-transferences and the perceived ways of connecting to the young people – or lack thereof – in our dealings with the young people during the team meetings. If necessary, we might also talk about recurring sensations of self-alienation and our own alien-like emotions as they occur with "recipients" of projective identifications. This is more difficult than it may sound: A highly effective barrier of shame and mistrust in our society, especially in the world of work, has to be overcome. But when it succeeded – and this was by no means always the case – then there was a chance for the team to get to the bottom of the "psychotic anxiety and [the] mechanisms of splitting off and projective identification" (Bion, quoted from Finger-Trescher, 1991, p. 110) that threatened to take effect here. Mostly, a feeling of ambiguity, of non-uniqueness of the gained insight (or interpretation) remained after such team discussions. But this alone represented a great advance over the standard fight-flight basic assumption of pedagogical teams, which is: "If we could only get rid of this one child, then everything would be fine" (Winnicott, 1988, p. 289). We became capable of action again and also curious, and thus for a time we were able follow the ideal path that Ogden draws for the mechanism of projective identification: "It may be that the essence of what is therapeutic for the patient lies in the therapist's ability to receive the patient's projections, utilize facets of his own more mature personality system to process the projection, and then make the digested projection available for reinternalization through the therapeutic interaction" (Ogden 1998, p. 20). This is not an easy task, but there is everything to suggest that it is as common in educational relationships as it is in psychotherapeutic ones, and that it can be managed. A functioning pedagogical team (which, in Bion's term, reaches the mode of the working group again and again) is enormously helpful and basically indispensable in this process.

6 Value of group self-structuring

This is also an essential prerequisite for the success of group self-structuring. Today's thinking in youth welfare means that the approach with individual cases and measures fails to address not only findings from relationship and bonding research, but also the socializing and personality-building value of group self-structuring, which is given no consideration in the system of "quality management". Apart from the age-related attractiveness described above, the peer group also plays a role as a training ground, as it were, for new approaches to coping with life. At first, young people get to know each other; profound conversations are held in pairs or threes, subgroups are formed for joint ventures, etc. The educators should only intervene here to regulate if it is clear that the young people have become bogged down or are trying to resolve a conflict in a destructive way (e. g., joint ventures with the goal of "Turk-slapping," etc.). We always had as few rules as possible, and even these could be negotiated if necessary. This concerned, for example, the rules for going out: On weekends, young people who were already well ensconced in the house were always permitted at night if they wished to visit the meeting places of their respective "crowd" or the like, with the condition that on their return (often at night) they should make themselves known to the educator on duty. If this worked, which was usually the case, then the boundary extension had proved successful. Moreover, the nightly excursion was freed from the odium of the boundary violation (secretly running away), and it was possible to talk openly about the experiences and their meaning; they thus became part of the group experience instead of acquiring a more or less destructive power in secret. Likewise, young people repeatedly sought to determine the limits of the educators' endurance. Above all, the question of whether it really made sense to undergo the hardships of school or training often played a role. Shrewd "lovers of ethical problems" (Makarenko), of whom there were more than a few, stylized this into the question of whether society owed young people something or could ultimately even demand something from them (given that, after all, they were so damaged). Battegay says of adolescent drug addicts: "They unconsciously have the attitude that those around them should understand everything and accept them unconditionally, however they behave. These young people expect those in authority in society to keep the gears turning, while they themselves – addicted – demand an everlasting understanding" (Battegay, 1987, p. 70). Once the matter had been discussed, it was still possible for a young person to simply stubbornly refuse. The fact that this never happened in a one-to-one constellation already made it clear that this was a group phenomenon.

For example, after a long group discussion in our office, a small scene occurred:
ANGELIKA (to the educator): You can say what you want, but I still don't feel like it and won't go to school tomorrow!
EDUCATOR (to a girl standing by): Alina, open the window!
ALINA: ???
EDUCATOR: I want to kick out Angelika.
Laughter.

It is clear to everyone that no one will be kicked out. But also that the limit of pedagogical talk has been reached. Whether Angelika will go to school tomorrow remains to be seen. The outcome remains open, and the entry of humor means the capitulation of every fantasy of omnipotence (that of the educator as well as that of the young people) and establishes the real distribution of responsibilities.

A large number of such everyday scenes constitute the effectiveness of the group, as can be seen from the fact that they are occasionally copied quasi-playfully by the young people themselves – and thus become elements of reality construction. Becoming an adult will only work if it is also pleasurable. Such steps into adulthood, into society, are often experienced as confusing, contradictory, and overwhelming, and this is where the group can help – it can withstand complexity better than the individual. However, this requires educators who are aware of this and who engage with the group and with their place "on the edge of the group".

An invaluable means of getting closer to the goal of self-discovery, self-reflection, and self-assertion for young people and employees alike is experiential education activities with the group. These do not necessarily have to be highlights such as rafting, canyoning, high mountain trekking, or similar. Practically every year we have organized a camping trip with as many residents as possible, usually on a Croatian island (distance over 1,000 km). The experience of being far away from the usual environment in a foreign country with a foreign language under rather simple conditions, but in a beautiful landscape and with attractive activities – swimming, snorkeling, stone-knocking, boating, socializing (there were also other young people), sometimes a disco in the evening, spending time together (two weeks) without the usual everyday demands – made the importance of the group more recognizable to all and likewise led to a boost in autonomy, self-reflection, and knowledge of others and of the whole group. This was true for young people as well as for adults. It had, one might say, a mentalizing effect.

David, a 15-year-old with a pronounced dissocial relationship pattern, found it difficult to fit into the group. Florian, 18, had already lived here for over two years and benefited well. He had come from the same previous facility as David and felt a responsibility to him. On the way to free time and on the way home, the two occupied the back seat on the bus and entertained the rest with original comments and sometimes extemporaneous dialogues in the style of "Waldorf and Statler" from The Muppet Show. At the campground, Florian also took David "under his wing" and went off with him again and again, armed with two hammers, to knock around on rocks somewhere nearby and uncover supposed treasures. In general, we have experienced again and again that "older" group members did a lot to facilitate the entry of those who came later.

After the return, it was regularly observed that coherence and bonds had been strengthened; the matrix had become richer and finer. The staff members who had accompanied the group were more self-confident, more respectful, and less fearful/avoidant with the young people afterwards.

In scenic understanding in the work with biographically heavily burdened adolescents, as we find them in educational assistance, it is particularly important to say goodbye to monocausal, dichotomous, or linear patterns of thinking and to allow for complexity. This means looking at things and conflicts in a dialogical way: acknowledging they can be complementary and antagonistic at the same time; seeing them as recursive – cause and effect can switch places; and finally, seeing them as hologrammatic – the whole is mirrored in one element of the group and vice versa (cf. Najmanovich and Lucano, 2012, p. 174). The group-analytical conception of the network with many nodes, of the social genesis and function of psychological structures and disorders, and of the dynamic group matrix is very congenial to these epistemological principles and helps in understanding even convoluted biographical, psychological, and social contexts.

In conclusion, for socio-pedagogical work in the context of residential youth care, group-dynamic self-awareness and group-analytical knowledge are of considerable importance. Thus, in the youth residential group, too, "providing brightness, enabling lasting adolescence, [...] can be an important function of group analysis" (Rudnitzki, 1996, p. 369). This is to be promoted.

At a glance:
In the social educational field of residential youth care groups, group analysis *enables:*
- a return to basic social educational competencies such as professional partiality and solidarity in teamwork,
- a gain in knowledge with regard to the social genesis of the clients' psychological processing problems and their effectiveness in the group network, and thus also a gain in room for maneuver,
- a broader view of the effectiveness of the group as a whole, and of the group of educators in particular.

The *gains* from group analysis in this field of work include:
- an extension of its application beyond the psychotherapeutic or supervisory field,
- potentially knowledge in looking at interlocking groups (client and educator groups),
- an expansion of effectiveness with regard to those group contexts in which a shared successful everyday life represents an essential criterion for success.

A necessary *precondition* for an adaptation of the group-analytical approach to this (as to any other) field of work is, first of all, mutual respect and recognition of the insights and standards of the respective other discipline. Thus, labels like "analy-

> tical, i. e., past-oriented" in relation to group analysis, or "un- or semi-professional" in relation to social pedagogy, are overcome.
>
> Both group analysis and social pedagogy can achieve a gain in knowledge and action in the sense of penetrating and coping with social complexity.
>
> In this sense, an expansion and deepening of joint group-analytical and social-educational work is urgently needed and desirable.

Bibliography

Arbeitsgemeinschaft Gruppenanalyse mit Kindern und Jugendlichen (Hrsg.) (2021). *Gruppenanalyse mit Kindern und Jugendlichen*. Göttingen: Vandenhoeck & Ruprecht
Battegay, R. (1987). *Die Hungerkrankheiten*. Frankfurt/M.: Fischer TB
Becker, S. (Hrsg.) (1995). *Helfen statt Heilen*. Gießen: Psychosozial
Bettelheim, B. (1971). *Liebe allein genügt nicht*. Stuttgart: Klett-Cotta
Brandes, H. (2008). *Selbstbildung in Kindergruppen*. München etc.: Reinhardt
Feuling, M. (2017). Verwahrlosung (in) der Jugendhilfe. *Kinderanalyse*, 25 (1): 42–61
Finger-Trescher, U. (1991). *Wirkfaktoren der Einzel- und Gruppenanalyse*. Stuttgart-Bad Cannstatt: Frommann-Holzboog
Foulkes, S. H. (1964). *Group Analytic Psychotherapy: Method and Principles*. London: Routledge
Internationale Gesellschaft für Erzieherische Hilfen (IGfH) (2020). *Forum Erziehungshilfen*, 26, 3
Makarenko, A. (1980). *Ein pädagogisches Poem*. Frankfurt/M.: Ullstein
Najmanovich, D., Lucano, M. (2012). Epistemología para principiantes. Buenos Aires: Era Naciente
Neumann, H., Zimmermann, S. (2010). Leitung als Paar in der analytischen Gruppentherapie. In Ch. Seidler, I. Misselwitz, S. Heyne, H. Küster (Hrsg.), *Das Spiel der Geschlechter und der Kampf der Generationen* (S. 197–202). Göttingen: Vandenhoeck & Ruprecht
Ogden, T. (1998). *Projective Identification and Psychotherapeutic Technique*. Northvale etc.: Jason Aronson
Rohr, E., Cogoy, R. (2020). "Wollt ihr einen VW-Käfer oder einen Mercedes-Benz?". *Gruppenanalyse*, 30 (2): 166–183.
Rudnitzki, G. (1996). Gruppenbilder der Adoleszenz. *Praxis der Kinderpsychologie und Kinderpsychiatrie*, 45: 362–70
Schröder, A. (2000). Fremdverstehende Zugänge und Jugendarbeit – Gruppendiskussionen mit Jugendlichen. In V. King, B. Müller: *Adoleszenz und pädagogische Praxis* (S. 157–174). Freiburg: Lambertus
Thiersch, H. (1986). *Die Erfahrung der Wirklichkeit*. Weinheim: Juventa
Winnicott, D. (1988). Residential Care as Therapy. In *The Collected Works of Donald Winnicott, vol. 9, 1969 1971*, Chapter 9. Oxford: Oxford University Press
Yalom, I. (1970/1996). *Theorie und Praxis der Gruppenpsychotherapie. Ein Lehrbuch* (4., völlig überarb. und erw. Aufl.). München: Pfeiffer

Group Analysis in Child and Adolescent Psychiatry – Experiences and Significance

Andreas Opitz

1 Psychiatry – a special place

What does this place mean for people who are in distress? What connotations does it have? It is very difficult for people to make use of help systems that are, in themselves, beset with fear, or which convey a certain stigma: madhouse, loony bin, mental hospital. Notions like forced medication, padded cells, straitjackets, or restraints come to mind and provoke fear. Furthermore, for many patients and their loved ones, this institution is often the last place that still can or must help, for example, as ordered by law. All this affects patients and impacts them psychologically, for example in their motivation and self-esteem. The matrix of the system that is psychiatry, with its current narrative as well as in terms of society, politics, but also history, affects treatment and the course it takes. My activity in the field of work with children and adolescents with specific needs began 39 years ago, so I am part of this matrix and bring this to bear in my work. In this field, I work as a social educator and a Gestalt and curative pedagogue, and since 2010 also as a group analyst. My employer is in Berlin; specifically, it is the Vivantes Netzwerk für Gesundheit GmbH.

The clinics for child and adolescent psychiatry, psychotherapy, and psychosomatics run by the Vivantes Network for Health Berlin GmbH are located at two sites: the Klinikum im Friedrichshain (KFH) and the Klinikum Neukölln (KNK). The two clinics provide psychiatric care for minors in the Berlin service regions of Mitte (Mitte, Wedding, Tiergarten), Kreuzberg-Friedrichshain, Treptow-Köpenick, and Neukölln. Sixty full inpatient units (four wards), including an optional protected intensive care unit, 52 partial inpatient treatment places (five wards), and two outpatient clinics provide treatment for all child and adolescent psychiatric disorders. At the same time, there are supra-regional care contracts for the treatment of substance abuse and dependency disorders in adolescents as well as for psychotherapy. In addition, the KNK specializes in infant psychiatry and provides outreach care to youth welfare facilities.

My area of activity is located in the Vivantes Klinikum Neukölln. There, I look after a group of children and adolescents aged between 13 and 18. At the same time, I lead an outpatient group of adolescent patients in the outpatient clinic there.

2   The day clinic group

In contrast to the inpatient setting, treatment in the day clinic takes place from 7:45 a.m. to 3:45 p.m. Afterwards, the patients return to their home environments or their care facilities. They do not have a room at the clinic and do not live together around the clock. There are eight young people who bring a wide variety of issues to the group, whereby the topics are also determined by the adolescents' ages, which range from 13 to 18. Within the group, conflicts arise, and issues get reenacted. In contrast to the stationary setting, in the day clinic there is consistency in the attending support staff. This allows for consistency in relationships, which is helpful for the work with the day clinic group.

3   The frame bears the image

Depending on the context, the question arises of the appropriate setting or framework. Among other things, the right framework, the safe framework, functions as a way to alleviate fear. There is a great fear of exclusion or dissolution among the individuals in the group. Such personal experiences are active, and the group remains unpredictable and strange. In my experience, it is important to create a stable outer framework. Wherever possible, this encompasses, on the one hand, a fixed and unchanging space, rituals, clear arrangements, and the safe and regular hosting of group activities. Continual changing of the space in which the groups are to take place and any lack of clarity in arrangements and rules very often lead to great insecurities and anxiety. Within the clinic, there is a regular assortment of groups and structured rituals, such as the weekly outlook group on Monday and the weekly review group on Friday. The weekly outlook involves each patient finding a personal goal for the coming week, which the patient then works on during the week. On Friday, at the weekly review, the patients then evaluate their goals together with the group. Each participant gives that person their own personal feedback on their weekly goal. For this purpose, a weekly skills group and another weekly social competence group are also hosted. These groups bring together emotionally unstable patients to train their perceptions and gain skills to regulate their emotions. Music therapy, communicative movement therapy, occupational therapy, sport, and the entire therapeutic milieu of nursing and educational services are further treatment tools. Schooling takes place in the in-house hospital school. Classes are held in small groups with a reduced number of students and are given by teachers who are trained in special needs.

4   The talking therapy group: "Space for inner being"

One important part of the week is the talking therapy group. This group takes place once a week and is hosted by me together with a colleague in psychology. This group is extremely important to the young people, and any cancellation or postponement of the group is met with resistance. There was one situation when I was absent due to illness and no replacement could be found. When I returned, the patients proudly informed me that they had kept the group appointment without me. There is no module or set topic for this group. The theme develops from the group and follows its own course. For many, time and again it is amazing and wonderful that their own, sometimes very personal, issues thus are the issue of the group and often of everyone in it. Their own difficult issues such as experiences of violence, fears, exclusion, conflicts over detachment, episodes of depression, etc., are reenacted and processed through the group. With the resulting feeling of resonance through the others and the various facets in which the individuals find themselves that are then gathered, problems are verbalized, and the young people often have a positive group experience for the first time.

This group supports the young people during the daily routine in the clinic and has an impact. The joint leadership with the psychologist, who also manages individual cases, proves to be useful. Here, too, it is important to me that there is continuity in the staffing.

5   What does the group tell us?

In the everyday work of group analysis, it is always fascinating to see how the individual patients' issues present themselves in a group topic. If one is open to seeing this issue with the group and giving it a name, then all those involved have the chance to recognize what is essential and to work on it together, as well as in individual therapy. The group topic emerges from the personal matrix of each individual patient, the people caring for them, and also the various institutions. Such issues might be the desire for autonomy, fears, anger, the desire for relationships, sexuality, splitting, or competition.

If you deal with these arising group issues openly and directly, there is generally a response and the sense that the group feels heard and taken seriously. In addition, it can show you why the group mood "suddenly" changes, or specific issues, such as bullying, suddenly become topical in the group.

6   The team as a mirror of the group/the group as a mirror of the team

In my experience, one strongly influential factor in work with children and adolescents is the behavior and existing dynamics within the care team. Unspoken conflicts in the team, inhibited aggressions, are reflected in the group. These suddenly arise within the patient group, which was so harmonious before. I have also seen how long-term illness among staff members in the group has triggered behaviors similar to those of children whose parents are separating. Issues of guilt and regressive behaviors increase, as do somatizing behaviors. Changes in the care team, such as a colleague's pregnancy, give rise to huge insecurities and anxieties, even though this is not officially known in the group yet. The group's fears about dissolution are activated. Similarly, the issues of the group are often transferred to the care team. A good example of this is the increasing divisions and communication problems within the team when it is caring for a group with several borderline patients. For me, it is very helpful to keep sight of the dynamics within the team and those of the patient group together. This really helps me to better understand processes and often saves me from having to chase after dynamics.

7   Leading and accompanying

In the day-to-day work with the group, I often see how important it is to question myself and to check how I am doing with each individual patient. How do I feel in their presence? When do I get annoyed or feel strong empathy or indifference?

The feelings change, just as the feelings of the patient group towards me change according to the situation. I find it very helpful to constantly situate myself in order to be authentic. I have seen how authenticity is appreciated by patients. Otherwise, there is soon a sense that this is not about a relationship, and the children and adolescents experience distance and defensiveness, as they so often do. It is astonishing how authenticity and transparency create resonance or enable a healthy culture of debate with the leaders.

During the group session, I generally take a back seat and allow the group to work. For me, it is important to intervene when there are destructive situations or the individual or the group needs to be protected. For the team, it is helpful to have supervision and, wherever possible, to establish a framework for appreciative exchange about individual patients within a specific protected setting. The main focus here should be on transference phenomena and nascent feelings. This interaction and a subsequent brainstorming session expand the scope for dealing with patients and are helpful for group leaders. In the clinic where I work, we use the medium of "in team" in this context, in which we meet regularly to talk about individual patients.

8   Leadership and transferences

Both in everyday group work and in the analytical discussion groups, I offer myself either alone or together with colleagues as a vessel for transference. This happens constantly and with different content. It is often very exciting and sometimes also tiring. Depending on the setting and the topic, you see many facets of a shattered mirror and are often confronted with patients' intense feelings. However, time and again it is astonishing how a transference situation can be worked through with and by the group when it is shared within it. The result is often very surprising and is internalized by the patients because it was worked out by them with the support of the leadership. Having a pair of group leaders expands the scope for transference for patients. Group fantasies about the leading pair's relationship with each other, desires of splitting and regression within the group can be reenacted and then worked on, among other things.

9   The group and sexuality

Dealing with the issue of sexuality in the patient group is challenging. With their frequently unfiltered or transgressive behavior, the young patients provoke the treatment team's own *(often)* conscious and also unconscious issues.

Their own taboo boundaries, defense mechanisms, or even massive insecurity in dealing with this topic are activated. In the group matrix, traumatizing, transgressive experiences of libidinous desires, questions about sexual prefer-ence, and much more accumulate. All this is shameful and leads to insecurity and anxiety. As a leader or a leading pair, you are part of the group and the dynamics. Here, too, I see a need to deal with this topic not only through pedagogical approaches. Rather, it is helpful to become aware of your own reactions and attitudes on this issue in dealing with the patients. If this happens, then the relationship with the group changes. Experience has shown that willingness among group leaders and also the entire team to address this sensitive topic in an open and approachable way has a stabilizing, reassuring effect on the group. This eliminates the often moralizing and punitive taboo-imposing attitude of society, e. g., that of the parents. For many patients, this is thus the first time in their lives that they experience a positive relationship with adults when dealing with the topic.

It is important to remain alert, since in the area of sexuality in particular, situations individual patients have experienced personally are reenacted. These will frequently be abuse, experiences of violence and humiliation, promiscuity, etc. Physical boundaries may be crossed or patients may unconsciously offer themselves as available victims in the context of reenactment. It is therefore important to notice the signs of the group and to pay attention to one's own feelings of transference and counter-transference in order to prevent the destructive retraumatizing of individual patients and to protect the group. In the context of group therapy, it is possible to face this issue in a limited way, as there is a need to pay attention and decide when it is better to discuss issues in individual therapy in order to protect individual patients. The clinic's toolkit principle is very helpful in this regard. In consultation with colleagues, there is also the possibility to work on topics, for example, in non-verbal therapies.

10 Chocolate makes you happy

I would like to present to you a case vignette. This is a record of memories from a group analysis session with a group of adolescents that I experienced some years ago in an inpatient setting. The names of the patients have been changed.

THEO, 18 years old: social phobia and depression; Kai, 16 years old: depression and trauma; Jörg, 17 years old: self-injurious behavior and depression; Bernd, 19 years old: somatization disorder.

BERND comes into the group room with a packet of chocolate candies. Kai sits down; he also has a candy in his hand and pops it in his mouth. Theo and Jörg take their seats in the circle. Kai shows the therapist his hand, which is shaking. The therapist welcomes the group. Bernd pops a piece of chocolate candy into his mouth and puts the packet away. (Silence.) The therapist tells the group he has noticed that two participants are eating chocolate candy.

THEO: "Well, Mr. Opitz, you do know that it is scientifically proven that chocolate makes you happy."

BERND: "There's never going to be enough chocolate for that; and it wouldn't stay down anyway. It's so fricking boring here, I can hardly stand it anymore."

JÖRG: "I don't think it's that bad; sometimes it just depends on you whether it's boring or not."

BERND: "Try being here for four months, then we'll talk about it."

The therapist addresses Kai's silence: "Kai, before the group started, you showed me your hand. Do you want to share something?"

KAI: "I'm not feeling very good. The weekend was OK, but then something happened that makes me furious. But I don't want to talk about it."

The others turn their attention to Kai.

KAI: "I'm so fed up of talking about everything all the time; today I just feel like letting it all eat into me."

JÖRG to Kai: "Do we have anything to do with your stress?"

KAI: "No, I'm just mad and angry at myself."

BERND: "I feel like that too. I can't quit the gambling, even though things were working out so well. But it's also fun! But then afterwards I feel bad about it again and my belly starts aching again."

JÖRG: "And then it's back dumped on the porcelain."

THEO, somewhat annoyed with Jörg: "Yes, yes, Mr. Sensible."

KAI: "I don't think he's that sensible."

JÖRG: "I couldn't help it that I got one in the face, it wasn't my fault *(he has a black eye)*. But I can also do things differently, I just don't trust myself to most of the time."

BERND: "I'm not afraid, but I can't put words to it when something's bugging me and then I my belly plays up again. Stupid trickery."

THEO: "You can't argue with my father. But when I hack his password, that makes me happy!" *(His father is an administrator.)*

The mood in the group becomes livelier.

BERND: "Man, I'm 19 years old and I can't even tell my mom when she's bugging me."

JÖRG: "But sometimes you have to look at yourself, too, and what you're contributing to the situation."

KAI, loudly: "But at some point enough is enough, Jörg."

Silence.

THERAPIST: "I notice that you've got an active discussion going. I was just wondering, what's the topic today?"

THEO asks Kai: "Is your hand still shaking?"
KAI: "No, it's better now."
BERND: "The frustration has to come out somewhere; you need an outlet somehow. I'm tired of stomach aches and all that crap."
JÖRG, thoughtfully: "I think, if you guys knew the other side to me, you wouldn't like me so much."
THEO: "I can well imagine."
KAI to Bernd: "Have you got another candy?"
BERND, loudly: "You have to do something good for yourself sometimes."
THEO to everyone: "And even if it's only chocolate."

The group, which I brought to life again through this session protocol, already knew each other very well due to a longer common inpatient treatment time. I chose this description of the group session because it illustrates how much the potential and abilities of each individual group member can be leveraged through the group analysis setting. I find my role as leader (conductor) clearly discernible here. It is hardly necessary to intervene, as the orchestra (group) plays as one and each instrument can be heard and finds its place. It's about self-support, attention, and care. Physical symptoms arise and are named. Behavioral patterns are reenacted. Traumatic and stressful situations are discussed. These shameful topics can be aired without the need for fear of exclusion or judgement, topics such as anger, the desire for autonomy, fear, and shame. Reflections from the other group members make it possible to recognize one's own patterns or to discover new things about oneself. The feeling of resonance carries the group and enables them to find the courage to open up new spaces. Each group chooses its own pace. Often, you have to be patient, but over time, you discover how valuable it is to allow topics to evolve in the group and work through them that way. Sometimes, you don't initially understand what is going on within a group, and you might be frustrated or perplexed. This feeling often reflects the feeling of the group, but if you recognize this, you can work with it. Trust your group.

11 The group – a boiling kettle

"Mr. Opitz, I think the group is like a kettle. At first nothing happens for a while, and then at some point it gets hot, and then it really starts to boil." This quote came from a former patient, who for some time refused to participate in the group therapy. It took her a long time to gain trust in it. At some point, the other group participants opened up the space to her and brought her issue to the group by proxy. Afterwards, things became very dynamic for her in the group, and she made tremendous progress for herself within it.

I think that becomes *(beautifully)* visible in the case vignette. Careful sharing of experiences with each other in the day-to-day group work, recounting difficult situations experienced outside the group, empathy and sharing, and recognizing new, positive things together – all that is very effective. This is the experience I have had and continue to have in the clinical group analysis work.

12   Group analysis and psychiatry

Working in child and adolescent psychiatry, I believe, is becoming ever harder in its complexity. The multi-professional work of therapists and educators of different shared orientations, and the interaction and exchange of individual and group therapies provide a wide and significant range of possibilities to help patients. The same goes for networking with other support systems, such as the youth welfare office. There too, the institutions work in groups and former patients from child and adolescent psychiatry contribute positive experiences from the clinic group. I find there is great appreciation for group therapy and recognition of the effectiveness of this method.

There is an ever-greater number of well-trained group therapists. The proportion of group training within specialist training programs is likewise increasing. This gives us reason to hope. Have fun with your group!

13   Some thoughts in conclusion

In my experience, group analysis work in the clinical area of child and adolescent psychiatry enables an opening and expansion of the patient's space for thought and experience. The shared experience of being together and getting to know the strengths and weaknesses of the individual group members and identifying with the experiences of the others strengthens individuality and the development of ego strength and generates a sense of trust that most patients have otherwise lost. Restoring the ability to communicate brings health. Such experiences are taken on board by the individuals and remain with them.

The group analysis approach, discovering issues that arise in the group and working with them, is different to many other forms of therapy and is often more unsettling for many therapists than working with modules, for example.

Nevertheless, I am confident because I am seeing that this method is gaining recognition and significance ever more in the clinical area, too.

At the same time, I find it significant and important that people wanting to work with groups are well prepared for it. The dynamics in groups are complex and are often hard to understand and sometimes even overwhelming. Confidence in leading such groups grows with experience and with seeing how exciting and enriching group analytic work can be.

At a glance:

In child and adolescent psychiatry, *group analysis enables:*
- an opening and expansion of the patient's space for thought and experience,
- the experience of being together and getting to know the strengths and weaknesses of the individual group members, as well as identifying with the experiences of the others,
- a strengthening of individuality and development of the patient's own ego strength.

In the psychiatric context, *group analysis gains* confirmation of its effectiveness through the visible and tangible positive development among patients in the overall group context outside of group therapy. The following methodological considerations are offered for the field of work depending on the age structure and context:
- use of media such as music or games,
- joint parent/caregiver groups.

Membership of a Range of Identities

What's it Like to Arrive in Germany? Experiences in Group Analyses with Unaccompanied Refugee Minors

Gerhild Ohrnberger

1   Introduction

I would like in this article to describe and reflect upon my work with group analysis with unaccompanied refugee minors (URMs) from Afghanistan. Since the spring of 2012, I have been leading therapy groups with Afghan refugees as a group analyst, together with B.[1] as interpreter, social counselor, and cultural mediator. Only young men are involved, since young women from Afghanistan almost never flee the country.

The group discussions take place in the participants' native language, so in Dari, Pashto, Farsi, and Urdu. This allows the young people to express themselves more authentically and freely. Since I am informed only secondarily through the interpreter, for me the emotional undertones of the discussion come to the fore. As they resonate within me, the emotional aspect is reflected more clearly than in what is said, as is, I assume, the unspoken intonation. I sense this, and through me it influences my actions. My observations focus on the effects of this unusual, "language-free" relationship on the setting, whereby I take my cue from the tenet that "unconscious to unconscious is understood without further ado".

About me: I have been working in a child and adolescent psychiatric practice in Frankfurt since 2001. It was in this practice that I began my expedition into the field of group analysis work with children and adolescents – I host group analysis sessions with children and adolescents both by myself and within the team. It is thanks to this that I have been able to participate in the GaKiJu (Working Group for Group Analysis with Children and Adolescents) since 2010.

From my own life history, I feel a connection with the group of refugees. My grandparents came from Haifa, in what was then Palestine, and my mother was also born there. As a child, I grew up with the Arabic language as well as with

---

1   For data protection, I am anonymizing the names of all those mentioned in the text by using capital letters in place of names.

Arabic food and everyday Arabic customs. I have retained an affection for the oriental culture and a familiarity with it all my life.

2   Child and adolescent psychiatric practice as initiator of the refugee group

One key area of the practice was and remains child and adolescent psychiatric and psychotherapeutic treatment for URMs from Afghanistan. B., with whom I lead the refugee group, has long been associated with it as an interpreter and cultural intermediary.

It was in spring 2012 that the idea was first mooted to work with URMs in a group. When I asked the psychiatrist about her reasons, she said: "My main motivation was the idea of equity of care. For years, we had been receiving a flood of enquiries about unaccompanied refugee minors from institutions and from the city health department, asking us about treating (questionably) traumatized refugees, so I was convinced that group therapy would mean a sense of home and promote identity and belonging. The loneliness of most refugees, the shared knowledge of the past, what it means to have been on an inflatable boat without knowing how to swim – I felt it all fitted better in a group than in individual therapies."

I was excited about the idea of a group for refugees, but also uncertain; I was excited, because I think a group like this is so meaningful in socio-political terms and because it was something new to try, a challenge to overcome; uncertain, because it was a journey into the unknown. An all-male, native-speaking youth group was planned, which B. and I were to lead together as a team. I was apprehensive about what it would be like to suddenly lead a group together with someone I didn't know and who had no experience of group analysis. Having only male participants wasn't a problem for me, but a group conducted exclusively in a foreign language? Who would I be within it? What role would I play? How foreign and superfluous would I feel? How would I establish a connection with the young people and find my place in the group? These questions and feelings seemed entirely to be countertransference reactions in advance. The experiment worked, and the group has now been running continuously since March 2012. It has become established and sought-after in the network of institutions for URMs. In 2015, for example, B. and I were hosting three refugee groups in the practice at the same time, each with eight or nine participants. The native-language aspect of the group marks it out as unique.

3   The group leadership in the team

B. is a somewhat older man. He radiates the warmth and dignity of his culture of origin. He came to Frankfurt as a political refugee from Kabul, Afghanistan, in 1983. He studied and built a livelihood for himself as a self-employed court interpreter and social counselor with a focus on cultural mediation for Afghan refugees. He is well-established in the institutions of the Rhine-Main region dealing with URMs (court, youth welfare offices, live-in facilities). He has made a name for himself in these fields.

B. brings with him group experience from his cooperation with FATRA (Frankfurt Working Group on Trauma and Exile) and from the various institutions. There, he is repeatedly asked to host pedagogical group discussions in which he explains to the young people in a nuanced way about socio-cultural coexistence in Germany and the expectations that are placed on them. B. recalls the foundation of our refugee group thus:

> "I was not familiar with group analysis as a method, but I was keen because I saw in the group a great opportunity for the 'children'. I am often called upon by the institutions to calm a conflict that has escalated or even a state of emergency. Here, a lot of the young people's questions are not answered sufficiently and simply persist. Now, with group meetings taking place continuously and that are also more intensive, it will probably be more about meeting and exchanging ideas personally. Because of my own history of flight and migration, I always have immediate access to the experiences of the refugees, can put myself in their shoes, and I've seen that as my contribution to the group discussions and as part of making them successful."

The theme – understanding and coping with the external reality – is present in the matrix of the group through B. as the group leader.

4   How do the refugees join the group?

The institutions responsible for the refugees register them with the practice for psychiatric evaluation and treatment. Mostly, they suffer from terrible sleep disorders, thoughts that forever circle, and have severe nightmares. In everyday life, that leads to somatic consequences such as persistent headaches, difficulty concentrating, and loss of appetite. These stress factors very often manifest themselves in behavioral problems such as emotional outbursts or depressive withdrawal. Again and again, the young men describe flashbacks and dissociative states, and occasionally also suicidal thoughts.

The psychiatrist compiles the initial case history with B. acting as interpreter, diagnoses the adolescents, and prescribes them medication – almost always a sleep-initiating agent, but the administration of antidepressants is not uncommon either. The primary diagnoses are adjustment disorders, nightmares, non-organic sleep disorders, depressive episodes, PTSD – all ICD-10 diagnoses.

The doctor recommends those young people for whom she feels there are due medical grounds attend the group. For me as group leader, that means that the participants are assigned to me. Generally, the first time I meet them is in the group. If, during the course of the group process, it emerges that someone is not suitable for the group, then it is my responsibility to terminate their participation. But in all these years, I have never needed to do so.

With B., it is different. He is familiar with the group participants from the first interviews with the psychiatrist, or perhaps from the institutions, from the youth welfare office, or similar.

In the scenic elements that characterize my situation with the group of refugees (being assigned to a socially alien situation, having to get to grips with it, facing the Foreign individually in their togetherness) my experience is like that of the refugees in reverse. Is there perhaps a chance for them to thus unconsciously identify with me?

B. has a real-life view of our participants:

> "Young Afghans are instructed to flee by their families, generally after the Taliban assassinates the head of the family and then threatens that the sons are next. Families often have to assume heavy debt in order to pay the traffickers. The journey, both on land and sea, is life-threatening. It is not unusual for it to take years for the refugees to get to Germany. Along the way, inhumane violence at the hands of smugglers, border guards, and police is simply the norm, and it is with these experiences that the young people arrive in Germany. And it's still the case that in Afghanistan people have ideas that Germany is some kind of paradise. The young people arrive with these kinds of fantasies and are shocked by what they find."

In the group, therefore, we meet young people who are marked by the deaths of their fathers and the fear for their own lives, who are depressed because their mothers and siblings have been left behind in terrible circumstances, who are damaged by the brutality and humiliation experienced while fleeing, and who are ultimately disillusioned by their place of hope, Germany, and find themselves all alone here. How is that manifested in the group?

5 The importance of the practice as a framework for the group and its process

The initial medical consultation is not only used for diagnosis, medication, and as a prerequisite for group participation, but in the initial presentation the refugees confide in the psychiatrist the events and problems that caused them to flee. They find that their history and hardships are in good hands with the psychiatrist, and so she remains an important, constant, and protective authority in the background for the group participants. They can, if necessary, turn to her for a personal discussion through the medium of an interpreter. I generally learn about their dramatic individual fates second-hand. Only occasionally do the young people bring their reasons for fleeing directly to the group. However, due to my role in the practice and through B., they enter the group's matrix unspoken.

Being a patient in the practice has another, eminent meaning for the refugees. In general, the psychiatric aspect in connection with the group therapy prevents their asylum application from being rejected and them being deported. The reason for this is that Afghanistan does not have adequate medical and psychotherapeutic treatment for psychiatric disorders. The opinions or psychiatric reports from the doctor protect the young people from the terms of their asylum status, which massively frighten and destabilize them. Only through this support can the group setting form the protected space in which the basic rule can work. Together, the framework and the setting provide a kind of bulwark. To the obvious question of whether this protective function performed by the practice counteracts the success of the group's treatment, B. and I would say no; on the contrary, the group proves to be a springboard for better integration into the German reality.

I am concerned about another contradiction: Young people typically revolt in a way that is not unfamiliar to us group analysts and which is exercised by rebelling against the setting, for example by determining "for oneself" whether to come to the session or stay away. Yet for the refugees, that would entail a threat to their connection to the practice, which itself guarantees their stay. Since they are financially unable to pay cancellation fees, they are threatened with the loss of their place in the group if their rate of absence is too high.

The issue of how young people deal with punctuality and commitment is a thorny one. I find it to be a problem that cannot really be solved, like a multi-layered skein of aspirations and emotions that I cannot quite grasp, and which entraps me. In the following, I examine this in more detail, helped here by a tenet of psychoanalysis: "The crucial conflicts play out on the margins."

6 How is the setting designed?

At an initial meeting about the group project in March 2012, B. and I agreed on the classic group analysis setting. The group is semi-open and fixed according to time and place. We arrange the chairs in a circle and sit and talk with each other for 90 minutes at fortnightly intervals. The vacation times are adapted to the school vacations, and during Ramadan the group is suspended. The target number of participants is a minimum of four and a maximum of eight young people. Together with B. and myself as the leaders, that makes ten people.

In reality, the number of participants is actually rarely consistent. Time and again, situations arise in which we are unexpectedly left with just two or three young people in the group due to external reasons – young people are transferred or change their place of residence for personal reasons, they have such severe mental breakdowns that they have to be temporarily admitted to a psychiatric ward for inpatient treatment, or they simply break off their participation in the group and go missing. The same applies to unexpected surges in numbers to more than eight because the demand is there.

We agreed to base the group discussion on the basic rules of group analysis – free communication, voluntary and binding participation, confidentiality and secrecy, abstinence. The roles that would take shape through the native-language communication in the group were something of which neither of us had any preconceptions or any experience. Given his dual role of interpreting the group discussion (indeed, not just for me but also sometimes among the young people themselves, who come from different ethnic groups within Afghanistan) and leading the group discussion with me at the same time, it stands to reason that B. could not interpret simultaneously. We were both entering uncharted territory.

Looking back on the years of group work with URMs, I can see that the setting has taken shape and morphed of its own accord. This was already evident with the very first meeting in March 2012.

7   Case portrait from the first group session

I recorded the initial scene that took place in March 2012 as follows:

"Three young people are registered. I don't know any of them, and I still don't really know B. yet either. Then only one of the three, N., turns up with B., and they are 20 minutes late. B. apologizes, saying that N. was hungry, and they just had to grab a bite to eat. Only later do I learn that B. is looking after N. as part of the youth welfare measures. I am currently frustrated by the contradiction between this need, presented as an absolute necessity, and my stance on enforcing the time frame of the group. Unsure what to do, I say nothing. I mull the matter over: Should the same rules apply to this unusual group as to my other youth groups? I don't reach any conclusion but rather decide to wait and see.

In the session, all three of us then carefully sound each other out by clarifying questions: What is a therapy group? What rules apply? What do they mean? Who are we? That is, N. and I need to get to know each other."

From today's perspective, I would interpret this initial scene thus: Is N. finding his way into the group? Does he recognize it as a space of possibility in which his hunger is symbolically satisfied? And applied to his real-life situation: Does Germany represent a chance for him to survive?

This short scene already encapsulates all the elements that will affect the setting and the group process in future. These are: provision of refreshments, the problem of commitment and punctuality (with which I have been constantly struggling since the first session), communication in the native language, and the manifold forms of personal contact B. has with the individual young people outside the group, all of which influence our roles within the group.

8   What are the goals associated with group therapy for URMs?

On the institutional side, there is the classic idea that therapy serves to enable people to come to terms with the past. The institutions associate this with overcoming the physical and psychological effects of the events that led to the URMs' flight and the experiences they made while fleeing and believe the conflicts in the day-to-day coexistence within the institutions are a result of these. It is true that the young people are psychologically injured by the violence they have suffered and that they have endured traumatic experiences. However, first and foremost what is true is that coming to terms with these terrible experiences is not only impossible, but even harmful while the refugees are not yet fully recognized and do not yet have solid ground under their feet.

On the psychiatrist's side, for B. and me the focus is on coping with and shaping the young people's manifest present and future. In other words, the group is geared to progression, not regression; it should be a place of growth, where support with the necessary adaptations serves to strengthen the ego. As B. emphasizes: "The group discussions help to reduce participants' anxiety and to calm them down about what is happening and what could happen to them in Germany."

From the perspective of the factors at large in group analysis, the group is a forum in which the refugees can talk about what it is like to be in Germany, what it does to them, how they find their way. It is also a development space for themselves where they can ask "Who am I as an Afghan in Germany and who do I want to be, who do I want to become?" and thus entails the typical aspects of identity formation. Other impacting factors are socialization and mutual help, including the correction of false perceptions, assumptions, and ideas, as well as shaping visions for the future.

For me, over time, the group as a whole has increasingly become a transitional space between the lives of the young people in Afghanistan and here in Germany, a space in which they share and bear together the experiences of the bitter parting and the arduous arrival, of fear and hope, of the loss of their previous way of life, of homesickness, of longing for their mothers.

9 The setting, its design, dynamics, and effect

9.1 Providing oral refreshments

The administration of the group is in my hands. Because I want to invite the refugees to the group, I always provide food and drinks. Initially, I provided Indian pastries in the hope that they would remind the young people of home. These were soon replaced by the almonds and cookies the Afghans love; water was rejected in favor of green tea, and I learned how it is prepared in Afghanistan. This welcoming gesture has been well-received and has now become something of a ritual over the years. The group often begins thus: While I take care of the refreshments, the men are already chatting. Despite all the cliches of gender roles, I find these scenes to be quite homely. I am presumably mimicking the pattern of an Afghan family, and that triggers a sense of ease among the young people without them saying so. To state this would be to destroy it –

that's my feeling. Feeding the refugees is essential for me – I can't imagine not doing so. It would seem to me as if I were cold-heartedly abandoning them to their misery; similar to the Croatian border guards, with whom some of our participants had the experience of being driven back across the Serbian border with rifle butt blows or into the ice-cold border river. Do my actions therefore banish their unbearable fears of annihilation? Does it contain them?

It becomes a real feast when B. brings his favorite Afghan dishes from home, Ih happens from time to time. Without exception, everyone eats heartily, laughs, and is happy. Home is in the space, the home-cooked food, the pleasure of being in a large family. The provision of food and drink symbolizes the family; through the food, the family is transferred onto the group, which becomes a substitute family. B. and I are cast as substitute parents.

9.2 Punctuality and commitment

For us as group analysts, punctuality and commitment are essential. They are fundamental for the formation of the group, and they guarantee that there is an inside and an outside to the group and that a safe space can form in which open communication and the group process can take shape. Accordingly, the time frame is discussed with each of the refugee group participants at their first group meeting. However, in reality when the group starts a lot of chairs are still empty and only fill gradually or not at all. This has been the case in a large number of the sessions for nine years, and it has troubled and plagued me the whole time, but my attempts to change it have all failed so far. The first paragraphs of my minutes from a group session in 2013 give an insight into the range of feelings I had on this matter, which remain comparable today:

"As always, at the start I am agitated and anxious about whether the young people will show up. At the same time, I'm annoyed because I reminded them by text message the day before. The institutions were also notified. I get the feeling that I'm calling out in vain, and no one is reacting.

After the first 10 to 20 minutes, A., S., and W. are there, while T. and the new guy are still missing.

B. is entirely unbothered by the delays; he remains relaxed and optimistic and tries to calm me down, assuring me they will turn up.

After half an hour T. arrives – alone, and he's in a bad mood. At Frankfurt Central Station, I., the new guy, wasn't fast enough, so T. just left him behind. I'm worried that I. is now just wandering around Frankfurt by himself."

In the minutes, I record my constant agitation across sessions: "The young Afghans come from somewhere that for me is unknown, unfathomable. They emerge and disappear again; it seems to me as if they could constantly be lost, relationships severed, without my knowing or ever discovering the reasons. Is something of their flight from their homeland being reenacted here? Is my fear and tension that of the refugees themselves? Or are my fears reflecting the young people's fear of losing their parents, their uncertainty of ever seeing them again?"

My discussions with B. about the lack of punctuality and the many unexcused absences of our participants always come to the same conclusion and never really resolve anything. B. emphasizes the current reality for the young people, noting how many of them have to travel a long way by bus and train to get to the group, how the public transport is often delayed, how they are likely to get lost in the city. They are also unfamiliar with German punctuality, he says, and they first need to learn it. But we also shouldn't blame them, he argues, irrespective of whether they prefer to do something else or are just being lazy; they always come back, after all.

B. is unable to understand my concern about the group disintegrating; he can't relate to my frustration that the group is not a space of its own but more like a passageway with lots of open doors. I am alone in my anxiety and agitation, which even I am unable to quite get to the bottom of. It drives me to take action. Just a short time after the refugee group started as a project, I begin to email the institutions regularly to draw their attention to the group appointment again each time, and I'm getting in the habit of sending a text message to the young people the day before the group as well. B. agrees that both are good methods. Yet they don't resolve the conflict.

I continue to address the lack of punctuality and reliability in the group, ask them in an approachable way what they are intending by it, whether there is a conflict with or in the group for them, whether they are somehow voting with their feet and no longer wish to attend. Always, the response is that the group is important to them. Then I get the same explanations that B. has already outlined, supplemented with "The supervisor didn't say anything", "I don't have any credit on my phone", "I had a headache". But I cannot shake the impression that the young people's explanations are rationalizations, that is, defenses – but from what? If there is greater incrimination in my voice when I speak to the young people, they react guiltily and withdraw from the conversation. The problem doesn't change. I am starting to doubt myself: Are my feelings coming from within me? Am I reacting out of my own unconscious and unresolved conflict?

I opt for a supervision session with a psychoanalyst and group analyst. He defines the matrix of the group as a coexistence and interconnection of external and internal reality. That means the matrix comprises two areas: one being that of pedagogical and social work, and the other that of group therapy. With regard to the two main topics of the group, recognition and independence, the processing of the manifest topics of asylum law, asylum procedure and its various processes, and the clarification of the rules, competencies, and responsibilities in the refugees' day-to-day lives falls within the B.'s ambit. The dimension of what these two topics trigger in the young people, how their adaptation to the German reality affects them emotionally, and how this process is reflected in them and changes them are all part of the domain of therapy, and that is what I am responsible for. I should understand their unpunctuality and unreliability, as well as my response, as indications of how the problems of recognition and independence are reflected in the young Afghans.

With this structure in mind, I now interpret my response thus: The ethnically homogeneous group of young Afghans with B. as their "uncle" (this is how they manifestly adapt him) seems to them like a little piece of home. This activates their memories of Afghanistan. When the young people in the group talk about their villages and their lives there, they seem happy, and it often then becomes so intense that I can almost feel the cool, clear mountain air, the wind; I can almost hear the far-reaching calls and the rushing of the water. Their longing for home, however, also brings to the fore the pain of loss, the unbearable experiences of violence both in Afghanistan and during their escape from it, the fears and uncertainty about their own future and that of their families. I understand my fears of loss and disintegration concerning the group as projective identification with the fears of the young people, their unpunctuality and unreliability as avoidance, that is, defense against these fears.

Another aspect of the young men's avoidance behavior also suggests itself to me. In a figurative sense, I represent the host society. B. represents the homeland and acts as the intermediary between the society of origin and the host society. I, by contrast, am insisting that they conform. This seems rigid and threatening, particularly since the "right to remain" in the group is preconsciously associated with the right to remain in Germany.

The pressure to conform that I exert puts the young Afghans in a dilemma. It calls them into question in a cultural sense. On that point, here is one episode relating to the matter of commitment: When I start probing as to why S. had not come to the group the last time, he told me that he had wanted to come but had met an Afghan friend on the way to Frankfurt who had asked him to go with him. He then asked the friend: "I have an appointment, so you tell me where I should go – to the group or with you?" The friend decided he should go with him. B. confirmed that this delegation of the decision in the event of a conflict is a form of courtesy for Afghans. This enables one to avoid having to dishonor the person one is immediately dealing with by saying 'no' and thereby losing face oneself. The group has taught me what it means to lose face in the Orient. It seems to have the same quality as a loss of identity does for us. Do my fears of disintegration reflect something of the threat to the identity of the participants?

The conflict has yet another aspect. Here, insisting on one's own identity and rebelling against the demands of adaptation (something, incidentally, which is typical of young people) go hand in hand with an existential threat. Because by refusing to adapt, the young people jeopardize their place in the practice, which is, however, what secures them the right to remain. From this point of view, the group becomes a place of negative dependence.

In one of the last group sessions, the dilemma took shape. Here I reproduce the relevant passage from my minutes of this group meeting.

"All participants except one arrive one after another. B. comes laden with pots filled with Afghan rice, mutton stew, sweet treats. His wife has been cooking since early morning. B. and I had thought about preparing a farewell meal before the summer break. I., M., H., and S. arrive. Everyone tucks in and there is a satisfied, good-humored atmosphere.

I speak to H. with a reproachful undertone about his multiple absences, explaining to him that everybody in the group is important, like a pearl in a necklace; that an absence is like the necklace breaking and the pearls falling off. H. apologizes, saying that the bus and train are unreliable. B. agrees with him. I stick to my argument that even if it is not his own fault but rather the circumstances that caused the absence, then participation won't work for this same reason. S. agrees with me, while I. and M. say nothing.

H. breaks off the contact with me and turns to B., addressing him in his mother tongue and seeking protection from him; next Wednesday he has his hearing. Despite having a good lawyer, he is worried. B. asks me to organize a certificate from the practice for H. And thus the old pattern of caring roles is restored.

S. starts talking about the strange health problems he has been having. He has an inflamed knee and allergic skin reactions for no reason. He has to get used to long waiting times at the doctor's, he says indignantly. I. mentions his sleep problems; he always lies awake for so long and is afraid of falling asleep. B. mentions the stress caused by the latest political developments in Afghanistan and his fear for his family. S. asks I. whether he spends a lot of time online looking at terrible things going on at home. That will get you upset and prevent you from sleeping, he says, adding that he avoids the internet himself for this reason. I. doesn't answer.

The conversation continues about the current events in Afghanistan. B. explains the geopolitical interests of the states around Afghanistan and the threat of civil war. I translate that into the question of their fear about losing their homeland. S. answers that they are threatened not only with the loss of their homeland, but also the loss of their families. They have already lost so much, he says, their youth, their childhood, and so much of what makes them what they are inside – feelings, dreams. Silence follows. I am utterly dismayed.

Then the conversation returns to mundanities."

10 Going forward

Many of the forces at work within the URM group are not covered in my paper. I am well aware of that. To cite just a few questions: How does the translation of the language, for example, shape my relationship with the group participants and theirs with me? What do I miss out on because of it? How does it structure the relationship between B. and me as group leader? Or: What is it like for the participants to be on an equal footing in a group with Afghan youths whom they would have rejected in their home country for ethnic or religious reasons? There are still a great many aspects to be examined. That is, the full complexity of refugee groups still awaits exploration.

> **At a glance:**
> The *group analysis* with unaccompanied refugee minors from Afghanistan *allows for:*
> - the staging of the specific cultural frames of the participants.
> - the clarification and management of specific processes and conflicts of adaptation to the host society and on entering it.
> - the exchange of personal experiences that take place as part of this and their modification through the group discussion.
> - self-correction and a change of perspective.
>
> The group analysis shows its effectiveness in the reduction of integration conflicts and to this extent a successful integration.

Psychotherapy and Psychoanalysis in the Counseling Center

Kadir Kaynak

We see educational and family counseling as a multiprofessional help, in which the child and its relationship constellations are in the center. Since we want to make ourselves useful for the affected families with our therapeutic focus and at the same time distinguish ourselves from other counseling services, the intrapsychic events and the interpersonal dynamics of the child usually become our focus.

Taking into account the reality of an intercultural society in Berlin, we have endeavored to form a multi-professional as well as intercultural team, which should thus serve as a role model for the families as well as reach their problem areas with the counseling-therapeutic offer.

Mixed cultural families with different ethnicities feel better accepted by public social institutions if they experience their representatives in important positions there. At the same time, this team reality also serves as a model for the German families to realize that we do not live and work next to each other, but with each other, without excluding anyone on the basis of their cultural or religious origin and declaring them to be "evil". In this context, it makes sense to present our ethnotherapeutic work in more detail, which is an important and indispensable focus of our services in Berlin-Kreuzberg. After the intercultural analytic/psychotherapeutic work in connection with the migration background with its content pillars has been explained, I will try to present one building block, namely the analytic group work with an adolescent group, as an example.

1 Prehistory

Around 1964, ideas for a "House of the Family" emerged in the Kreuzberg district. The basic idea was to strengthen the parenting and relationship skills of the parents, which could not be accomplished with the conventional methods of social work. The interesting thing was that this project was to be set up in the Kreuzberg district of Berlin, which was the most socially difficult district at the time, and such an institution had not previously existed in Berlin or anywhere else in Germany. It was therefore not possible to profit from a body of experience; the project took on a model character. After the idea was positively received at the political level, a house was conceived which, with its facilities, was to serve important needs of Kreuzberg families beyond the area of youth welfare. Thus, in addition to the facilities planned by the youth welfare office, health care offices and the registry office were also included in the building space program.

However, it was not until 1972 that a majority in the Berlin House of Representatives was found in favor of its inclusion in the building plans, after concerns about an untested advisory institution of a special kind had been dispelled in the main committee. The Berlin House of Representatives finally emphasized the model case of the project in its approving resolution and welcomed the fact that the Parent Center, which was to be built in the conveniently located "House of the Family," was also to be open to visitors from the neighboring districts.

2 Present situation

Today, the former Parent Center exists under the name Family Center, is managed in cooperation with the Kreuzberg District Office and the Pestalozzi-Fröbel-Haus and is visited by many young families with children up to three years of age, both for leisure activities and for specifically offered educational courses. There is a constant contact as employees in the same house between our team as Education and Family Counseling (EFB) and the Family Center for joint consultation and support of citizens.

In the meantime, former facilities such as the registry office and a daycare center, which were part of the joint building complex, have moved to other parts of the city. Instead, there are new facilities such as a police library and a department of the responsible tax office.

Meanwhile, there are three EFB teams in different locations of Friedrichshain-Kreuzberg (the merger of both districts took place after the reunification), which try to meet today's complex needs of the district's population with their multi-professionalism as well as with multiculturalism. These three teams meet for regular so-called internal training sessions, resulting in a lively exchange both on a professional and personal level.

In our team, which has its rooms in the "House of the Family" described briefly above, six colleagues of Arab, German and Turkish origin are employed with different numbers of working hours and different professional focuses. For this very reason, it is a fundamental basis for our work to meet regularly twice a week for a team meeting, in order to be able to profit from each other both on an organizational and on a professional level. This internal working method has proven to be an enriching tool, so we would like to keep it going on a regular basis.

In one of the teams that take place, we carry out the "case distribution". This means that the registrations of families who have been taken in the office or by individual colleagues are discussed together in order to understand their concerns and at the same time to ensure that someone from the team takes the main responsibility for the counseling. Since EFB is a municipal facility, we must accept all applications and offer people an appointment to talk as soon as possible. However, especially in the winter months, the number of registrations increases enormously, so we have decided from experience to make people aware of a possible waiting period of three to six weeks if needed. If they are in urgent need of a consultation, we help them in that they can switch to the other surrounding psychological counseling centers. As far as possible, no one should feel alone or abandoned with their concerns.

In our district, the multicultural proportion is high, which is also evident in the families registering. With a small excerpt from our internal statistics I would like to present the development in this regard:

While in 2012 56.64% of the registered families had mothers of German origin, in 2013 this figure showed 59.32%. On the other hand, 41.34% of mothers had migration origin in 2012 and 38.58% in 2013. Among them, mothers of Turkish origin were in the first place with 17.79 and 20.47 % respectively. Again, in percentage terms, with 21.55% as well as 22.83%, children between 10 and 13 years of age formed the strongest group. The number of single mothers with 29.82 % and 33.33 % respectively also represented the highest group on the statistical scale of family status.

3   What problems or symptoms do we learn about?

About 50 % of the problem spectrum consists of educational and developmental problems. Neurotic or psychosomatic reactions showed an increase of 16.1 % among all problem areas in 2013. Based on our previous experience, I would like to put forward the thesis that families with a migration background have also adapted to the reality of Germans with their symptom development in their now over fifty-year history of integration. There are no more disturbance fields, which belong only to the life habits of the Migrant:innen, and also vice versa there are no symptoms, which we could define as typically German abnormalities. Nevertheless, in the many years of work we have found some personal, collective-cultural as well as psychodynamically important peculiarities (psychological and social component, culture-specific component and the development in migration), which I try to explain with the focus of our work with migrants. There are different patterns of thinking and behavior that play a role in the development and maintenance of problems and can be used in diagnostics, counseling and therapy:

The psychological and social components are an important field in educational counseling, which receive attention and treatment through the cooperation of psychological as well as socio-pedagogical specialists in a multidisciplinary team. Through the regular exchange in the team we believe to acquire an up-to-date psychosocial competence.

As a result, we feel increasingly able to deal in depth with the *culture-specific component,* which is clearly evident in the counseling-therapeutic work with foreign-cultural families, but which also plays an important role in contact with native German families. Culture-specific issues as well as problems arise not only from religious, ethnic or linguistic differences, but also from the different upbringing of girls and boys, from generational conflicts as well as from the different lifestyles of social classes. Our profession, with its own ethics and tradition, and its influence on the counseling and therapy process, also influences the professional work with the affected families, sometimes favorably, sometimes unfavorably. We also come from a certain family upbringing, which we work on through our training and self-experience in order to understand who we are, so that we can respond as clearly as possible to the client/patient. Here the mutual transference processes are of elementary importance, which are already set in motion during the telephone call for the purpose of scheduling and develop in later sessions. An example: I am a migrant who grew up in Berlin and who, in his developmental years, felt compelled by the social conflicts to make the strongest possible adaptations in order to be accepted in this society. The host country is seen in the spirit like an "ideal mother" who welcomes her new children benevolently and enables every single immigrant to live a decent life.

With this background, I sit in the counseling center where a separated young German father of a four-year-old child gets in touch with us. He wants to have contact with his child, who lives with his mother. In conversation, he states that he is unemployed and jobless, does not think much of customs and traditions, and is very concerned about his individual freedom, which is why he often moves around the apartments of his circle of acquaintances, where people often smoke pot and use other drugs. I will of course discuss this case in the team to get adequate help. But I must first check in my own world whether I can and want to support this man in his desire for contact with his child, despite his different way of life, which may be completely unfamiliar to me personally. I have learned in my professional career that every human being is equal before the law and that my work can have emancipatory influences that help personal growth. But for this I must first accept him as a fellow citizen with the same rights as well as duties and be able to make him feel accepted in the meeting. After all, his child has a right to see him. However, I might create associations in me about his way of life to the effect that he is a slacker who lives off "our taxes." Therefore, I could make his right of contact with the child more difficult, even thwart it, through my discretionary powers.

With regard to the psychological development *in migration, it* is important to note that the initial studies on this tended to crystallize the deficits of the migrants and the factors of migration that make them ill. Only through the presentations of the interculturally designed work teams, through the reports of the experiences of the "affected" as well as the native-speaking psychotherapists who emerged from their ranks, could it gradually be made clear that migration can be a difficult, stressful process on the one hand. On the other hand, however, it can also lead to enrichment, in that the individual or an ethnic minority can broaden the horizon of life and develop new perspectives through the possibilities of comparison of different ways of life.

My parents belonged to the first generation that emigrated to Germany in the 1960s in order to improve their earning potential, but also to leave behind their disputes in the family of origin, jealousies, the feeling of disadvantage among their siblings or their feelings of pain due to the death of their parents. They tried to deal with their complex issues and problems mainly by believing that they had to make the enormous effort to adapt, not to attract attention with their existence. They lived modestly, withdrawn and uninvolved in their experiences here and in social processes. Accordingly, they also tried to influence the second generation growing up here, from which I emerged. We had to learn to work diligently without interfering in what was happening here. As we grew up, so did the energies to differentiate and problematize the different attitudes to life between the generations. This development was also influenced by the wind of social change desires from the 1970s and 1980s in the sense that the transgenerational relationship conflicts increased and the new generations increasingly took over, or had transferred to them, the unresolved and repressed conflicts of their parents' generation.

In this context, the native-speaking psychotherapists' explanations of the conditions of migration as well as of the relationship dynamics in the migrant family at the beginning, during and after migration promoted an interaction between the arrival in the new host country and the increasing public acceptance of immigration.

Through our previous counseling and therapeutic work, we can describe that each affected family is in a different stage of their migration phase, both psychosocially and psychodynamically. Accordingly, they are engaged in their own coping strategies of the prevailing conflicts.

There are families who seem so entangled in *their traditional behavior and beliefs that* they hardly seem accessible to outsiders. One of the reasons for this state of affairs may be that the members of the family concerned may have embarked on their migration with a traumatic experience of separation. This background can have such a negative impact on their arrival, settlement and further stages of life in the new country that people feel unaccepted and isolated, and may even develop paranoid fantasies. A consequential reaction from this would be that they become entangled in their tradition in order to be able to exist at all, even if this means that their inner life and their external perception do not match and they react in an emotionally split manner.

In another group of families, I experience the *inner split in the* form that they show strong ambivalences with regard to both their inherited values and ideas of life and their new life experiences in the host country and react to the experiences without clear points of view. They can jump back and forth between the traditional values and the newly experienced life concepts to such an extent that in some individual cases one can speak of psychological dysfunctions with borderline characteristics. In such cases there are enormous conflicts between the generation of the parents and the adolescents, because the children feel "driven crazy!" by ambivalences. The famous sentence of such parents towards their children is: "I have confidence in you, but not in the environment, my child. That's why you can't go out!"

Then there are families that obviously come from extremely patriarchal structures and have not managed to get a grip on their individual possibilities under the new living conditions, because individual development is capitalized in the advanced industrial society and a so-called group individuality cannot hold out for long in this country. The members of such families are often threatened by "*disintegration*", by destruction, because they are under the fantasy that they can compensate for their individual undesirable developments (weak as individuals, no profession, no recognized education, little self-esteem, many complexes) by drug abuse (Güç, 1991). This is, of course, a mistake, because self-destruction takes its course and is difficult to stop the more addiction takes its space in people's lives.

These briefly described models of psychological development of families with a migration background are basically those who have presented themselves at the counseling center. Most of them, who integrate in every way and manage to become a useful part of society, do not become a topic of conversation because they manage their lives on their own and do not need help from counseling centers and independent therapy practices.

In our therapeutic work with migrants, we can explicitly emphasize the experience that the success rate both in the counseling centers and in clinics is increased by the cooperation of native-speaking psychotherapists as well as by the cooperation in intercultural teams. Through constant mutual discussion in intervision groups and cooperation in casework, each staff member achieves an intercultural competence that enriches the overall work. Compared to other institutions that have no experience with different ethnic groups or find it difficult to deal with them, we achieve greater self-evidence in everyday contact with the people concerned.

The transference processes that we use in the therapeutic process do not usually run In the direction of an exaggeratedly positive evaluation of the "foreigner", as otherwise happens consciously or unconsciously in many social institutions, in order to be able to suppress the inner contradictions or fears of the "foreigner". On the other hand, through our several times reflected attitude we also reach the confrontation with our own prejudices as well as racist parts.

Our applied systemic as well as analytic depth psychological methods, which are, however, reviewed from case to case with regard to their viability in the family or reference group, show themselves to be useful therapeutic attitudes. In this professional approach we also consciously perceive our model character for the families, who are in various personal as well as interpersonal development processes. A public counseling center, which presents itself to the families through employees of different cultural and ethnic origins, builds trust in the professional work as well as in its own existence. The affected family feels taken seriously and important by their "representatives" in the group of employees of the counseling center, so that they like to attend and cooperate. In most cases, they bring along some acquaintances or relatives who would like to provide a better mental and spiritual understanding with their "bridging function". In this case, it is advisable to involve these people in the process by mutual agreement instead of excluding them for any formal reasons. This experience of cooperation will be passed on by the people concerned through rapid word of mouth, so that it will be known fairly quickly in migrant circles whether this particular counseling center is to be trusted or whether one should stay away from it. Finally, two case studies follow in order to be able to describe the psychotherapeutic work in the counseling center in concrete terms, after the knowledge gained so far and culture-specific phenomena have been explained in the above chapters.

4 Case examples

The first case study is about a physically and mentally well-developed twelve-year-old girl whose mother comes from the former GDR and has been living in Berlin-Kreuzberg for a long time. Here she had met a Kurdish migrant from Turkey. The above-mentioned daughter was born from this relationship. The child's parents separated when she was still a small child because the child's father had been unreliable in his attitude and had neglected the family. After that, the daughter grew up in the care of the child's mother.

The presentation at the educational and family counseling center occurred because the daughter had swallowed pills, had been admitted to the Child and Adolescent Psychiatric Clinic (KJP), where, however, she had felt unwell and had urged her discharge. The clinic in charge had insisted on therapeutic follow-up in case of her discharge for legitimate reasons. The child's mother was very pleased that we both came into contact because she hoped for a better understanding on my part of the family background, since I would come from the same cultural background of the child's father. Both the daughter and the child's mother agreed with the clinic that they would like to come to EFB, so the discharge took place.

At the same time, in consultation with the family, a telephone call was made to the clinic psychologist to arrange everything necessary for the child's discharge and to ensure her follow-up with our therapy services. Meanwhile, I made the case a team topic, because I needed the support of all colleagues if I was to take over the therapy and the associated parent meetings for a longer period of time (for probably two to three years). In the counseling center, new registrations arrive every week for various family reasons, which also need to be taken over. If someone from the team is to work therapeutically with a person or with a family for a longer period of time, clarification in the team is necessary so that the required time commitment can be organized for the therapy and this can be supported as a useful offer of the EFB. It is clear that due to time constraints we can only offer our therapeutic qualifications as a therapeutic process in individual cases, so that most of our time and energy remains dedicated to therapeutic counseling work.

I was in contact with the child and its legal guardians for three years. Therapy took place regularly on a weekly basis with one or two appointments.

The child came regularly, unfolded in a therapeutic framework that conveyed trust and security, with an analytic depth psychological focus. She was very silent in the beginning, which required a very patient therapeutic approach. She painted a lot. During his long silent phase it was elementarily important to stay in contact and to comment on what she was doing. During this time, I could clearly perceive on the transference level that she was strengthening her introjections until she began to talk first about her everyday life, then about internal family matters. Parallel to this, regular parental meetings took place, in which both the separated Kurdish father and the new partner of the child's mother participated over time. The new partner also came from the former GDR and had been imprisoned for 15 years in the city of Bautzen for resistance against the socialist republic. It became clear that the girl did not feel emotionally accepted by the child's mother and therefore spontaneously attempted suicide by taking pills – not to die, but to send a cry for help.

The child's mother worked for a long time to open up emotionally to her daughter and to develop understanding for her gradually emerging adolescent traits. To this end, she became more aware that her child lacked real contact with the child's father and his family of origin. In the common interest, she was able to gradually involve the child's father more consciously in the daily life of the daughter and perceive this for herself as a relief in her responsibility for upbringing and relationships. The daughter became much more relieved and satisfied since she met with her father and also got to know his family of origin. This increased her desire for her Turkish/Kurdish side and she felt much more secure in everyday life.

In the final stage we met fortnightly for individual sessions with the intention of ending the therapy by the next summer. The child's mother became more self-confident in her parental attitude and in her behavior towards the new partnership and approached our parting slightly sad, but well prepared. Through therapy, the young patient grew into a cheerful adolescent who was preparing for the transition to secondary school.

In conclusion, it was very useful that I, as a psychotherapist from the Turkish culture, who also knows the German reality, took over the treatment. For those affected, this was well supportive for both personal positive development and clarification of family connections, as well as acting as a role model (Kohte-Meyer, 2000).

Overall, the entire counseling center took on a role model character as a cooperating team in which respectful interaction is possible among each other, which was able to relieve and successfully support this family in clarifying their psychodynamics with stressful fixations as well as repression mechanisms.

In the course of the years, the need and the question arose whether the offer of an analytical group therapy within the framework of the work presented above could benefit the interested young people to discuss and work on their conflicts in the group and thereby also gain experience with their cultural backgrounds. Because we made the experience that they live in the same district, attend the same schools, but shy away from personal experiences for various reasons. Therefore, Team Mehringdamm (EFB) decided to adapt the concept to the circumstances of the young people and offered an analytical therapy group in addition to the counseling activities. This is described below and supplemented with an account of a session of this group as an example of how analytic thought in the group can provide clarifications as well as progression.

The second case study is about a therapy group that consisted of adolescents and existed for a total of four years from 2012 to 2016. Naturally, there were different stages in the overall process. What is expressed in the session below is the positive outcome of two years, the further development of which, as already indicated above, took another two years.

All the young people came from severely disturbed relationship constellations in their parental homes. They had massive proximity-distance-ratio-problems, which the group member Seyfi[1] in particular expressed or acted out on behalf of all of them with his frequently transgressive manner. The oral as well as anal neediness was another central theme in the group, whereby of course oedipally unresolved conflicts as well as their age-appropriate pubertal sexual difficulties and desires in this regard were dealt with in every session. However, they are particularly expressed in the session described here. The adolescents had German, Polish, and Turkish roots, all of whom were born in Berlin and whose current youthful existence represents Germany's future intercultural society. All were either in school education or in vocational training. On the one hand, they were very combative, avoided no confrontation, but at the same time supported each other enormously. No matter how bad the individual behavior was, no one was excluded, each member stayed in contact with the person in conflict and dealt with it in their own way. The group was accepted as a symbolic, nurturing, holding and caring mother for growth, and in the process internalized that confidentiality gives each member a security for their behavior and encourages the deepening of their thoughts and feelings.

The fact that the importance of secrecy is particularly great for the young people with Turkish roots must be mentioned separately here. They benefited enormously from the dynamic process in this analytical framework because they had the certainty that their parents' homes were not allowed to find out anything about group events and their statements without their knowledge. They explained several times that in the Turkish community, everyone knew each other and would quickly inform each other about the actions of the young people, exaggerating and therefore causing "a lot of gossip". It is just remarkable that the young people concerned in the analytical group have sought and found exchange and clarification processes despite this strongly prevailing social control in their own cultural circle. They developed the necessary courage and confidence for a good prognosis together in the group and built up various pas-

---

1   All names appearing in the text have been anonymized by the author.

sageways between the cultural barriers. This process with culture-related difficulties is to be particularly emphasized because there are people in the German majority society as well as multipliers who claim that one cannot work with migrant youth because of their "different cultural affiliation".

In their exchanges as well as quarrels, the young people benefited a lot from each other. Towards the end, it could be experienced that both their tolerance limits had been expanded and their fighting spirit had grown. They approached each other more courageously in order to question their mutual ideas, to criticize, to reduce their inhibitions, but also to respect each other.

The whole development and the process of experience resulting from it could be a good model for our society. Encounter creates understanding, tolerance and empathy. Distance and lack of contact cause fear, hostility, strong prejudices and accelerate projections of one's own parts, which have remained strangely repressed in the dark, onto the people with other cultural habits.

Group on the last Thursday before the Christmas holidays 2014 at 18.00 h
ANGELIKA again talks about her graduation from high school and her new plans to study psychology, complaining that her children's parents still reproach her and cannot even appreciate her success.
SEYFI says that she will never get recognition from her parents, she is trying in vain because they would be very unhappy in their own lives. They would always dump their feelings of unhappiness on Andrea to make themselves feel better at her expense.
ANGELIKA thinks for a moment and says that there would be something to this explanation.
MERVE and THOMAS observe the scene very attentively, but are silent.
SEYFI describes his quarrel with his father because he wanted to force him to return to Turkey.
THERAPIST: "This is the first time you've reported this in such detail, I think it's a big step for you because, after all, dad was considered very powerful and untouchable for you for a long time."
SEYFI: "Yes, by now I have checked that respect is mutual."
Then he gets restless and praises Thomas' hairstyle.
But ANGELIKA and MERVE think he's exaggerating, as if he's "taking the piss" out of Thomas. Then ANGELIKA tells about Seyfi's call. She told him that she wanted to take a shower, whereupon Seyfi offered to go to her place and take a shower together.
ANGELIKA adds that she found this offer absurd.
SEYFI: "What's the big deal if I want to shower with you?"
ANGELIKA and MERVE: "You can't do that, it's something intimate. Besides, you're actually thinking about something else when you say "shower". How can you think something like that?"

SEYFI: "Well, we are allowed to talk openly about everything here, aren't we? Besides, if you flirt with others and get into bed, why not with me? You know me better than that."
MERVE: "That's just it. You're too familiar, too close."
ANGELIKA (slightly annoyed): "You only see me as a sex object. You know that this is my most difficult subject, and here you hit me with it."
SEYFI becomes silent. I then ask what he feels about this statement.
SEYFI: "Yes, I do; now I say what I believe, there are women for sex, for banging, and there are some for marriage."
The girls get loud, protesting, "It's impossible how you think."
Seyfi laughs, enjoying the situation.
THERAPIST: "I think you wanted to provoke now, certainly to bring some more action into the group. Because I remember, for you it was often boring here, so sometimes you wanted to sleep."
SONER: "You can't categorize women so badly. Marriage, love, sex belong together, don't they?"
SEYFI: "Come on, don't act so sanctimonious. You have two faces. Here you speak like this, outside differently. You're just as horny as I am. At least I admit that and talk about it openly." Then he shows me and the group the picture he has painted in the meantime and laughs his head off.
THERAPIST: "I continue to think that you want to provoke the group. This picture is also a provocation or a product of your fantasies."
SEYFI: "Yeah, dude, I met a cute 27-year-old girl at work. She wants to fuck me."
MERVE: "Come on, don't brag, if you had a girlfriend and had sex more often, you wouldn't talk about it so aggressively. You're missing a girlfriend."
SEYFI: "Well, at least I talk about it. But Thomas not at all."
ANGELIKA: "Sex and aggression are often the same with you."
SEYFI pretends to be embarrassed, as if he felt caught, turns solemnly to me, "Kadir Bey still hasn't said how many times and with which women he did it."
THERAPIST: "I think you like to dodge now because you felt pressured by the girls."
SEYFI: "I'm thinking, what's actually going on with Thomas? You're not getting involved again. Before I go out of the group, I want you to finally have a girlfriend."
THOMAS: "Seyfi, you're annoying. You don't get a girlfriend on order. This has to come about. Then I can build a relationship."
SEYFI: "Well, hopefully before I'm retired." Everyone laughs.
Then SEYFI continues, "Tell me Thomi, if you're gay, you can tell here. We are a closed group."
THOMAS: "We'd better discuss that calmly next week. We are already over the time. But I can reassure you, I'm not gay. But I can hear your aggression on the subject, as if you have something against gays."

SEYFI laughs sheepishly.

I say that we have to finish the session and we can continue next week. Then, as always, there will be a farewell ceremony.

> **At a glance:**
> Group psychotherapy plays a major role in the psychotherapeutic care of the population. Statistically, about one third of all treatments in analytical psychotherapy take place in groups. Group psychotherapy has many advantages over individual therapy:
> - it can represent the social reality of our lives in ongoing group psychotherapy.
>
> Because of the presence of several people, the likelihood of transference developing is much higher than in individual therapy.
>
> The therapeutic potential is greater because all group members are active, able to perceive and interpret more than the group therapist alone.
>
> This achieves a stronger persuasive power when discussing a current topic or an individual state of mind, expression.
>
> I have a personal as well as professional identity with a migration background.
>
> Therefore, it was clear to me to lead an analytic therapy group in which young people from different ethnic backgrounds could come together and gain experience in working through their brought-in intrapsychic as well as interpersonal conflicts (Bianchi Schäffer, 1996)
> - Above all, they should be able to experience sitting together and understanding each other while developing an awareness that they can have cultural, intellectual as well as social differences,
> - but still experience a healthier, more humane relationship with themselves and with group participants through the tolerance of the analytic treatment process.
> - In this context, it seemed necessary to me to investigate the effect of the protected and silent group setting on the young people regarding the experience of mentalization and symbolization of their life conflicts.
> - The goal should be to achieve positive developmental steps as a group experience and to feel inwardly strengthened by the group.
>
> The central idea behind this was that the psychological development of a person takes place in relationship, i.e. in the group, and that we move in different social groups throughout our lives. Therefore, the analytic group as a section of this could offer the possibility to repeat and process the previous life experiences.
>
> Further, the approach was a basic element whether also in group therapy through transference and countertransference the restoration of the original problem situation is possible, which we know from the individual analysis and whether the

> symptom of the individual can be perceived and worked on as a kind of "group relationship disorder".
>
> In this context, *Foulkes* speaks of the "cultural matrix", that the constellations of relationships in the group represent society and, among other things, are reminiscent of Freud's culture-specific reflections (von Lüpke, 1996).

Bibiography

Bianchi Schäffer, M. (1996). Ausländische Therapeutinnen, Fremdenhaß und die Auseinandersetzung mit der eigenen Nationalität. In D. Kiesel, S. Kriechhammer-Yagmur (Hrsg.), Gestörte Übertragung. Ethno-kulturelle Dimensionen im psychotherapeutischen Prozess (S. 197–108). Frankfurt/M.: Haag und Herchen

Güç, F. (1991). Ein familientherapeutisches Konzept in der Arbeit mit Immigrantenfamilien. *Familiendynamik. Systemische Praxis und Forschung,* 16 (1), 3–23

Kohte-Meyer, I. (2000). Ich bin fremd, wie ich bin. Migrationserleben, ich-Identität und Neurose In U. Streeck (Hrsg.), *Das Fremde in der Psychoanalyse. Erkundigungen über das Andere in Seele, Körper und Kultur* (2. Aufl., S. 119–132). Gießen: Psychosozial

Lüpke, H. von (1996). Weitere Überlegungen zur Entwicklung der Fremdenrepräsentanz. In D. Kiesel, S. Kriechhammer-Yagmur (Hrsg.), Ethno-kulturelle Dimensionen im psychotherapeutischen Prozess (S. 16–25). Frankfurt/M.: Haag & Herchen

Further recommended reading for in-depth work with intercultural topics:

Akgün, L. (1991). Strukturelle Familientherapie bei türkischen Familien. *Familiendynamik* 16, S. 24–36

Erim-Frodermann, Y. (1998). Schwierigkeiten beim Einstieg in die psychotherapeutische Behandlung türkischer Migrant:innen. In E. Koch, M. Özek, M. W. Pfeifer, R. Schepker (Hrsg.), *Chancen und Risiken von Migration* (S. 249–260). Freiburg: Lambertus

Opening Transcultural Spaces in Group-analytical Processes with Refugees

Beate Schnabel

"The sun of social prestige renders the firmament of the unconscious invisible."
(Erdheim, 1986, p. 200)

"Confronted as I am by radical uncertainty, I mostly stumble in the dark. All I can think of doing is try to find and meet with others."
(Dalal, 2018, p. 76)

It may seem odd to use these two quotes to accompany us in the transcultural space. Farhad Dalal might seem more readily accessible, but the sun of social prestige? What is the sense of this quote in the transcultural context? Join me in the following as we embark on a voyage of discovery.

If children and adolescents fleeing their homes make it to a host country after a long, arduous, and dangerous journey, they are still, by a long way, not there yet. In urban regions, unlike in rural areas, they encounter societies that reflect diversity and yet deviate from the hopeful images they have formed of these places. An application for asylum, the initial welcome center, the housing group, learning the foreign language, school, and the wait before gaining a hearing at the Federal Office for Refugees (BAMF), which decides whether a stay in the host country is granted or not. All these can be endured in the first few months by the relief of having survived the journey, which combines with the hope of prospects in life and a secure future. Yet soon the challenges in the host country, which are often accompanied by irritations, experiences of alienation, and real threats, begin to mix with the experiences of loss, profound shocks, and traumatizing events in the country of origin and on the journey to escape it. Paralyzing memories that come with fears of being lost, forgotten, and abandoned. The painful loss of developmentally necessary attachments intensifies the accompanying feelings, and the young people are not prepared for them. To make matters worse, they are unable to gauge the representatives of the host culture on whom they have pinned many hopes and who, at the same time, are associated with troubling experiences (police, foreigners' registration authority, youth welfare services, and the welcome facilities). The young people remain cautious, skeptical, and distrustful of such people. Above all, their communication with the authorities is encumbered by political experiences in their countries of origin, arbitrariness and violence on their escape routes, and uncertainty about what spoken words may lead to. The professionals who accompany the refugees on their different paths (youth welfare office, youth support institutions, school, etc.) in turn adopt different attitudes in their roles. In addition to a benevolently supportive humane approach that does not come across as uncritical, in times of crisis among the young people such professionals may show pronounced reservations, resentments, or even open rejection, in which the power relations are nevertheless clearly defined. Within the trap of unquestioned Eurocentric convictions, the chances of transcultural encounters are closed; they become repetitions in which whatever is forgotten, repressed, marginalized, demonized, etc. all mixes together. Some of these impasses were addressed in a project that set itself the goal of developing a transcultural psychosocial group for unaccompanied refugee minors in order to support and empower young people in crisis with the help of the group.

Over a period of two years, a group of female refugees of adolescent age was supported by group analysts and cultural intermediaries. The girls and young women came from Eritrea and Ethiopia and were aged between 14 and 19. They had been forced to flee for social, religious, or political reasons, and almost all of them had journeyed for months, some for up to two years, before they made it to Europe. They had been in Germany for between six months and two years by the time they joined the group, so the languages used for communication were their respective mother tongues and German. The plan was to create a semi-open group, so new members joined when other group participants left after a longer or even shorter period of time. Network meetings were held at regular intervals, attended by professionals from youth welfare institutions, youth welfare offices, and a psychiatrist, in order to incorporate the experiences of the professionals into the pilot concept, which was in a state of constant ongoing development. The group processes in the pilot group as well as the network meetings were monitored in both a supervisory and scholarly capacity. The project was financed by Aktion Mensch and supported by the UNHCR and the Software AG Foundation in Darmstadt. The following recalls some key experiences and findings in this project (Schnabel, 2020, p. 125 ff.).[1]

---

[1] The article "Erkundungs- und Erzählräume. Konzept einer transkulturellen psychosozialen Gruppenarbeit mit unbegleiteten minderjährigen Geflüchteten an der Schnittstelle zwischen sozialem und medizinischem Bereich" ("Exploratory and narrative spaces. Concept of transcultural psychosocial group work with unaccompanied refugee minors at the interface between the social and medical fields"), published in: Kerschgens, A., Schnabel, B., Frankfurter Institut für interkulturelle Forschung und Beratung e. V. (2020). Psychosoziale Arbeit mit jugendlichen Geflüchteten. Transkulturelle Übergangsräume und Verstehensprozesse. (Psychosocial work with young refugees. Transcultural transitional spaces and processes of understanding.) Frankfurt/M.: Brandes & Apsel. The use of content from this text is by kind permission of the publisher.

1 Initial observations on situating transcultural processes in space and time

The forms and structures of life in postmodern societies and the metropolises of the world have developed into heterogeneous, ethnically intermixed, culturally hybrid forms of society as a result of accelerated globalization and worldwide displacement and migration movements. The worldwide interconnectedness in all fields (the economy, technology, politics, science, art, environment, and health) has partially led to rethinking in different areas of research such as migration studies, cultural studies, sociology, literary studies, ethnology, and anthropology, where prevailing cultural theories and their essentialist and domination-centered understanding and its consequences are now being critically questioned. Stuart Hall, one of the important cultural theorists and co-founder of the Centre for Contemporary Cultural Studies (CCCS 1964–2002), at a very early stage critically engaged with the essentialist notion of culture prevalent in the Western world (Hall, 1989, 1994; Hörter, 2016). He countered this notion by offering a concept of culture that is not stable, homogeneous, and tightly knit, "but is characterized by openness, contradictions, negotiation, conflict, innovation, and resistance" (Hörning and Winter, 1999, p. 9). Culture is understood as something "that permeates all 'social practices'" and is always contextual and "embedded in historically specific and socially structured contexts" (Hörning and Winter, 1999, p. 9) with their implicit power relations. Identity from this perspective is "not a fixed entity; it is a becoming and not a being" (Hall, 2020, p. 89) – something that is existential for migrants in the diaspora. With postcultural studies (Bronfen, Marius, and Steffen, 1997; Bhabha, 2000) the focus has been placed on the effects of social processes, examining the way "in which the 'colonized' are made a defined, explorable part of this world against the background of Eurocentric, colonial, and racist discourses" (Hörter, 2016, p. 344). The interest lies in "overcoming colonial and anti-colonial thought patterns" (Rehbein, 2010, p. 223). Especially for Homi K. Bhabha, the best-known representative of postcultural studies, cultures are not closed, not homogeneous; rather, they are hybrid, constantly in motion, without fixed representations. Through discourses, new meanings and interpretations are forever evolving. "Cultural hybridity," which he sees as the essential concept of culture, is what he understands to be the possibility of creating interspatial transitions in which there is a place for difference without an assumed hierarchy, a constantly changing space (Klein, 2008a). After all, "in an integrated world system of nation states," according to Homi K. Bhabha, "there is no 'free space' – no scope for individual actions and opinions – for the stateless, the refugees, the minorities, the displaced" (Bhabha,

2012, p. 36). The research and insights of cultural studies and postcultural studies can offer guidance and food for thought when we explore transcultural spaces, and this reflection is an intrinsic part of transcultural processes. Transcultural processes can become, as Adelson puts it as regards creative thinking, "'places of rethinking' – imaginative spaces" in which "cultural orientation can be radically rethought" (Adelson, 2015, p. 129). Maya Nadig compares Bhabha's concept of "Third Space" to Winnicott's transitional space, a "vital important life space" (Nadig, 2000, p. 93) of experience. A potential space where "creativity, symbols, and difference can develop" (Nadig, 2000, p. 93). She emphasizes that the spatial concepts of psychoanalysis and cultural studies could complement each other. It is the "perspective on the dynamics of cultural complexity" (Nadig, 2006, p. 70) that calls for a "concept of social space" in order to grasp transcultural processes more precisely, although it should not be overlooked here that Winnicott's understanding of culture (embedded in space and time) differs from Bhabha's concept of culture. Dialogue about this difference could, in my opinion, be fruitful for practice. Bhabha's concept of Third Space stands for a place of transcultural understanding; he conceptualizes it as a communal place that goes beyond the "established dual entities in concepts, in minds, and in reality," "where new meanings, ways of seeing, and ways of drawing boundaries emerge" (Bhabha, 2000, p. 71). In meeting and experiencing, in shared action, reflection, and exploration, our culturally shaped patterns of perception, evaluation, and action are always present. We have learned them through action, and only the least of them is consciously accessible to us (Bourdieu, 1993). "Social orders thus become ingrained self-evident facts and embodied lifestyles" (Klein, 2009, p. 455). If cultural taboos touch each other in this process, they usually trigger intense affects such as shame, disgust, anger, hatred, and others; due to their ambivalent structure, they are also seen as anxiety-ridden threshold phenomena (Gutjahr, 2008; Klein, 2020). In transcultural spaces, precisely because of their group and cultural specificity, cultural fracturing of taboos can become an opportunity for development. The search for the misunderstood, the differences, and the necessary words for them, is characterized by the impression of being stuck, of ending up in dead ends, a turning back and forth, a closeness and distance, an effort to keep the door open for a process that will not be completed and yet allows the way for a beyond. What emerges in this Third Space out of this uncertain, indeterminate balancing act are transcultural mixtures, overlaps, shifts of the different cultural influences (Klein, 2022).

Just such a communal place of polyphony and mobility, reminiscent of Winnicott's transitional space and Bhabha's Third Space of transcultural understanding, has, I believe, been created by Tobi Nathan at the George Devereux

Centre, Paris, and by Marie Rose Moro at the Avicenne Clinic, Department of Child and Adolescent Psychiatry, Bobigny, with their ethno-psychiatric treatment. Moro, founder of the Association Internationale d'Ethnopsychoanalysis (AIEP), has built on ethnopsychoanalysis to develop a specific parent-child ethnopsychoanalysis in which she sees the possibility of overcoming transcultural risks. For group analysis, a rich source of findings is treatment in multiethnic treatment teams and with the whole family, which includes not only parents and children but all members who can contribute to the understanding of the existing problem. These forms of treatment, which take place in groups and often involve up to 20 people, usually favor families from attachment-oriented societies, who feel more protected in the group. The "language and culture intermediaries", who provide support in emotionally translating interpretive patterns, i.e. for culturally shaped ways of thinking, concepts of normality, and action patterns, come from the cultural circles of the patients and are part of the treatment team with additional training as "mediateurs". The work by Nathan and Moro has strengthened and encouraged us to attempt to develop a concept for pedagogical practice in this sense through our experiences with young refugees.

2 Adolescents and their psychosocial positioning in society

The transition from childhood to adulthood has always preoccupied all cultures and has led to the most diverse, sometimes subtle, forms of transition, rites, and rules applied by adults to adolescents in order to introduce them into the social community. It is this "culturally typical sequence of adolescence," as Erdheim (1984, p. 290) put it, that affects the ways in which "a society transforms itself."

In Western societies, which are characterized by rapid change, the push toward individualization has contributed to the dissolution of traditional systems of order and values, and has also led to a change in the notion of stable identities and identity trajectories. What is needed, above all, is individual activity and initiative as well as a high degree of autonomy and less predefined, intergenerational models. Individuation and, above all, the promotion of autonomy are central to child development. In adolescence, the phase of upheaval, change, and reorientation, detachment from the authority of parents is required in order to create visions of the future that differ from the ideas and expectations of the parents. Ideally, young people are granted a prolonged adolescence that provides both personal and educational and ultimately professional development opportunities over longer educational trajectories (King, 2002; Erdheim, 1984; Günther, 2020). The creative potential of young people becomes a socially necessary and indeed desirable skill required for social change, so that utopian potential can unfold here. This sociocultural change and the fragility of social self-constructions that goes hand in hand with it harbor both opportunities and risks. On the one hand, the dissolution of traditional order and value systems offers the opportunity for individual freedoms, but it also increases the risks in managing the desire to locate oneself in space and time (Giddens, 1996). Identity as a becoming rather than a being, as Hall puts it, remains a permanent performance of balancing the demands of the social environment, external specifications, and one's own needs, impulses, and desires (Klein, 2019).

Whether and how adolescents think about new orders and are able to transform them into visions is to a large extent subject to processes of cultural change. They are shaped and influenced by social place, families and their conditions, the social environment, and the power structures of society. When potential spaces for adolescent processes emerge, it is not equally possible for all adolescents to participate in them. In addition to gender, socially shaped access to educational systems, conditions on the training market, and – most significantly for our context – ethnic affiliations are among the factors that can open up potential spaces, but also close them off.

In societies in which collectively regulating forms of behavior structure and hold together people's ties to the community, the focus is on belonging to the social group and the ability to bond with others. Desires for individualization are encouraged in their attachment to the group, but aspirations of autonomy among adolescents are inhibited by attachment to social roles. These are roles that take on community-promoting functions and ensure group cohesion. Through identification with the associated gender- and generation-bound prescribed behavior and the attachment to the ideas and values of the community, coexistence is regulated and organized through tight social controls. Desires for change and rebellion are relegated to the hidden realm in order to keep development and change at bay (Erdheim, 1984), with religion often taking on a central, stabilizing function here. These forms of society offer their members security, clear roles, and structures that apply equally to everyone (Rohr, 2016).

Social change in the process of globalization means that even in these societies, traditional forms of life and security no longer endure. On the one hand, family ties scattered throughout the Western world nourish hopes; on the other, they tug at the close-knit bond of families, in which, among other things, the efforts required to survive in the "new" world are usually kept quiet. Digital networking also brings youth cultures and adolescents closer together (via music, films, political and social movements, and more) as they strive for greater self-realization and thus drive the process of change. The different experiences as well as forms of cognition, which have long ceased to exist in isolation from one another, influence, overlap, and intersect one another. With them, the identifications with socially prescribed roles are shaken, and they intensify the tensions between the generations and the sexes. Processes of change develop that do not coexist on an equal footing, but are equally permeated, limited, and oppressed by dominant power structures.

3   Escape and adolescence

The challenges facing young refugees are formidable. On the one hand, they spend a long time living in an in-between state, neither here nor there. On the other, their particular vulnerability in a transcultural situation poses risks for their development (Rohr, 2017a, 2017b, 2020a). Adolescents socialized in a society more committed to traditions and supportive of community develop a more "interdependently structured self, which leads to a different way of dealing with emotions" (Kotanyi, 2018, p. 157). "The tightrope trodden between individual and internalized group" is a matter of individual positioning, "which in non-Western cultures, especially in Africa, is constituted as a multiple and is not understood as decisively singular" (Kotanyi, 2018 p. 157). Thus, for example, individualizing demands in terms of Western patterns of thought and action, without taking into account the multiple constitution of young people, can overwhelm them. What they then feel is the loss and denial of connectedness in decisions to be made, which they experience as rejection and exclusion from the community. Acting self-responsibly in terms of the interdependent structure can be translated as a constant process of the ego seeking to reach a consensus with the internalized group, an inner dialogue between an "us without you"[2], in which the others are always included. Being a refugee leaves deep cracks in the experience here, which can shake one's "faith in humanity," as one young person put it. She comes to the group, in spite of her great anxiety, to learn to be with people again. It is the close interconnectedness between psyche and culture, and the consequences of the shocks that are so enormously important. In attempting to adopt the perspective of the interdependent self, we encoun-

---

2   The formulation of an ego in the presence of the group was explained to me during my studies by a student from Ecuador, who belonged to the Quechua people. He learned the word "I" as a pupil in a Spanish school in the lowlands. His story was shrouded in a sadness that touched me and evoked associations with my departure from the village community, which was necessary for my survival and confronted me with the feeling of loneliness for the first time.

ter limits of understanding due in part to different emotionally invested language games. The aspect of the dialogical in relationships takes a different form, one in which the emotional relational experiences are bound close to the body. Desires are communicated in narrative descriptions, while fears, illnesses, and ideas about where these come from and what they relate to are mentioned in comparative stories, metaphors, in life lessons, which at the same time communicate to others desired forms of action and relationships. Misfortunes are likewise interpreted in connection with others. One small example: One of the young people repeatedly dropped something from her spoon while eating and appeared startled in her response to this. When asked about it, she revealed shyly and sadly that this mishap told her that her mother was suffering from hunger. Being here, she explained, she was not able to help her. It is one's own experience that is constituted in relation and in reference to others. We must always ask ourselves how, from this perspective, the young people translate the individualizing demands made on them, which do not give priority to others, but to individuals. Furthermore, we need to examine what psychological and social meanings these different perspectives may have on adolescent processes among the young refugees. The following describes experiences from the group process in narrative form, with the addition of reflections on pedagogical practice.

4   The group

On the assumption that the group can be seen as a social microcosm which reflects and re-reveals time and again the way the individuals deal with their environment, their fellow human beings, their family and life group, and ultimately their culture (Klein, 2020), it is important to explore, for example, how the young refugees imagine their life in Europe: What wants and needs have they brought with them? How do they explain their experiences and ordeals, which, in the host country, are largely determined by the society to which the young people belong. It is possible to find meaningful sense that shapes the togetherness through joint exploration with culturally mediating guides who accompany them as they approach, sample, and discover what is shared and what is distant, as well as through verbal and non-verbal communication and the interactions that play out against the background of the respective socio-cultural context of all participants. It is the physical experiences and the ideas that the young people have of Europe and that we have of them which shape the way they deal with their own matters and with others, as well as the way we deal with ourselves and with them. The togetherness, the atmosphere that is created, what can be exchanged with one another and what cannot be discussed – all these become important conveyors of meaning with regard to the refugees' experiences and their attempts to process them. The use of languages, the alternation between the mother tongue, a foreign, different language, and German also becomes important. At the heart of it all is everything that concerns, moves, and worries the young people, their wishes, their fears and experiences, all with the knowledge that they are still a long way from arriving emotionally, despite demands to the contrary: their own, those of their families, and those of the host country.

To put our finger on ethnocentric judgments, we strive to explore cultural patterns of meaning and action and to understand how they operate. We encounter them in tensions, insecurities, and fears; in the attempt to make what is different, unfamiliar to us, equal to our ideas; in the struggle to recognize and acknowledge otherness, and in the effort to deny ambivalences and evaluations. In all of this, the way we speak takes on a special significance (Klein, 2008b). A pictorial language, a more narrative form, and a less rationally direct speech, rather than "blundering straight to the point" (Waldenfels, 1999, p. 76), creates the openings for accessible spaces "in which new meanings, ways of seeing, and boundary-setting emerge" (Bhabha, 2000, p. 71).

5   Sketches from the group process

The group begins with the absence of virtually all participants; only one of the young people has turned up. Her trusted cultural intermediary forms the link to us, the German group leaders. For the young people, the intermediary is the anchor, the connection to familiar feelings that binds the past and that which is lost, as well as the homesickness inherent in the present, to a place to which there is no will to return. Neither here nor there. After this group meeting, it is still unclear whether we will manage to create a space with and for the young people.

We make an effort with each individual participant, and at the second group meeting they are almost all present. Two of the young people arrive too early; two others are brought by their counselors and arrive on time; three of them are picked up from the nearest subway station, and three more get lost. Thanks to a few photos of street signs and various voice messages, they manage to find their way to the group. The different ways of arriving are reminiscent of the mistaken and roundabout routes they took as refugees making their way to Germany. The session is filled with the attempt to position the group in space and time. Opposite an "us" (and it includes the cultural intermediaries), there is a "them", the two Germans. It is towards the "them" that the us direct their initial mistrust and caution. Later we learn that it took a short consultation with one of the cultural intermediaries to clarify whether we two Germans can also be trusted. The oldest participant in the group is the first one to speak. She wants to know what kind of accommodation everyone has and what are the group participants' hopes for the future. Also significant are the questions about what goals we have in mind for our meetings and the expectations everyone has coming to the group. What they want from us is to learn to better know and understand "this here" with our help and for us to guide and support them in becoming stronger, to come together as a group. With a youth group, this is not easy.

In many of the subsequent group sessions, the young women share with us how they perceive and understand their immediate environment. They talk about their astonishment, amazement, and irritation, about behavior that is foreign and incomprehensible to them, about the efforts and psychological burdens that life in the institutions means for them. They stumble over a lack of compassion in many everyday situations and want to know how we understand what they are experiencing. They talk about overly strict rules and confrontations in the institutions, about the severe sanctions for non-compliance. They see for themselves young people in need and can tell "what the young people need. The girls need more human connection", they tell us with conviction. Destructive behavior, meanwhile, is something they can no longer tolerate: "We have survived so many dangers, we know when we are at risk."

Sometimes important thoughts and messages are hinted at fleetingly, in passing, in the transition between coming, staying, and going. The girls stand in the hallway, talk to one another, and seek proximity to the cultural intermediary. After some months, they hint at what they have seen and experienced in the respective countries along their long, arduous journeys. These journeys they survived only because of the group; without the group they would have died psychologically, they say. Even temporary loss triggered panic and profound horror. The experience was that of being utterly alone, their survival fragile and only possible with others whom they didn't even know. Repeating it would be unbearable. The fact that not everyone always comes or simply stays away is unsettling to them, as for all of them the days are exhausting and reassurance only possible to a limited extent. Many of them wake during the night, their hearts throbbing. The vivid memories are so powerful that falling asleep is no longer an option. These weigh heavily on the young people, and the increasing exhaustion makes the demands on them burdensome. With the experiences we have together, the memories and the notion of who they are takes on a special significance. The only thing is: How do they deal with memories they no longer want to have, which they desperately want to forget? Memories that separate their lives into a before and after and which they can't and won't talk about? Memories that don't disappear, recollections that won't fade away. Feelings that pursue them, impress themselves upon them, and frequently dominate their nights. Lessons absorbed in transit. A humiliation. They have desires and dreams that they are able to pursue for the first time, and they are shocked at how difficult it Is for them. The body and the mind need rest that won't come. Not arriving, being in the wrong place, being taken everywhere. Experiences on their refugee journeys that have been overwhelming for the psyche. It is the experiences between life and death that have left deep cracks and scars, additionally reinforced by a feeling of "nothing remains" because real mementos (children's pictures, favorite music, and others) have been lost on these journeys. They served as reminders that "I am", where I come from, and that I have a history. In many group sessions, it is the fragmentary translations that we share: We struggle, understand a little, and yet not too much. It is exhausting. We endure the repeated experiences of fearing death settling within us as feelings of profound powerlessness when they hint at violence and sexual assault, mention deaths, and tell of the dangers of drowning. A kind of unburdening. Other unburdening moments are those in which they are amused by our astonishment when they characterize people from their close environment in such a nuanced way. Moments when they enjoy how impressed we are by them. Another unburdening is when they are able to talk about their anger and rage because they do not feel heard or even taken seriously. We are to understand that in order not to be rude, they then withdraw from the adults. If they become overwhelmed by anger and shout back, they feel ashamed. It is then easier for them to become quiet and say nothing more, or to resist in other ways. We encourage them to maintain the contact by trying to understand how the different worlds of thought struggle with each other and seek understanding. Between powerlessness and wanting to understand, between being at the mercy of and dependent on others, there are moments when it becomes clear that we discover the world together because we sense it, experience it with our feelings, and explore it with the stories we hear and the images we see. Moments that quickly pass and leave the young people alone with their own thoughts.

With the increasing familiarity, the languages start to mix, but profound emotion can still only be expressed in the mother tongue. The girls have a longing for familiarity, for provision and security; yet at the same time, the existing obligations and responsibilities to those left behind weigh heavily on them. Emotionally, they are alone. They do not talk to their families about what they experienced on their journeys, nor do they tell them if they are sick. They do not want to worry the family. It takes time, a lot of time, in which we, too, have to learn to abide by certain social rules, for example what is said publicly and what is not. Non-public talk involves topics that can only be discussed within the family if at all, or topics that were too dangerous politically to address in public. Even within the group, a person can lose face and dishonor their family. Social rules continue to have an effect in the host country, and with them they maintain a bond with the family. They provide orientation and solidity, even though they are restrictive. The existing networks among the refugees also make the question who knows whom and who is related to whom or comes from the same village highly pertinent.

6   The unspeakable in the group

Pregnancies, abortions, and the painful consequences of circumcision – still affecting between 70–90 % of women in Central, East, and West African countries – are also taboo topics, as are emerging intergenerational conflicts. The severity of the burden carried by young people here is onerous. For one thing, cultural expectations and evaluations are at work, since the young people assume the adults here think like their family and social environment in their countries of origin – and therefore judge and condemn them. This applies particularly to a relatively common occurrence, namely abortions. The significance of these painful procedures for the young people is unclear. Generally, they are alone with this experience, disembedded, alienated, distanced from themselves, even though they strive for the opposite, longing for connection, to no longer be alone, for a "safe" survival. Seen in this light, the frequent abortions could also stand for the punishment of their own desires, which distance them from the family whose closeness they so painfully miss. Possibly, however, it is also about the unconscious repetition of bodily experiences (the bloody circumcision), the meaning of which remains hidden.[3] On the other hand, when it comes to the subject of circumcision, the young people encounter the attitudes and judgments of women in the host country, which make it difficult for them to talk about these cultural practices and the consequences they have for them. With their close ties to their family, the young people's ambivalence is suspended in their strict rejection of the Western world.

An either/or that prevents them from coming to terms with all the contradictoriness that this culturally legitimized violence against women means for them. Even merely perceiving it as violence inflicted on them is a psychological effort, and integrating this even more so. To summarize, the cultural corset (of the country of origin and the host country) is what guides, restricts, and at the same time offers orientation and provides the basis for new development. A new development that can interweave with the individual limitations and possibilities that serve a dual purpose: On the one hand, it can bind the fear of being overwhelmed by one's own fantasies and feelings, while on the other, it can allow these fantasies new freedoms.

---

3   Attempts at interpretation that were developed in the supervisory research support provided by Prof. Dr. Elisabeth Rohr in 2018 and 2019.

7 Transcultural orientation in pedagogical work

7.1 Pedagogical support

Sandwiched between institutional requirements and the goal of rapid integration, professionals have little time in their daily pedagogical routine to emotionally catch up and arrive let alone to understand dynamic processes. Feelings of helplessness and powerlessness, the experience of differences that cannot be bridged, make cooperation difficult. Differences between expectations and what happens, between agreements and refusal, between what they see and think they understand and the inadequate answers to this; between their own self-image and the incongruent perception of the others; between an approaching attitude and rejecting gestures, and much more. These are the hard-to-bear feelings that lead many pedagogical professionals to freeze and ultimately to turn away from understanding the young people. Not infrequently, the powerlessness and hopelessness of the professionals mirror the feelings of the young people, who are psychologically overwhelmed and, in the worst case, suicidal. The speechlessness is onerous for the professionals as well as for the young people. All of this can easily lead to our Western concepts and ideas of individualization being imposed on the young people without closer examination of whether they are right for them. Without careful consideration, colonial power relations can creep into relationships. Talking about the differences, like and unlike, and experiencing the constellating power relations could allow professionals to discover their own and others' contexts of meaning (Klein, 2022).

7.2 Networking of professionals in work with young refugees

The youth welfare office as the representative of a socio-politically relevant social institution and the institutions as a socio-family structured environment form a triangular network with the young people, albeit a coarse-meshed one, through whose support the complicated confrontation with reality can be furthered but also prevented. The adolescents, existentially dependent on both institutions, relatively quickly grasp the nature and design of the working relationship between the staff members of the particular institution into which they are woven, and adjust according to their assessment. Recognition of the possibility for the young people to turn to the staff of the respective institution trustingly in complex, hard-to-bear moments without having to fear negative consequences would be relieving and could also prompt the young people to brave more self-determination. Such participatory involvement by the young people would create spaces for transcultural processes. Nadig understands transcultural processes as "processual relationships that influence each other, are interconnected, interdependent" (Nadig, 2016, p. 207). This never involves "the view of two dual perspectives" (Nadig, 2016, p. 207). Transcultural processes go beyond intercultural, ultimately dual perspectives that start from cultural differences and sometimes get stuck "between the chairs."

Transculturality focuses on the dynamic process of transcending; it blurs and erases the supposedly different boundaries between the self and the foreign, the ego and the other, and creates space for the formation of new intermixed cultural forms and ways (Klein, 2022). Transculturally oriented work is guided by a willingness to engage with one's own culture-specific perceptions and attitudes, which also involves reflection on the institution's pedagogical assumptions, norms, implicit rules, and symbol systems (Rohr, 2020b). Fundamentally, this way of facing oneself can trigger insecurity and anxiety and thus the desire ultimately to counter the condition of uncertainty, instability, insecurity, and confusion with order and clarity in order to re-establish stability and comprehensibility. It remains a constant requirement to resist this closure through understanding. It can be exciting to observe the situations in which we fall back on demarcation and limitations; when we begin to think in binary categories (us – the others, etc.); or ultimately to retreat to familiar, conformist explanations of the world, of society, of demands and necessities, without noticing that we have long since lost sight of the other. Without careful reflection, discriminatory and even racist thinking can creep into explanatory approaches, interpretive patterns, and judgments. They can find their way unnoticed into relations between generations, between the sexes, into how the relationship between African and Asian countries and Western Europe is described and understood. Where the journey will take us remains unclear, although we know full well that we, too, will change in the process (Rohr, 2020b).

And so back to the starting point of our little voyage of discovery: Even if we wander around in the dark for a long time and do not escape this state with hasty explanations, it is the brief moments, the moments of revelatory encounter, that are touching and valuable. In the eagerness to understand, the desire for recognition and belonging can obscure the view of what is essential. This interdependence remains a challenging tightrope walk on this path of knowledge.

At a glance:
Transcultural spaces in group analysis mean:
- entering into a discussion and asking what cultural understanding implicitly underlies group analytic assumptions.
- keeping encounters open in transcultural spaces.
- fostering a deeper understanding of the dynamics of transcultural processes.
- at the same time offering research spaces that invite us to "places of rethinking" and create transcultural spaces of recognition and exploration: spaces of experience in which, above all, quasi-"natural" as well as theoretical certainties are shaken because we also discover in them discriminatory or the confirmation of colonialist-influenced relations of domination.
- overcoming and critically questioning unexamined Eurocentric beliefs.

It remains a moot question to what extent group analysis, will be able to open up to this process more than before; indeed, the process itself shakes up the very understanding of group analysis.

Bibliography

Adelson, L. A. (2015). Against Between – Ein Manifest gegen das Dazwischen. In A. Langenohl, R. Poole, M. Weinberg (Hrsg.), *Transkulturalität. Klassische Texte* (S. 125–138). Bielefeld: transcript

Bhabha, H. K. (2000). *Die Verortung der Kultur.* Tübingen: Stauffenberg

Bhabha, H. K. (2012). *Über kulturelle Hybridität: Tradition und Übersetzung.* Wien: Turia + Kant

Bourdieu, P. (1993). *Sozialer Sinn. Kritik der theoretischen Vernunft.* Frankfurt/M.: Suhrkamp

Bronfen, E., Marius, B. (1997). Hybride Kulturen. Einleitung. In E. Bronfen, B. Marius, T. Steffen (Hrsg.), *Hybride Kulturen. Beiträge zur anglo-amerikanischen Multikulturalismusdebatte* (S. 1–29). Tübingen: Stauffenberg Verlag Brigitte Narr

Dalal, F. (2018). Zurück zum Ursprung – Von der Vorhersagbarkeit zur radikalen Ungewissheit. *Gruppenpsychotherapie und Gruppendynamik – Zeitschrift für Theorie und Praxis der Gruppenanalyse*, 54 (2), 76–93

Erdheim, M. (1984). *Die gesellschaftliche Produktion von Unbewußtheit. Eine Einführung in den ethnopsychoanalytischen Prozeß.* Frankfurt/M.: Suhrkamp

Erdheim, M. (1986). Fritz Morgenthaler und die Ethnopsychoanalyse. In F. Morgenthaler (Hrsg.), *Der Traum. Fragmente zur Theorie und Technik der Traumdeutung* (S. 187–211). Frankfurt/M.: Edition Qumran im Campus Verlag

Giddens, A. (1996). Leben in einer posttraditionalen Gesellschaft. In U. Beck, A. Giddens, S. Lash (Hrsg.), *Reflexive Modernisierung. Eine Kontroverse* (S. 113–194). Frankfurt/M.: Suhrkamp

Günther, M. (2020). Adoleszente Entwicklung im Kontext von Fluchterfahrungen. In A. Kerschgens, B. Schnabel (Hrsg.), *Psychosoziale Arbeit mit jugendlichen Geflüchteten. Transkulturelle Übergangsräume und Verstehensprozesse* (S. 25–43). Frankfurt/M.: Brandes & Apsel

Gutjahr, O. (2008). Tabu als Grundbedingungen von Kultur. Sigmund Freuds Totem und Tabu und die Wende in der Tabuforschung. In C. Benthien, O. Gutjahr (Hrsg.), *Tabu. Interkulturalität und Gender* (S. 19–50). München: Wilhelm Frank.

Hall, S. (1989). *Ideologie, Kultur, Rassismus. Ausgewählte Schriften 1.* Hamburg: Argument
Hall, S. (1994). *Rassismus und kulturelle Identität. Ausgewählte Schriften 2.* Hamburg: Argument
Hall, S. (2020*). Vertrauter Fremder. Ein Leben zwischen zwei Inseln.* Hamburg: Argument
Hörning, K. H., Winter, R. (1999*). Widerspenstige Kulturen. Cultural Studies als Herausforderung.* Frankfurt/M.: Suhrkamp
Hörter, K. (2016). Die Konstruktion der Anderen. (Ethno-)psychoanalyse aus Perspektive der Cultural und Postcolonial Studies. In Reichmayer, J. (Hrsg.), *Ethnopsychoanalyse revisited. Gegenübertragung in transkulturellen und postkolonialen Kontexten* (S. 342–361). Gießen: Psychosozial
King, V. (2002). *Die Entstehung des Neuen in der Adoleszenz. Individuation, Generativität und Geschlecht in modernisierten Gesellschaften.* Opladen: Leske + Budrich
Klein, R. (2008a). Pädagogische Absichten und ihre Aushandlung – eine symboltheoretische Skizzierung des sozialpädagogischen Handlungsraums. *FQS – Forum Qualitative Sozialforschung,* 9 (1), Art.52. DOI: 10.17169/fqs-9.1.318
Klein, R. (2008b). Kultur erinnernd verstehen – der Versuch einer reflexiven Begegnung zwischen Psychoanalyse, Biographieforschung und Cultural Studies. In M. Dörr, R. Klein, H. Macha, W. Marotzki, H. von Felden (Hrsg.), *Erinnern – Reflektion – Geschichte. Erinnerungsarbeit in psychoanalytischer und biographischer Perspektive* (S. 49–62). Wiesbaden: VS-Verlag
Klein, R. (2009). Raumbildung in der Sozialen Arbeit – vergessene Zusammenhänge. *Neue Praxis – Zeitschrift für Sozialarbeit, Sozialpädagogik und Sozialpolitik,* 39 (5), 452–466
Klein, R. (2019). Wie geht es Dir heute, Toni? – Soziokulturelle Perspektiven auf Kind(er)leben. *Feedback 1 & 2 – Beiträge zur Kulturtheorie, ÖAAG,* 8–26.
Klein, R. (2020). Transkulturelle Übergangsräume und andere Bruchlinien der Erfahrung. In A. Kerschgens, B. Schnabel (Hrsg.), *Psychosoziale Arbeit mit jugendlichen Geflüchteten. Transkulturelle Übergangsräume und Verstehensprozesse* (S. 45–70). Frankfurt/M.: Brandes & Apsel
Klein, R. (2022). Prekäre Zwischenwelten – Transkulturelle Streiflichter auf Transiträume und Grenzgänge. In M. Günther, A. Kerschgens, P. Meurs (Hrsg.), *Geflüchtete Familien und Frühe Hilfen.* Weinheim: Juventa
Kotanyi, S. (2018). *Einführung in die französische Ethnopsychiatrie. Die therapeutische Behandlung von Migrantenfamilien am Centre Georges Devereux und im Krankenhaus Avicenne.* Gießen: Psychosozial
Nadig, M. (2000). Interkulturalität im Prozess. Ethnopsychoanalyse und Feldforschung als methodischer und theoretischer Übergangsraum. In H. Lahme-Gronostaj, M. Leuzinger-Bohleber (Hrsg.), *Identität und Differenz. Zur Psychoanalyse des Geschlechterverhältnisses in der Spätmoderne* (S. 87–101). Wiesbaden: Westdeutscher Verlag
Nadig, M. (2006). Transkulturelle Spannungsfelder in der Migration und ihre Erforschung. In E. Wohlfart, M. Zaumseil (Hrsg.), *Transkulturelle Psychiatrie – Interkulturelle Psychotherapie. Interdisziplinäre Theorie und Praxis* (S. 68–79). Heidelberg: Springer
Nadig, M. (2016). Begegnungen mit anderen Welten deuten. Über das vermeintlich Fremde in uns und in der ethnopsychoanalytischen Forschung. In J. Reichmayr (Hrsg.), *Ethnopsychoanalyse revisited. Gegenübertragung in transkulturellen und postkolonialen Kontexten* (S. 200–231). Gießen: Psychosozial
Rehbein, B. (2010). Eine kaleidoskopische Dialektik als Antwort auf eine postkoloniale Soziologie. In J. Reuter, P.-I. Villa (Hrsg.), *Postkoloniale Soziologie. Empirische Befunde, theoretische Anschlüsse, politische Intervention* (S. 213–235). Bielefeld: transcript
Rohr, E. (2016). If you want to go fast, go alone, if you want to go far, go together. *Gruppenpsychotherapie und Gruppendynamik – Zeitschrift für Theorie und Praxis der Gruppenanalyse,* 52 (3), 308–322
Rohr, E. (2017a). Kinder auf der Flucht. Die Traumatisierung einer Generation. In K.-J. Bruder, C. Bialluch (Hrsg.), *Migration und Rassismus. Politik der Menschenfeindlichkeit* (S. 83–100). Gießen: Psychosozial

Rohr, E. (2017b). Forcierte Autonomie und keine Zeit zum Trauern. Transnationale Kindheiten in Ecuador. In H. Schnoor (Hrsg.), *Psychosoziale Entwicklung in der Postmoderne. Psychoanalytische Perspektiven* (S. 109–124). Gießen: Psychosozial

Rohr, E. (2020a). Transit nach der Flucht und vor dem Ankommen. In A. Kerschgens, B. Schnabel (Hrsg.), *Psychosoziale Arbeit mit jugendlichen Geflüchteten. Transkulturelle Übergangsräume und Verstehensprozesse* (S. 13–24). Frankfurt/M.: Brandes & Apsel

Rohr, E. (2020b). Supervision in einer traumatisierten Postkonfliktgesellschaft. Ein Fallbeispiel aus Guatemala. In V. Duque, E. Rohr (Hrsg.), *Supervision in Mesoamerika. Herausforderungen in einer traumatisierten Postkonfliktgesellschaft* (S. 195–216). Gießen: Psychosozial

Schnabel, B. (2020). Erkundungs- und Erzählräume. Konzept einer transkulturellen psychosozialen Gruppenarbeit mit unbegleiteten minderjährigen Geflüchteten an der Schnittstelle zwischen sozialem und medizinischem Bereich. In A. Kerschgens, B. Schnabel (Hrsg.), *Psychosoziale Arbeit mit jugendlichen Geflüchteten. Transkulturelle Übergangsräume und Verstehensprozesse* (S. 125–163). Frankfurt/M.: Brandes & Apsel

Waldenfels, B. (1999). *Topographie des Fremden. Studien zur Phänomenologie des Fremden I.* Frankfurt/M.: Suhrkamp

To finish with a story

Christina Selle

An everyday school situation in a second-grade class at a special school for the speech-impaired

A morning of lessons is behind us. The twelve pupils left the classroom a few minutes ago. There is an unusual silence. I have time to put some materials in order. Tidying up the room, I find dolls' furniture in several places in the room. It belongs in the dollhouse, which is easily accessible on a low windowsill and can be used freely. Chaos reigns in the dollhouse. With each new item I find, I become more annoyed, and I decide to talk to Jana about it the next day. I had seen her playing with the dollhouse during the morning. The idea that comes to my mind on seeing the state of it is that of an explosion in an apartment building. Then I remember Jana in the morning circle on Monday. She told us, "Dad moved out over the weekend. He took the sofa and the chairs with him. But Mom has already ordered new furniture. We have to wait a little while for it to be delivered."

With that reminder, my anger fades. I am very relieved that I haven't yet done any damage to the student with my planned rant. After all, she was just very impressively portraying her momentary life situation in the game, so I could easily put things back in order and continue. It helps me understand her situation better. Over the following play sessions with the dollhouse – and outside – I am witness to the changes in the family.

That was 18 years ago. On my birthday and at Christmas, Jana's mother still writes to me and tells me what has been going on in her daughter's life in the meantime – and of course, I make sure I always answer her.

The name of the student has been changed.

Word of Thanks

The translation of this book into English has been a joint effort and I would like to thank everyone involved for their contributions!
- The authors who with great personal dedication and financial commitment have made it possible to bring out this publication in English.
- The delegates of the 48 Institutes in the European Group Analytic Training Institution Network (EGATIN – https://www.egatin.net) and its Executive Board at the time – Jutta Gliem, Tija Despotovic, Alex Collins, Marina Brinchi, Taras Levin, Egle Pauzine – for their great interest in the publication of the German edition of this book in 2022 and the numerous invitations to present excerpts on group analysis with children, young people, and their carers at the EGATIN and PrEgatin 2023.

  It was the strong favorable response from many of my international colleagues that motivated and encouraged me to bring out this English edition of the entire book.
- Deutsche Gesellschaft für Gruppenanalyse und Gruppenpsychotherapie (D3G – https://www.d3 g.org), are represented by its Board (Martin Pröstler, Patrizia Gerhardt, Thomas Schneider and Hermann Storm). In the form of a generous donation, they really helped drive the project to bring the book out in an English edition. I would like on behalf of a large number of the colleagues who participated in the project to thank D3G for this recognition of the many years of dedicated work to establish group analysis with children, young people, as carers.
- The members of the association Arbeitsgemeinschaft Gruppenanalyse mit Kindern und Jugendlichen (GaKiJu – https://kindergruppenanalyse.de) who at their General Meeting in September 2023 unanimously agreed to donating a generous sum by way of support for the publication of this book project.
- The entire team at publishers Brill Deutschland/Vandenhoeck & Ruprecht – Sandra Englisch program director for Psychology, Imke Heuer as editor of the German edition, and Ulrike Rastin as editor of the English edition, as well as Ingeborg Lüdtke from the Contracts Management section.

  In 2019, Sandra Englisch first gave me the idea of editing a book on the topic of group analysis with children and young people. She immediately

welcomed the concept I tabled and brought all her expertise and optimism to bear supporting the project and providing further encouragement.
- Maria Hagl (mh@mariahagl.de) was a source of great inspiration in her function as external editor for me as author of my texts in the German edition.
- My profound thanks also goes to all those who supported the translation of the essays, all the family members and friends of the authors who I do not know in person for their help in realizing this book.
- My special thanks go to Jeremy Gaines (office@gainestranslations.de). He is well-versed in psychoanalytical literature and thought and with great personal dedication translated my own essays and subsequently agreed to act as the native speaker editor for the entire volume, ensuring it its linguistic homogeneity.
- Last, but most certainly not least, I would like to thank all the children, young people, and adults who have placed their faith in me in the 27 years of my work as a group analyst. Each group process with them convinced anew that such work is so profoundly meaningful. During times of crisis, to find the space and time (in the sense of Kairos[1]) to reflect on oneself, the others, and current social contexts forever lays new foundations for dreaming, for joy, and for a lust for life.

---

1   Joke J. Hermsen (2017). Kairos Castle: The Art of the Moment. Lannoo: Tielt, Belgium

Information on authors

Birgitt Ballhausen-Scharf, MD, specialist in psychosomatic medicine and psychotherapy and group analysis trainer, has been active in one-on-one and group psychotherapy in her own practice. She is a founding member of the Working Group for Group Analysis with Children and Adolescents (Arbeitsgemeinschaft Gruppenanalyse mit Kindern und Jugendlichen e.V., GaKiJu).
birgitt.ballhausen@gmail.com

Kadir Kaynak, qualified social pedagogue, analytical child and youth psychotherapist, group analyst for children and adolescents, works in his own practice in Berlin.
kaynak.kadir@t-online.de

Dr. Furi Khabirpour, a pediatrician and psychotherapist, lecturer, and group analysis trainer at the Institute for Group Analysis in Heidelberg (Institut für Gruppeanalyse Heidelberg e.V., IGAH), and runs his own practice in Speyer. He is a member of the German Society for Group Analysis and Group Psychotherapy (Deutsche Gesellschaft für Gruppenanalyse und Gruppenpsychotherapie, D3G) and on the board of the Working Group for Group Analysis with Children and Adolescents (Arbeitsgemeinschaft Gruppenanalyse mit Kindern und Jugendlichen e.V., GaKiJu). furi@khabirpour.de

Dr. Anja Khalil, specialist in psychosomatic medicine and psychotherapy, specialist in child and adolescent psychiatry and psychotherapy, group teaching analyst (D3G), and supervisor, has her own practice in Bremen. She is chair of the Working Group on Group Analysis for Children and Adolescents (GaKiJu), a member of the German Society for Group Analysis and Group Psychotherapy (D3G), and a lecturer at the Bremen Working Group for Group Analysis and Group Psychotherapy (BAGG), the Bremen Psychoanalytic Association (BPV), and the Psychoanalytic Institute Bremen (PSIB). She publishes on the topic of online group dynamics.
praxis@khalil.de

Dietlind Köhncke, M.A., studied Literature, Sociology, and Philosophy and worked as a teacher and teacher trainer. She is a group analysis trainer, Balint group leader, group-analytical supervisor (IGAH, D3G), and has published, among others, on the topic of play and creativity, the short story "Die Wörtersammlerin", and the novel "Grenzwege".
d.b.koehncke@-online.de

Hans Georg Lehle, qualified educationalist, analytical child and adolescent psychotherapist, group analysis trainer, supervisor, and lecturer, has a private practice in Ulm. He is a founding member of the Working Group for Group Analysis with Children and Adolescents (Arbeitsgemeinschaft Gruppenanalyse mit Kindern und Jugendlichen e. V., GaKiJu) and co-chairman of the Stuttgart Working Group for Group Analysis (Arbeitsgemeinschaft Gruppenanalyse Stuttgart e. V., AGS)
h.g.lehle@praxis-lehle.de

Anke Mühle is a state-certified social educationalist and social therapist who trained in group therapy, which she completed in Göttingen and Berlin as part of her affiliation with the Working Group for Group Psychotherapy and Group Analysis (Arbeitsgemeinschaft für Gruppenpsychotherapie und Gruppenanalyse e. V.). Since 2010 she has been working in Potsdam at the Family and Competence Center for Early Childhood at the University of Applied Sciences in Potsdam (Familien- und Kompetenzzentrum "Frühe Kindheit" an der FH Potsdam) as part of a multidisciplinary team focused on families with multiple challenges and parents with mental health issues, along with their infants and toddlers aged up to five years old. Anke Mühle is a member of several professional associations, including the German Society for Group Analysis and Group Psychotherapy (Deutsche Gesellschaft für Gruppenanalyse und Gruppenpsychotherapie, D3G), the Federal Association for Psychoanalytic Couple and Family Therapy (Bundesverband Psychoanalytische Paar- und Familientherapie, BVFFP), the German Association for Social Therapy (Deutscher Fachverband für Sozialtherapie e. V., DFS), and the Working Group for Group Analysis with Children and Adolescents (Arbeitsgemeinschaft Gruppenanalyse mit Kindern und Jugendlichen e. V., GaKiJu).
as1.muehle@t-online.de

Christoph F. Müller, MD, specialist in child and adolescent psychiatry and psychotherapy, psychotherapist, psychoanalyst, and group analyst, has his own practice in Zurich. He is a lecturer and supervisor in educational and therapeutic contexts and a founding member of the Working Group for Group Analy-

sis with Children and Adolescents (Arbeitsgemeinschaft Gruppenanalyse mit Kindern und Jugendlichen e. V., GaKiJu).
chris-f-mueller@gmx.net

Gerhild Ohrnberger, graduated in Sociology. She is a group analyst, a supervisor in group analysis and organizational consultant (IGA, D3G) and instructor in group analysis (D3G). Moreover, she is a founding member of the GaKiJu working party, and a member of the staff of a psychiatric practice in Frankfurt/Main specializing in therapy for children and adolescents, wherte she leads groups of children and young people.
g.ohrnberger@gmx.de

Andreas Opitz, curative teacher, Gestalt pedagogue (TU Berlin), social pedagogue, and group analyst (D3G), is a member of the Berlin Institute for Group Analysis (BIG) and a founding member of the German Society for Group Analysis and Group Psychotherapy (D3G). He works as a social pedagogue and group therapist in child and adolescent psychiatry, psychotherapy, and psychosomatics at Vivantes Klinikum Neukölln (Berlin). He is also in demand as a lecturer and leader of workshops and seminars.
andreas.opitz60@gmx.de

Ursula Proebsting, born in 1967, is the head of an open all-day elementary school in Wuppertal. In 2015, in addition to full-time school management, she began working as a conflict moderator and supervisor at schools in the Düsseldorf administrative district. She completed further training in group analysis at the Institute for Group Analysis Heidelberg (Institut für Gruppenanalyse Heidelberg e. V., IGAH). As a non-medical practitioner for psychotherapy, she works part-time in her own practice for children, adolescents, and adults.

Christoph Radaj is a graduate social worker, child and youth psychotherapist (VAKJP), a registered psychoanalyst for children and adolescents (DGIP), and group analysis trainer (D3G) with his own practice in Hamburg and at a children's clinic. He is also a supervisor and lecturer at the Academy for Psychotherapy, Psychosomatics, and Psychoanalysis Hamburg (Akademie für Psychotherapie, Psychosomatik und Psychoanalyse Hamburg, APH gGmbH), is affiliated with the Alfred Adler Institute Munich, and serves on the board of the Working Group for Group Analysis with Children and Adolescents (Arbeitsgemeinschaft Gruppenanalyse mit Kindern und Jugendlichen e. V., GaKiJu).
Info@praxis-radaj.com

Beate Schnabel, graduated in Sociology and in Social Education. She is a qualified group analyst, an in instructor in group analysis (IGA), a supervisor for group analysis (D3G), and a member of the staff of the Frankfurter Institut für interkulturelle Forschung und Beratung e. V. She also freelances providing supervision.
Beate.Schnabel@online.de

Thomas Schneider holds a degree in social pedagogy. He also studied philosophy, Catholic theology, and psychology and completed his individual psychology training as a psychotherapist for children and adolescents at the Alfred Adler Institute in Munich and his qualification as a group analyst for children and adolescents at the Institute for Group Analysis in Heidelberg. He has further completed training as an EMDR therapist for children and adolescents and in social therapeutic role-play. He is a group analysis trainer in the D3G and in the German Society for Individual Psychology (DGIP) as well as a trainer-analyst in the Association of Analytical Child and Adolescent Psychotherapists (VAKJP). He is a member of the Professional Association of Licensed Group Psychotherapists (BAG), founding board member of the GaKiJu working group, and expert group speaker on child and adolescent group analysis in the D3G (together with Susanne Dittrich). He is a lecturer, board member, and treasurer at the Würzburg Institute for Psychoanalysis and Psychotherapy.
www.tschneider-praxis.de

Franziska Schöpfer is a qualified educationalist, certified art therapist, analytical child and adolescent psychotherapist (VAKJP), group analyst, and group analysis trainer (D3G) and supervisor with her own practice in Berlin-Charlottenburg. She is a member of the Berlin Institute for Group Analysis (Berliner Institut für Gruppeanalyse e. V., BIG), the Working Group for Group Analysis with Children and Adolescents (Arbeitsgemeinschaft Gruppenanalyse mit Kindern und Jugendlichen e. V., GaKiJu), and the German Society for Group Analysis and Group Psychotherapy (Deutsche Gesellschaft für Gruppenanalyse und Gruppenpsychotherapie, D3G).
franziskaschoepfer@gmx.de

Christina Selle studied special education in Frankfurt/Main and Marburg, specializing in speech and language therapy education and graduating with a degree and diploma. She lives in Berlin and has taught for over 30 years at a school in Berlin's Kreuzberg district with a special focus on language. After advanced training at the Berlin Institute for Group Analysis (Berliner Institut für Gruppeanalyse e. V., BIG), she took on the joint leadership of groups together with a

psychotherapist for children and adolescents. She has since begun working with a child and adolescent therapist in her practice, initially with groups of children and currently with adolescents.
christina-selle@web.de

Tilman Sprondel, Dipl.-Päd. (Tübingen 1977), Group Analyst (IGA Heidelberg), has 39 years of experience in social educational work in residential youth care facilities, of which 34 years have been spent in leading functions. He was a resident leader of a small facility in an average neighborhood of a small town in South Baden (Germany) until December 2015. Lecturer on the Group Analysis with Children and Adolescents foundation course, Heidelberg (since 2021).
tilmansp@aol.com

Katrin Stumptner graduated as a music therapist from the University of Music and Performing Arts Vienna and also studied theater and film studies in Berlin. She has been a registered psychotherapist for children and young people since 2000 and is a group analyst and a supervisor for group analysis, as well as an organizational consultant. She also lectures and is a group analysis trainer (D3G) and supervisor (D3G) at the Berlin Institute for Group Analysis (Berliner Institut für Gruppenanalyse e.V., BIG) and at the Institute for Group Analysis Heidelberg (Institut für Gruppenanalyse Heidelberg, IGAH). She is active in the BIG, the EGATIN (European Group Analytic Training Network), and the GASI (Group Analytic Society International). Her particular focus is on scenic understanding in small and large group sessions in connection with transgenerational and transcultural contexts. She is a founding member of the Working Group for Group Analysis with Children and Adolescents (Arbeitsgemeinschaft Gruppenanalyse mit Kindern und Jugendlichen, GaKiJu e.V.).
Katrin.stumptner@t-online.de

Carla Weber, academic speech therapist (Univ.), special educator for behavioral disorders, psychotherapist and psychoanalyst for children, adolescents, and young adults, and group analyst, has her own practice in Munich and publishes on the topics of psycho-dynamic treatment techniques and transgenerational traumatization. She is a member of the German Society for Group Analysis and Group Psychotherapy (D3G) and the Association of Analytical Child and Adolescent Psychotherapists in Germany (VAKJP), member and lecturer of the Munich Working Group for Psychoanalysis (MAP), and lecturer at the Medical Academy for Psychotherapy of Children and Adolescents, Munich.
carla-weber@t-online.de

Dr. Harald Weilnböck studied in the field of qualitative-empirical Cultural, Media, and Social Sciences, Narratology, and Psychology, and these are also the focus of his research. He has worked as a visiting scholar at both the Sigmund Freud Institute in Frankfurt and at the Giessen Graduiertenzentrum für Kulturwissenschaften. He has trained and worked in group-analysis-based psychotherapy and supervision (DGSv). As a cofounder of Cultures Interactive e. V. he has for many years been active in conceptualizing content for and applying intensive educational techniques in the field of the prevention of extremism and the promotion of dissociation (so-called deradicalization).
weilnboeck@cultures-interactive.de

Dr. Matthias Wenck is a consultant for pediatrics and adolescent medicine, a consultant for psychosomatic medicine and psychotherapy, a psychoanalyst for children, adolescents, and adults, and a trainer analyst for group therapy registered with the German Society for Group Analysis and Group Psychotherapy (Deutsche Gesellschaft für Gruppenanalyse und Gruppenpsychotherapie, D3G). He runs his own practice in Markt Schwaben.

Horst Wenzel is a qualified social worker (university of applied sciences), educational advisor, and group analysis trainer (D3G) and supervisor (EKFuL). He works at a psychological counseling center run by the Diakonisches Werk and lectures at the Institute for Psychoanalysis and Psychotherapy in Kassel *(Institut für Psychoanalyse und Pyschotherapie)*.
ho.wenzel@t-online.de

Dietrich Norman Winzer, graduate psychologist, works as a psychoanalyst for adults, children, and adolescents in Munich. He is a lecturer and head of an outpatient clinic for children and adolescents in Munich. Winzer is a founding member of the Working Group for Group Analysis with Children and Adolescents (Arbeitsgemeinschaft Gruppenanalyse mit Kindern und Jugendlichen e. V., GaKiJu). One focus of his work is the treatment of French-speaking patients, which includes group therapy with refugees from Africa.
dietrich.winzer@web.de

> "The foreignness of the other person decreases proportionately to the increase in shared ground and the degree to which you transgress the boundaries of your own form of living."
> (Waldenfels, 1997, p. 117).